Japan and Protection

Recently, the extent of Japanese export penetration into other Western economies, particularly the USA, has become a matter of great international concern. There have been increasingly strident demands for Japan to reciprocate on imports, for the Japanese market to be 'opened up' and, by some people, for sanctions or a trade war if the Japanese do not respond.

This book examines the growth of protectionist sentiment and the Japanese response to it. It examines in detail the debates within Japan and discusses the measures which the Japanese have actually taken, including the voluntary export restraint measure in the automobile sector. It concludes that, broadly, the Japanese are indeed responding to world demands for their market to be opened up but that successful exporting to Japan depends equally on efforts by Western companies to service that market, which they have so far been relatively slow to do.

The author: Syed Javed Maswood is a lecturer in the Division of Asian and International Studies, Griffith University, Brisbane, Australia.

THE NISSAN INSTITUTE/ROUTLEDGE JAPANESE STUDIES SERIES

Titles in the series:

JAPAN AND PROTECTION

The growth of protectionist sentiment
and the Japanese response

SYED JAVED MASWOOD

ROUTLEDGE
London and New York
and
NISSAN INSTITUTE FOR JAPANESE STUDIES
University of Oxford

First published 1989
by Routledge
11 New Fetter Lane, London EC4P 4EE
29 West 35th Street, New York, NY 10001

Reprinted 1990

Printed in Great Britain
by Antony Rowe Ltd

British Library Cataloguing in Publication Data

Maswood, Syed Javed
Japan and protection : the growth of
protectionist sentiment and the Japanese
response.
1. Foreign trade. Protection. Policies of
Japanese government. Japan. Government.
Policies on Foreign trade protection
I. Title
382.7′0952
ISBN 0-415-01030-6

Library of Congress Cataloging in Publication Data

Maswood, Syed Javed.
Japan and protection : the growth of protectionist sentiment
and the Japanese response / by Syed Javed Maswood.
p. cm. – (Routledge Japanese studies series)
Bibliography: p.
Includes index.
ISBN 0-415-01030-6
1. Japan – Commercial policy.
2. Free trade and protection – Protection.
3. International trade.
I. Title. II. Series. HF3826.5.M37 1989
382.7′3-dc19 88-18286

ISBN 0-415-01030-6

To my mother and in memory
of my father

Contents

Figures

Tables

General Editor's Preface

Almost imperceptibly, during the 1980s, Japan has become 'hot news'. The successes of the Japanese economy and the resourcefulness of her people have long been appreciated abroad. What is new is an awareness of her increasing impact on the outside world. This tends to produce painful adjustment and uncomfortable reactions. It also often leads to stereotypes and arguments based on outdated or ill-informed ideas.

The Nissan Institute/Routledge Japanese Studies Series (previously the Nissan Institute/Croom Helm Japanese Studies Series) seeks to foster an informed and balanced – but not uncritical – understanding of Japan. One aim of the series is to show the depth and variety of Japanese institutions, practices and ideas. Another is, by using comparison, to see what lessons, positive and negative, can be drawn for other countries. There are many aspects of Japan which are little known outside that country but which deserve to be better understood.

One of the greatest achievements of the post-war world was a liberal trading regime, permitting far freer international trade than before the war, and great consequent increases in prosperity for those nations able to benefit from it. Some have argued that a liberal international economic order is typically maintained by a single nation that is sufficiently dominant to act as 'hegemon', and that where no nation is dominant, such an order is likely to be threatened. During the 1980s the emergence of a huge and unprecedented Japanese trade surplus over the United States (hitherto the 'hegemon') suggested that a liberal regime in world trade might be under threat. Dr Maswood carefully examines the evidence for and against this, and makes valuable suggestions for preserving and reinvigorating a liberal international economic order. He argues that both Japan and the United States need to change policies if this is to be achieved.

J. A. A. Stockwin
Director, Nissan Institute of Japanese Studies,
University of Oxford

Acknowledgments

This book is a revised version of my Ph.D. thesis submitted to the Department of Political Science, Carleton University, Ottawa, Canada. My biggest debt is to my three supervisors at Carleton; Professors R. Bedeski and M. Dolan of the Department of Political Science and Professor H. English of the Department of Economics. I received much needed encouragement from Professor Bedeski who, at times, had more confidence in the project than myself. Professor Dolan read through successive drafts of the dissertation and saw it through to completion. I also wish to register my thanks to Professor J. A. A. Stockwin, Director, Nissan Institute of Japanese Studies, for his many helpful suggestions during the dissertation writing stage and then for encouraging me to continue and get it ready for publication. Professor Barry Buzan, Department of International Studies, University of Warwick, read through the first part of the book and offered several helpful suggestions and improvements.

The research contained in this book would never have been possible without a generous grant from the Japan Foundation, Tokyo. I am most grateful to them for the grant which allowed me to spend 14 months at Hitotsubashi University in Tokyo. At Hitotsubashi I benefited from the helpful supervision and advise of Professor Hiroshi Tanaka of the Faculty of Social Science. During my stay in Japan I interviewed many individuals both in the government and the private sector. They gave willingly of their time and patience. Their co-operation facilitated both data collection and analysis. However, since it is not possible to name all of them individually, I hope a collective thank you will suffice.

Much of the final revision of the manuscript was done while I was attached to the Institute of Southeast Asian Studies as a Research Fellow and I would like to acknowledge their help and support. Finally, it remains for me to mention that I alone am responsible for any remaining errors and omissions.

1

Introduction

In 1985, the historian Theodore White wrote a scathing critique of Japanese trade policies in the *New York Times*. In jingoistic terms, he warned Americans of a grand Japanese conspiracy to choke American society slowly and to deindustrialize its economic structure. He asserted that unless the United States awoke to the dangers, Japan would soon succeed, through peaceful means, in what it had set out to achieve during the Second World War. Inspired by mounting economic difficulties at home, it only added fuel to the fire and increased the level of anti-Japanese sentiments and the demands for protectionism. Of course, 'Japan bashing' did not originate with Theodore White, but he epitomized it perfectly. According to this perspective, the cause of American economic problems could be traced to external sources and the unfair trading practices of others.

Although this book does not seek to provide a definitive explanation of the American economic malaise, we disagree with the notion that the final cause, and therefore the cure, can be found in America's trading partners. However, we do not also subscribe to the popular Japanese view that 'Japan bashing' is simply making a scapegoat out of Japan for internal policy issues. Simple mono-causal explanations should be avoided, but it is important to identify the different areas of problems in a problem-solving exercise. We do acknowledge that a relatively closed and export-oriented Japanese economy did contribute to industrial dislocation in the United States and subsequently to the destabilization of the international trading regime. In this, our purpose is to understand what was being done by the Japanese government to improve access to their market and

1

contribute to regime stability. We do not suggest, however, that liberalization of the Japanese economy can be the sole mechanism for balancing international trade. A liberal, open economy, by itself, cannot achieve much unless there is concomitant effort on the part of foreign manufacturers to penetrate the market and to modify their products to meet local conditions. American businesses must become more aggressive in their export strategies. We also do not suggest that Japan's efforts in the macroeconomic sphere alone can ensure stability of the trading system. The US government cannot continue to insist that its policy choices were free of blame.

In so far as the American trade deficit in the 1980s was reflective of the problems confronted by American policy makers, it should be pointed out that it was not the result of a general increase in tariffs or non-tariff barriers in Japan. The trade imbalance cannot be separated from the reckless spending splurge in the United States during the 1980s, particularly in the public sector. Fiscal spending and budget deficits continued to expand at a rapid pace even as other countries, confronted with similar deficits, introduced stringent fiscal discipline. The deficit was financed through foreign capital inflows which appeared to be a relatively cost-free way to continue the economic boom of recent years. That is, until 'Black Monday', 19 October 1987, and the stock market crash. The boom had busted and many 'whodunnit' scenarios were quickly circulated. Some blamed it on the computerization of the New York stock exchange and programme trading; others blamed Treasury Secretary James Baker for 'unwise' remarks on the value of the dollar; and a few more blamed Chairman of the Federal Reserve Board Alan Greenspan for sending out mixed signals. Even though a few, including President Ronald Reagan, were initially hesitant to acknowledge, most analysts were agreed that the basic problem was the consumption spree and fiscal deficits. It could not possibly have gone on for ever, but the question still remains why the stock market crashed when it did, and why not much earlier or later. The immediate cause, perhaps, was the shift to a tight monetary policy in West Germany. The Bundesbank, instead of stimulating economic expansion, raised interest rates on four separate occasions, the last one only a week before the stock market crash. This was done for the selfish reason of keeping inflation at zero per cent, but its international conse- quence was to put upward pressure on American interest rates at a time when the US administration would have liked to keep interest rates low to boost economic growth.

Despite the pain and suffering caused by the stock market crash, it might still prove to be a blessing in disguise. For one, Congress and the White House have started discussing the problem of federal deficits and it is expected that meaningful measures will be taken to restore fiscal balance. A meaningful deficit-reduction plan would have to go beyond what would be automatically required under the Gramm–Rudman–Hollings budget-balancing act of the US Congress.

In so far as the private sector consumption pattern is concerned, the stock market crash resulted in reducing the wealth of a great many Americans and eroded the savings of many more. Without wishing to appear callous and insensitive to the misery of others, we may say that it is likely that the crash will have some positive outcome. In particular, it is likely to alter the consumption patterns and generate more savings as individuals try to rebuild their capital stock, and this should, over time, reduce the market for imported goods but also help to bridge the gap between domestic investment and savings. In the long run, this could prove beneficial to the growth and vitality of the American economy and contain the centrifugal pressures on the world trading system.

The blame for the present crisis of the liberal trading system lies both with the United States and Japan, and both countries have to take corrective measures if regime stability is to be restored. Having said that, we will, however, focus on the Japanese contribution to system stability and argue that recent Japanese foreign economic policies can be interpreted as attempts to strengthen the resilience of the trading order. Those who impute a sinister meaning to Japanese economic policies ignore the fact that Japan as a large trading nation is completely dependent on the maintenance of a liberal trading system. If there was an economic conspiracy to destroy the economic might of the United States, we could easily extend the argument to suggest that Japanese decision makers had consciously decided to self-destruct. Still, there did exist some problems and Japan could rightly be accused of not doing enough to contribute to regime stability. We argue that the shock of protectionist retaliation was sufficient to galvanize Japanese decision makers to alter the future role of Japan within the trading system. We do not argue that everything that was

3

possible or necessary had been done, but simply that a start was made to play a more positive role. This, in itself, is significant, although the full realization of Japanese potential will, no doubt, require a longer timeframe.

Even though our focus will be on the concept of regime stability, we do not necessarily wish to raise it to the level of the ultimate good, or to deny the importance of issues of equality and justice. The concerns of the Third World and those who would seek to introduce changes in the system are real, but perhaps not realistic. Essentially, the question of justice has been approached from two different perspectives: one that assumes that justice can be achieved through modifications in the system and the other that raises fundamental doubts as to the viability of achieving justice within the existing system. In the former stream of thought, we have the growing literature on the new international economic order (NIEO), which aspired to work within the system to bring about changes that would take into consideration the developmental interests of the Third World. In the latter, we have the dependency theorists who regard the system itself as repressive, with little possibility that the dominant interests would acquiesce to anything more than token concessions.

We have decided to keep issues of value separate partly because of our scepticism about the success of protest within the system, as attempts to shape a NIEO over the past decade have shown. The entire question of economic justice and equality not only relates to the system as a whole, but also the internal conditions of many of the Third World countries where experience has shown a clearly discernible trend toward greater inequality in income distribution. Whatever benefits the Third World derives from participation in the system are inequitably distributed within their societies. Thus systematic modifications alone may not have the desired egalitarian effect. A perfectly egalitarian society may not be possible, but the gap should at least narrow, not widen as it has in the past.

A related question is whether the demand for justice had the potential of undermining the stability of the liberal trading order, either by withholding support for the system or through the pursuit of autarkic policies, as is advocated by some dependency theorists. Given the Third World's small share in total trade, its withdrawal would probably not have the effect of undermining the system, although it would certainly narrow its domain. The system might not continue as the 'global' system, but it would continue to function within a more restricted boundary. It is, at the same time, highly unlikely that there would be a mass exodus from the system, which again is not to make a value statement.

In terms of structure of the book, the next two chapters provide a theoretical framework for analysis, a general overview of the attributes of the system, and a definition of the problem. The next four chapters discuss particular issues in Japanese trade policies with an emphasis on their systemic impact. While the theoretical chapters are not essential to an understanding of what follows, it is hoped that the reader will benefit from them. We should also stress the fact that the book provides an interpretation, not necessarily the definitive explanation. We are aware that there are other explanations as well, but we hope that we make a plausible argument to lend credibility to our thesis. While this book focuses on Japan's foreign economic policies and its attempts to stabilize the liberal trading system, we do not wish to suggest that Japanese initiative alone can prevent the collapse of the system. As such, the concluding chapter goes beyond the narrow focus of this book to consider some of the other factors that need to be considered as well, and to make some recommendations. The purpose of the book is to point to the inadequacy of arguments that suggest that Japan is shirking its international responsibility and/or taking a free ride on the system. These, and others that present a more negative interpretation of Japanese policies, overlook not only the genuine efforts being made by Japanese policy makers, but also fail to appreciate the objective constraints and the policy-making environment in Japan.

In keeping with Japanese customs, all Japanese names are given with the surname first. Unless otherwise indicated, all translations of Japanese-language material are this author's.

Part One

Theoretical framework: regimes and system support

2

Political Realism
and International Regimes

INTRODUCTION

The trade problems between Japan and the rest of the world have attracted considerable attention from scholars seeking to analyse the source of the frictions and to suggest solutions. These studies have been important in furthering our under-standing of the decision-making process within particular Japanese bureaucracies, the many vested interests impeding trade liberalization, the work ethics of the Japanese worker, and the frugality of the Japanese consumer, etc. Most also highlight the important fact that this island country of 120 million people is crucially dependent on international trade for its continued well-being and prosperity. This, too, is a study of Japanese trade policies, but with the added dimension of the present threat and the future viability of the world trading system as it has existed in the period following the Second World War.

Japan was the principal beneficiary of the post-war liberal international economic order (LIEO) and the future viability of its economy will depend on whether the principle of easy access to foreign markets is preserved. The importance of this becomes obvious when we consider the structure of Japanese tade. The near-total lack of raw materials domestically has forced a reliance on foreign sources of supply which could only be financed through foreign exchange earned from export trade. Commenting on this vertical nature of Japanese trade, Krause and Sekiguchi wrote that

Even though Japanese growth in the main has not been export led in the analytical sense, it does not mean that

9

exports were unimportant to growth. Export expansion has been of strategic importance principally because it has financed the growing import of raw materials and capital goods that embody new technology.[1]

Problems arose not only because Japanese exports were concentrated in a few manufactured products, but also because suppliers and buyers, for imports and exports respectively, constituted two generally distinct sets of countries. Naturally, therefore, trade accounts tended not to balance on a country-by-country basis. Broadly speaking, Japan ran trade deficits against the raw-material-exporting countries which, in turn, were balanced with surpluses against the developed industrialized countries. Trade frictions have mainly involved the latter group of countries – the United States and West European – and increased in intensity with the deterioration of the state of the world economy.

The chronic persistence of Japanese trade surplus has been a major irritant in US–Japan relations because it was perceived, by the United States, to arise largely from imperfections in the Japanese economic system and the legacy of past policies that denied foreign manufacturers 'open' access to the Japanese market. Whether real or otherwise, this contributed to an increased demand for reciprocal protectionism. This was the main threat confronting the LIEO during the 1980s. The danger was that if the American administration gave in to this protectionist sentiment, it could become the start of an unravelling process for the world trading system. Although, to its credit, the US administration remained firm in its support for liberal trade, it also was unlikely that this commitment could be sustained indefinitely without support from other 'able' and 'willing' regime members.

This crisis within the system presented Japan with some crucial choices to make about its future economic policies. At one extreme, the decision would be to continue with the present policies without any significant change in the market liberalization programme, regardless of whether or not this worsened the strains on the system. Alternatively, it could consciously seek to reorient its role in the international system as a supporter. The second alternative contains the assumption that systemic costs had drained popular support for liberal trade in the United States and that Japan, by partially relieving the United States, could help to strengthen the foundations of the regime. We will argue that recent Japanese foreign economic policies can be explained as attempts by Japan to play a stabilizing role within the trading regime.

Within the realist school of thought in international relations, the notion of regime stability has been studied by Robert Gilpin and Stephen Krasner, among others. The central idea was borrowed, with modifications, from C. P. Kindleberger's hegemonic-stability thesis. Kindleberger, on the basis of his study of the depression years of the 1930s, had concluded that regimes required the leadership of a hegemon for stability. The economic nationalism and the depression of the 1930s seemed clearly to be the result of the refusal/inability of the hegemon, the United States, to provide effective leadership. He argued that, contrary to the teachings of classical economics that free trade required only the realization of self-interest based on comparative advantage, a 'free trade system' really was brittle and, therefore, required the presence of a strong and large economy, with a natural preference for open trade, to provide leadership. According to the hegemonic-stability thesis, it could be argued that a fragmentation of power would result in a fragmentation of regimes, and instability, and that only a hegemonic actor had the capabilities to maintain an international economic order that it favoured.[2] In other words, the potential for order was seen as a direct derivative of the concentration of power within the system.[3] It is easy to see, therefore, why the realists attribute the relative stability of the LIEO for much of the post-war period to the presence of strong control and domination by the United States. The doctrine of hegemonic stability has an instant appeal for the realists, so used to explaining outcomes and behaviour in terms of power configurations within the system. In contrast, the interdependence approach denies that the success of the post-war LIEO can be attributed solely or simply to hegemonic control. It points to the declining utility of force which allegedly stands out in sharp contrast to the realities of the nineteenth century. It suggests, instead, a pattern of interest-based agenda-setting, of bargaining and negotiations. Exemplifying this alternative approach, Robert Keohane argued that while creation of liberal economic regimes may require hegemonic direction, once established such regimes could be maintained on the basis of 'shared interest' of the regime members.[4]

The two different perspectives on regime maintenance have led to different prognoses for the liberal trading order. While the realists despaired of American hegemonic decline, leading to and making difficult the management of conflict, the interdependence approach solved the problem not by denying any role for the hegemon, but by making it redundant under the present circumstances. The latter, more optimistic prognosis was possible because, Keohane argued, since co-operation becomes institutionalized over time, regimes, too, gradually become autonomous of the conditions of creation.

However, the approach taken by Keohane is less logical in its argumentation and more ideological in its commitment to a preferred outcome. It posits a distinction between the originating and maintaining conditions, but instead of demonstrating this to be true, it is taken as an assumption. Thus rules, once created, to support a regime become, with the passage of time, norms not requiring enforcement. The transformation of the essential rules into norms is possible because a regime, allegedly, serves both as a school of good behaviour and as an enlightening institution.

The theoretical arguments will be fleshed out further below, but first we must define some of the terms and concepts that we will be using. Like most concepts in the discipline, regimes have been used to mean several different things, from informal rules of international interaction to formalized institutions. Most, however, appear to accept a definition that includes a degree of order and regularity, not necessarily institutionalized but which, nevertheless, constrained state behaviour in an anarchic setting. This is clear from the writings of authors like Ruggie, Stein, Keohane, and Kratochwil. For Ruggie, a regime is composed of principles, norms, rules, and procedures; and Stein, concurring with this, wrote that a regime manifested itself when the interaction between the parties was not based on independent decision making.[5] The difference between rules and norms, according to Kratochwil, was that while rules became norms over time, not all norms displayed a rule-like characteristic.[6]

In addition to the autonomy-restricting nature of regimes, a time dimension must also be included in the definition of it. For a regime to acquire recognition as such, it must display an element of permanence, that is, it must be seen as having long-term viability. This, as will become clear later, explains why regimes appeal to the members. The literature on regimes identifies two primary functions that they serve:

1. simplify situations of choice, that is, make environmental complexity more manageable; and
2. reduce bargaining costs by providing templates for wholesale advance co-ordination.[7]

The term hegemon incorporates both political and economic potential although there exists some disagreement as to how to rank the two criteria. In the interdependence approach, a hegemon could conceivably be defined largely in terms of its economic potential, given the assumed ascendence of 'low politics' over 'high politics'. In the realist tradition, however, both the economic and the political–military aspect of hegemonic power remain intact. As Gilpin wrote, there are 'two dimensions to a hegemon's power: economic efficiency and political–military strength'.[8] First, with regard to the economic element, it should be pointed out that the absolute size of the economy, while important, is not the only critical factor, for as Kamijo Toshiaki observed, it is quite possible that in the nineteenth century both France and China had a larger absolute GNP than Britain.[9] A hegemon's economic strength, according to Keohane, depended on four factors. Thus, he wrote that, 'Hegemonic powers must have control over raw materials, control over sources of capital, control over markets, and comparative advantages in the production of highly valued goods'.[10]

Control should not be used to mean physical possession necessarily, but rather the ability to affect outcomes. Keohane suggested that this was true for the United States in the first twenty years after the Second World War, with respect to oil resources. The loss of control, thereafter, did diminish US economic strength, but it should be pointed out that OPEC, for example, had considerably less impact on the United States than on Japan or Western Europe. At the same time, the United States still possessed enough power potential to deny OPEC the ability to create an alternative oil regime, both through the creation of the International Energy Agency in 1974 and through the development of a 'special relationship' with Saudia Arabia.

The fourth prerequisite of hegemonic strength, cited by

Keohane, should be given the greater weight. An uncompetitive hegemon can hardly remain a hegemon in the long run. Competitiveness is important because it makes possible the long-term viability of a liberal trading order. This is so because it is in having an efficient economy that the hegemon could be said to have a natural preference for relatively free trade.

Under normal conditions, regime maintenance would not require the hegemon to wield its political power and it is the non-use of political–military force which makes regimes attractive. The post-war trading system was not based on overt coercion and any members was free to opt out of the system at any time, although there were just enough benefits spread around to ensure that this did not happen on a large scale. One such positive inducement to the weaker members was the Generalized System of Preference (GSP) under which the developed countries granted duty-free status to specific exports of the developing countries. At the same time, the GSP also became a mechanism to exercise influence within the system. For example, in 1985, disgruntled with the hostile and negative attitude of the less developed countries (LDCs) to the new round of multilateral trade talks, United States Trade Representative (USTR) Clayton Yeutter threatened to withdraw American GSP privileges unless the LDCs agreed to the American agenda for the trade talks and the inclusion of services trade.[11] Thus, although, according, to Kratochwil, regime members agreed to abide by the norms and rules because their 'impersonal' character distinguished them from the immediate and blatant exercise of power[12], we should be careful not to push this point too far. Rules and norms are not always of an impersonal nature.

The hegemon's military potential serves as a useful back-up tool through, at least, an implicit linkage of issues. According to Keohane, however, 'American military power served as a shield protecting the international political economy that it dominated, and it remained an important factor in the background on economic issues; but it did not frequently impinge on such issues'.[13] Directly, military power may have limited utility in dealing with other regime members and no one would go so far as to suggest that the US might use its military advantage to press for trade concessions from the other members. The US could, and did, force the Japanese market open with the 'Black Ships' of Commodore Perry off the Tokyo

Bay in the nineteenth century, but the US 7th Fleet can hardly be used in a similar manner. This is not because the utility of force *per se* had declined, but because Japan's position with respect to the United States had changed. At the same time, a total delinking of miltiary and economic issues is also not possible. The military factor may not be explicitly stated but does influence decision making. Thus, at the Washington Energy Conference in February 1974, the United States used its security commitment to Europe to secure consent for an International Energy Agency (IEA). After the first day's negotiations had ended in a deadlock, President Nixon addressed the delegates at the state dinner and clearly stated that if Europe persisted with unilateralism on energy issues, the United States might not be able to resist the growing pressure for isolationism and withdrawal from Europe. He stated that, 'Security and economic considerations are inevitably inter-linked and energy cannot be separated from either'.[14] For the Europeans, so dependent on the United States for their security, the implication was clear. The creation of the IEA was not the result of co-operation but of coercion, and without the exercise of American domination would likely have been still-born. It was also not inconsequential as a narrow reading of the effectiveness of 'stocks' policy might suggest. The IEA was instrumental in preventing a consumer–producer dialogue in which OPEC would have a dominating influence.

Furthermore, it should not be forgotten that the liberal trading order is only a subsystem operating in a 'hostile' environment. It is necessary, therefore, for the hegemon to possess sufficient capability to ward off external threats and disturbances that might affect the stability of the system. To cite Keohane, 'Sufficient military power to protect an international political economy from incursions by hostile powers is indeed a necessary condition for successful hegemony'.[15] Of course, he is not convinced that hegemony itself is necessary for regime maintenance. We will, however, argue that hegemony is required both for regime creation and regime stability, although the present condition of relative American economic decline calls for hegemony to be supplemented with regime support.

HEGEMONIC-STABILITY THESIS AND ITS CRITICS

The role of a supporter is not necessarily inconsistent with

15

hegemonic stability, but not all are agreed on the validity of the hegemonic-stability thesis itself. It has been argued that a liberal trade regime could be maintained in the absence of a hegemon and, indeed, that it was being so maintained today. The mechanism for stability, in this alternative framework, is system-wide co-operation, and it should be obvious that this makes no special provisions for the role of supporter, since all members are cast into a supporting role. In what follows, we will first outline the key features of the hegemonic stability thesis, followed by the alternative model, and finally argue in favour of modifying the hegemonic-stability thesis to incorporate a system supporter.

As mentioned, the hegemonic-stability thesis is associated with C. P. Kindleberger and his study of the Great Depression.[16] That study had led him to conclude that a liberal trade regime could only be established when a hegemonic power assumed leadership in the system. At other times, protectionism reigned supreme with the consequent danger of the creation of economic blocs and competition between them bordering on or resulting in conflict. This was readily incorporated into the realist literature. Ruggie summarized the realist position saying that

> If economic capabilities are so concentrated that a hegemon exists, as in the case of Great Britain in the mid- to late nineteenth century and the United States after World War II, an 'open' or 'liberal' international economic order is hypothesized.[17]

Kindleberger's study, however, had amply demonstrated that there was no autocorrelation between the presence of a hegemon and the creation of a liberal trading system. In Britain, free trade did not follow automatically from its economic supremacy but rather was the result of a long and hard struggle between the agricultural interests and the industrial capitalists. The process itself began well before the repeal of the Corn Laws, which was only the culmination of a lengthy process. The United States, too, only accepted leadership after domestic conditions had changed sufficiently to enable this, and leadership did not flow unhindered from its hegemonic potential.

The presence of a hegemon merely creates the conditions for

the establishment of a liberal trade regime, but it does not guarantee that this will, in fact, take place. In the inter-war period, for example, the United States, by all accounts, could provide leadership but, instead, it chose to stay outside the system due to constraints imposed by domestic political considerations. Thus, even though the United States was instrumental in securing the Versailles Treaty and in the establishment of the League of Nations, it was forced, by Congressional opposition, to remain outside the system it had helped to create. By its decision to steer clear of 'entangling alliances', the United States forfeited the opportunity to maintain order. We could blame Woodrow Wilson for failing to secure Congressional approval for the Versailles Treaty and Herbert Hoover for precipitating disorder (Smoot–Hawley Tariff Act), but Kindleberger was particularly critical of Franklin Roosevelt for failing to assume leadership at the World Economic Conference of 1933 and for displaying, what we called, 'world economic irresponsibility'.[18]

Barry Buzan highlighted the voluntaristic nature of regime creation when he wrote that

> So long as the international political system remains anarchic, it seems most unlikely that a liberal system could be created by any mechanism other than a hegemonic actor. The interesting question is whether or not an already existing liberal system can be maintained by other means when the originating hegemonic power no longer has sufficient relative strength to act as underwriter.[19]

The first part above fits neatly into the realist framework with its emphasis on anarchy as the essential characteristic of international politics. It is the presupposed anarchic nature of international politics that forms the basis of the theory that only a hegemon, with vastly superior capabilities, could impose order and create a regime based on its preferred norms of international conduct. The second part of the quotation from Buzan contains the crux of the present controversy – whether or not the originating conditions must also, and always, be the sustaining conditons. For the realists, the answer is derived very simply from the assumed anarchy of international politics. The act of 'maintaining' is no more than the act of 'recreating' and a regime, therefore, is unlikely to assert its autonomous existence.

Their critics, however, make a distinction between the two and, below, we will consider some of the main points.

David Lake challenged the realist position with the assertion that, 'there is no axiomatic relationship between hegemony and free trade or declining hegemony and protectionism', and that a non-hegemonic system could have several variants in regime structure, including the liberal order.[20] He argued that it was possible that when a hegemon faced decline, the members of a given regime would negotiate on the rules and norms so as to compensate for hegemonic decline.[21] We can well appreciate why regime members *should* act to preserve the regime, but this general interest may not be sufficient to arrive at the desired outcome and to override invididual interests. Also, it is debatable whether regimes are based on some abstract notion of general interest unless it can be shown that a regime is composed of members that are roughly equivalent in terms of economic potential. This condition, however, does not obtain and it is the economic disparity between states that makes it difficult to establish liberal trade on a non-hegemonic principle. Regimes embody the interests of the hegemon and are, therefore, more beneficial to the strong than to the weak. We must introduce the caveat, however, that a hegemon may not, as mentioned above, act on those interests either because the interests are not accurately perceived or because of domestic political constraints.

The benefits of regime leadership should not be narrowly equated purely with the gains from free trade. From the viewpoint of neo-classical economics, it might be suggested that the relative trade gains for the weaker countries were greater than for the larger countries simply because of their greater dependence on foreign trade. Larger countries, because of the size of their domestic market and better resource endowments, are usually more self-reliant and, therefore, less dependent on trade. However, the cost–benefit analysis cannot be done on purely economic terms. According to Bruce Russett,

> The gains from an open global economy surely exceeded the costs to the United States. Despite what ultimately proved to be heavy burdens that the United States shouldered to maintain an open economy, the balance sheet for Americans looks favourable when compared with the costs that other powers accepted in decolonization . . . . The major goods

provided by American postwar hegemony – 'stable peace' within much of the industrialized world, a *cordon sanitaire* around the major perceived security threat, a relatively open, expanding, and largely predictable world economy – were obtained in degrees that were not markedly sub-optimal from the American point of view.[22]

Returning to the notion of common interests, realists, like E. H. Carr, dismiss all arguments for the general interest as attempts to disguise the interest of the strong.[23] To suggest, therefore, that a regime could be sustained on the basis of the general interest through some co-operative agreement was like asserting that regime members would willingly make themselves subservient to the interest of the hegemon, in the absence of hegemonic control. As well, Lake himself pointed to the weakness of a non-hegemonic regime when he added that a non-hegemonic regime would be both more prone to protectionism and more fragile; the latter because of the incentive to cheat arising from the increased uncertainty levels in the operating environment, making empty promises of agreed rules. Every member may agree to the rules and yet few may adhere to them. In the 1920s, the European countries consistently and solemnly promised to lower tariffs and all the while raised them to still higher levels.[24] Lake, nevertheless, maintained that there was no *prima facie* evidence for firm linkage of LIEO to a hegemon, paticularly if the following two conditions were satisfied:

1. existence of moderate certainty and predictability of others' behaviour, particularly on compliance with established rules and norms; and
2. existence of successful rule-making to compensate for and to replace the hegemon.[25]

It must be pointed out, however, that it was, in fact, the hegemon that facilitated rule making and ensured rule enforcement. Also, it was the hegemon that provided relative certainty in the system, which could, otherwise, break down for lack of positive inducement or negative sanctions. Given the anarchic nature of international politics, co-operation and collusion among the regime members can hardly be taken for granted even where it can be demonstrated to be in their interest. We

19

need only to recall the analogy of the 'deer hunt' to grasp this principle. The former West German Chancellor, Helmut Schmidt, was only being realistic when he observed that, 'Neither trilateral co-operation nor worldwide co-operation is imaginable at present without American leadership'.[26]

In his book entitled *After Hegemony* Robert Keohane, using case studies of several international regimes, attempted to demonstrate the (increasingly) weak relationship between regime stability and hegemonic control. Even following the observation that, 'As American power eroded, so did international regimes',[27] he argued boldly for the possibility of regime stability in the absence of hegemonic control. This was of crucial importance because, as he stated, 'Hegemonic leadership is unlikely to be revived in this century for the United States or any other country'.[28] If, therefore, the liberal trade regime was worth saving, other mechanisms, besides hegemonic control, had to be found to ensure regime stability.

Unlike in his earlier work on complex interdependence which attempted to break away from the past because increased cross-national interdependence had, allegedly, made past patterns irrelevant to the conditions of the present, Keohane's latest book tried to find firm footing on what he called, the 'legacy' of the past. Yet, even if the past was important, the old route of regime creation and maintenance was no longer available because hegemons, in the past, had arisen from the ashes of 'world wars'. Since a world war in the nuclear age would bring about catastrophic results, it was unlikely that a new hegemon could take the old route. Thus, while emphasizing the legacy of the past, he was forced to reject it. Co-operation became the key word in his analysis and he wrote, 'If we are to have cooperation . . . it will be cooperation without hegemony'.[29] Alluding to the difficulty of this process, he was, nevertheless, optimistic that the institutions left behind by the US would continue to function because states would find it convenient to interact within regimes than outside, since uncertainty reduction was a major foreign-policy objective. Not only did this redefine regimes largely in terms of institutional structures, but missing from the analysis, also, was any discussion of what values such a non-hegemonic regime would pursue. He gives the impression that regime members would continue to abide by values cherished by the former hegemon, for example, on trade with the Eastern Bloc countries, and the role of the Third

World within the regime. Values are important because the LIEO is not based on the principle of perfect free trade. The rules are not value free, and as Gilpin pointed out, the interests served by existing regimes will reflect 'the interests of the most powerful members'.[30] Besides being utopian in his conclusions, Keohane's position is, at least subconsciously, ideological: 'it is easier to maintain them [regimes] than it would be to create new ones'.[31] Therefore, an American hegemony could be maintained, even when the basis for that hegemony no longer existed.

In game-theoretic language, it can be safely assumed that in a two-person prisoner's dilemma, the outcome of each game will be different in terms of whether or not the game was single play or iterative, with co-operative behaviour more likely in the latter case. Theoretically, the case for co-operation within a regime is strengthened because, as we said, regime maintenance could also be viewed as regime reproduction and, therefore, as an iterative play of the game of prisoner's dilemma. However, although co-operation may obtain in an iterative two-person prisoner's dilemma, if we increased the number of players, the same pattern may no longer be observable. In a regime composed of many players, the configuration of behaviour patterns is rarely symmetrical and while a co-operative behavioural mode may be present, defection, too, is not unlikely. In any large group there is an inherent tendency to free-ride, which the hegemon, it is assumed, helps to keep in control. If the mechanism of control became weak or non-existent, it would be reasonable to assume that the problem of free-ridership would increase sufficiently to threaten regime stability.

If the difficulty of maintaining non-hegemonic regimes was that the absence of hegemon reduced long-term certainty and predictability of the actions of others, Keohane made the counter-argument that the presence of institutions set up during the period of American hegemony and which generate and disseminate 'high-quality information' served to enhance the levels of certainty and that these institutions could function independently. Thus, he asserted that realism needed 'to be reformulated to reflect the impact of information-providing institutions on state behaviour, even when rational egoism persists'.[32] Functional institutions aside, Keohane assumed that all, or most, institutions would continue to function efficaciously even under the changed circumstances. This, however, needs to be demonstrated rather than assumed. Realists do not deny the usefulness of these institutions but question their ability to modify state behaviour. Institutions like the World Health Organizations would, probably, continue to function, but could we confidently say the same for the General Agreement on Tariffs and Trade (GATT) or the International Monetary Fund? GATT is already confronted with a challenge of sorts from France and the, so-called, 'Gang of Four' – India, Brazil, Egypt, and Venezuela – over the new round of trade talks. Also, it seems unreasonable to impute to information a rationalizing role. Robert Jervis showed that misperception was not an uncommon phenomenon and John Steinbruner, too, persuasively argued that decision makers tend only to accept information that conforms to preconceived views and that the cognitive belief systems act as a mental block against conflicting information.[33] The point is not that misperceptions in a non-hegemonic system are more prolific, but simply that they may be more difficult to manage.

Keohane's excessive faith in rational state behaviour is also reflected in his discussion of regimes under the assumptions of bounded rationality. Bounded rationality is a concept which relaxes the assumptions of strict rationality to suggest the possibility that, given time constraints, decision makers may exhibit only utility-satisfying behaviour rather than utility maximization. He argued that, even under bounded rationality, states would inevitably realize that the 'alternatives to regimes are less attractive than they would be if the assumptions of classical rationality were valid'.[34] This, he suggested, was because regimes freed decision makers from the costs of constant certainty calculations, but this is essentially an argument for why states prefer to work within regimes rather than outside. It does not really enlighten us as to how a non-hegemonic regime may be maintained over time.

In criticizing the non-realist approach, the intention has not been to suggest that the realist formulation of the hegemonic stability thesis is without fault. A well-founded criticism was that of Duncan Snidal who wrote that the theory of hegemonic stability contained a 'virtually hidden assumption: *Collective action is impossible*'. This, however, is hardly a hidden assumption but rather fairly obvious, which he, himself, found to be 'well demonstrated in Kindleberger's negative assessment of the likelihood of Japan and West Germany overcoming their private interests to collaborate with a (less than dominant) United States in providing collective economic leadership'.[35] The notion of collective leadership, it should be pointed out, is different from that of co-operative management because, while the former retains the concept of leadership, the latter finds leadership to be an obsolete concept. Our argument is precisely that Japan, at least, is moving beyond its early mercantilist policies to assume a greater responsibility for regime stability and that this became possible because of a convergence of interest between the United States and Japan. This convergence of interest, however, should not be taken to mean perfect harmony and we do not rule out the possibility of conflict, particularly on procedural matters.

It is true, as Snidal pointed out, that we have tended to view the hegemon as a unitary actor, whereas present conditions may demand that we assess the possibility of collective leadership. In Japan, several authors, including Okita Saburo, have argued for both its desirability and inevitability. Okita Saburo, a former foreign minister, suggested that the current system of American leadership be replaced with collective leadership because stability could not be entrusted solely to the United States and, especially, because factors internal to the United States had emerged as the principal threat to the system. Similarly, Stoga argued that the future stability of the LIEO required careful consideration of a system of collective leadership. He wrote that, 'Reinvigoration of the free trade and payments economic system with US or shared US–Japanese–West German leadership holds the greatest promise for the world economy and indeed, probably for the US economy'.[36]

Although collective leadership can take various forms, not all the variants have an equal likelihood of success. An important determining factor would be the size of the decision-making structure. Evidence from group theory suggests that decision making in small groups is more effective than in larger groups which are often paralyzed by inaction. This is because in a large group there is little incentive for individual action, since the outcome would, in any case, be a public good. A public good is characterized by non-exclusivity and jointness of supply, which essentially means that the benefits cannot be denied to any member whether or not cost sharing is enforced. This particular feature of public good is why free-ridership becomes a natural

23

tendency in large groups. Thus, it is easy to see why the annual summit meetings between the leaders of the industrialized countries have been less than effective. Rhetorical protestations of unity and amity can be found in plenty, but actual agreements have been difficult to reach. The paucity of meaningful achievements has made the exercise of summitry a hollow affair of pomp and pageantry. The Bonn summit of 1985 was the first one in six years to specify, in the most general and non-binding terms, the role expected of each of the seven participating countries in the field of growth and employment for the stability of the global economy.[37]

A more successful variant would be a smaller group with a demonstrable convergence of interest and willingness to share the costs, but which still retained the concept of a powerful core. We argue that a leadership structure incorporating Japan and the United States could be effective. Even so, Sakamoto Masahiro argued that the United States would still have to retain veto powers because, despite its relative decline, it was still the most powerful country as well as the provider of military security within the system.[38]

Accordingly, our notion of collective leadership is based on a leader and system supporter. The concept of system supporter is borrowed from David Lake. Expanding on Kindleberger's classificatory scheme, Lake suggested that there were four state categories that could be discerned within an international system: leaders; supporters; spoilers; and free-riders.[39] Using this classification system, we will apply the concept of supporter to Japan and try to understand its explanatory potential in reference to recent Japanese foreign economic policies. The supporter should not be regarded as a blind follower of the hegemon, and this leaves open the possibility of conflict. But what makes a regime member a supporter, besides its economic potential, is a demonstrable interest and an apparent lack of political power to assume leadership. Formally, Lake defined supporters as countries that, 'because of their high relative productivity, value export markets more than protection at home, but will sacrifice the latter only if necessary to obtain the former'.[40]

In borrowing the notion of system supporter, we wish to differentiate it somewhat from the meaning given to it by David Lake. He suggested when a regime had an effective leader, the supporter would tend to free-ride and that when a leader was no longer present, their interests would force them to change their past free-rider policies. This would assume that a regime either had a robust leader or had autonomy. This assumption cannot be given too much credibility, although Stephen Krasner did take this position arguing that the constraint on American protectionism was the existence of a liberal trading regime, even if this was of a temporary nature and the results of 'regime inertia'.[41] The linkage, however, is difficult to substantiate and to disprove, but it should be pointed out that protectionist pressures have always been a part of American domestic politics. If American decision makers have, indeed, been constrained by the regime, then it becomes important to show that they would otherwise prefer to take the protectionist route. There is no evidence of this and, on the contrary, Judith Goldstein argued that, 'American central decision makers continue to be as committed to liberal trade today as they have been in any previous period in American history'.[42]

That may be somewhat overstating the American commitment to free trade, for it cannot be denied that the United States has had a chequered history in foreign economic policies. However, in the post-war period, there is little evidence to suggest a dramatic change in the professed free trade principles. This is not to suggest that there is no threat to the system, but if we accepted the autonomy thesis it would become difficult to rationalize the role of a supporter, since that would be a natural outcome in the absence of a hegemon. Instead, we argue that a supporter's main role is when the hegemon confronts relative decline in the system and is unable to provide effective unitary leadership as before. The role of the supporter is to take on an additional burden of cost sharing and to adopt measures that mitigate the domestic pressures on the hegemon to renounce its position as leader. Yet, just as the hegemon has to contend with domestic political factors, the supporter, too, cannot ignore the domestic variables that may impinge upon their ability to provide systemic support. As such, we do not wish to imply a causal relationship between interest and system support. Interest constitutes a necessary condition that must be obtained as a precondition to successful support, but it becomes a sufficient condition only when the domestic factors so allow. In the case of Japan, interest and economic capabilities are sufficiently present to make a reasonably sound argument for Japan as system supporter. However, the enabling conditions must also be considered and a significant portion of this study will try to address the problem of internal constraints.

We need to reiterate, also, the importance of keeping 'system-supportive' and 'leader-supportive' acts separate. This is particularly important in the context of US–Japan relations because Japan, in the past, was excessively dependent on the United States both for its military security and economic survival. As it consolidates its position as a supporter, it should be more able to assert its independence and this might become the source of conflict between it and the United States in the future. The new leadership structure would require the United States to be more attentive and responsive to the interests of Japan, unlike in the past when it could enforce its own interests. If Japan is to accept a greater share of the burden of regime maintenance, it would be natural to expect it to want a greater say in the distribution of benefits.

The role of a system supporter can be justified on the basis of structural changes within the system. In the interdependence approach, the structural changes made co-operation inevitable if the system was to remain stable, but we will argue that these same structural changes have created an opening for system supporter which we consider a more realistic outcome as compared to co-operation. According to Kenneth Waltz, a system is composed of the structure and the interacting units of the system. The relationship between the structure of a system and the units – agencies – is explained in the following terms: 'Agents and agencies act; systems as wholes do not. But the action of agents and agencies are affected by the system's structure'.[43] The structure of a system is largely defined by the ordering principle or the hierarchical positioning of the units in terms of power and capabilities. The concept of system supporter is developed on the basis of relative changes in the positioning of states, that is, in the structure. The structural change is presumed to be the result of the decline of the United States as compared to Western Europe and Japan. Since structure affects interests and, subsequently, the behaviour patterns, we argue that changes in the relative positioning of interacting units within the system which may be linked to the rise of protectionism in the United States may also be seen as the determinant of Japan as system supporter. Japan's interest in the stability of the LIEO can be easily seen in the importance of liberal trade to its economic survival. Japan was the principal beneficiary of the LIEO in the past and the continued stability of the LIEO will be equally important in the future. There may be other gains as well, if the Japanese yen should become an international currency. As Stoga observed, Japan stood to gain from a '. . . loosening of constraints on economic policy that results from the reserve-currency status'.[44] Not only for Japan, but the structural changes have also, as is to be expected, altered the role of the United States within each regime area.

Thus, with respect to the oil regime, although the United States no longer had the capabilities to deny the creation of an alternative regime dominated by OPEC. The present role of the United States in the international oil regime could be analysed using the concept of 'system spoiler'. It denied Mexico the option of joining OPEC under the threat of withdrawal of its GSP privileges and effectively prevented independence in energy policies within the oil-consuming countries, through the IEA. One US source acknowledged the success of American policies saying, 'The United States uses its bilateral relations with producing countries, particularly Saudi Arabia, to support IEA decisions.[45]

Within the trading regime, the relative decline of the United States undermined the domestic consensus on liberal trade on the grounds that the costs of regime creation had brought on the relative decline. At the same time, it created opportunities for other countries to play a more active role in buttressing the stability of the system. Even so, the American role remains crucial because its relative hegemonic position gave it an effective power of veto in the system. The continued importance of the United States to system stability explains our focus, though not exclusively, on the US–Japan nexus. Much of American protectionism can be traced to its trading relations with Japan and this makes it particularly interesting to examine this aspect of intra-systemic interactions.

One example of the new leadership principle can be seen in the agremeent reached in September 1985 (the G-5 agreement), at a meeting of the finance ministers of the five Western industrialized countries, to lower the value of the American dollar. The two key elements of the G-5 agreement were, first, to lower the value of the dollar and, second, to restore fiscal balance in the United States and demand expansion in Japan. As a result of this agreement, as of late 1987, the dollar had declined approximately 70 per cent against the Japanese yen.

Not only the implementation, but the very process of achieving the G-5 agreement revealed the principle of collective leadership at work along with the powers of veto retained by the United States. For several years prior to the agreement, Japan had consistently argued that it was largely an overvalued US dollar that was responsible for Japanese trade surpluses and American deficits. The United States, however, consistently refused to accept a lower dollar value fearing that such a step would force it to lower domestic interest rates, diminishing its capacity to fund the huge federal budget deficits, and undermine the anti-inflationary policies of the administration. Despite repeated calls from Japan and its other trading partners, the United States adamantly stuck with its position. In the February 1984 Economic Report of the President to the Congress of the United States, Reagan, even after admitting that the high dollar value had exacerbated the trade deficits, went on to state that, 'I am . . . firmly opposed to any attempt to depress the dollar's exchange value by intervention in international currency markets'.[46] Yet, a year later, he had no misgivings about intervening in the markets to lower artificially the dollar value. There were a number of factors behind the shift in policy, but one was the ability of the then Japanese Finance Minister, Takeshita, as he himself insists, to convince the US government on the imperative for exchange-rate adjustments if protectionism was to be contained.

In essence, we argue that a supporter, defined as a state with demonstrable interest in the stability of the LIEO but lacking the political power to provide leadership, is consistent with the basis elements of the hegemonic-stability thesis. The interest-power disjuncture, which forms the basis of supportership, applies well to the case of Japan and is unlikely to change significantly in the near future. We will, accordingly, argue that a realization of this basic dilemma invigorated Japanese leadership to chart a new direction in economic policies and take on a more positive role in the maintenance of the liberal trading order.

3

The Post-war Liberal International Economic Order

COSTS AND BENEFITS OF REGIME MAINTENANCE

According to the hegemonic-stability thesis, the maintenance of a liberal trading regime imposes costs as well as accords benefits to the hegemonic leader. Drawing upon the historical decline of *pax britannica* as well as the more recent decline of *pax americana*, many analysts have assumed and argued that the long-term costs associated with leadership outweigh the potential benefits. Indicative of this viewpoint, Andrew Mack argued that, 'neo-Marxist claims to the contrary, America's globalist policies were never self-financing – let alone profitable'.[1] The Nixon Doctrine of 1971, therefore, he stated, was a response to the unbearable costs of hegemonic control, an attempt to achieve 'hegemony on the cheap' that was, however, laden with contradictions because, 'It was illusory to believe that America's allies would be prepared to bear an increasingly larger share of the costs of *pax americana* while allowing the US to continue to play its traditional role unchallenged'.[2]

The contention that costs exceed benefits is difficult to reconcile with the realist perspective in which states are seen as engaged in a single-minded pursuit of the national interest and altruism, too, is only a disguised form of national interest. It becomes impossible to explain why self-serving states should follow policies which lead to their ultimate decline. It may be possible to suggest that states are, perhaps, not too prescient or rational in the calculations of the long-term consequences as they are of their short-term benefits. Stein, for example, distinguishing between absolute and relative gain to the hegemon from liberal trade wrote that, 'To maximize one's own return requires a commitment to openness regardless of what others do. To maximize one's relative position, on the other hand, calls for a policy of continued closure irrespective of others' policies'. Thus, he argued, hegemons 'do not impose openness, they bear its costs'.[3]

This may explain a relative decline of the hegemon but does not resolve the issue of whether relative decline necessarily undermines the leadership abilities of the hegemon. Logically, relative decline should not, by itself, be a cause for series concern. As we would expect, Britain did experience a relative decline in the nineteenth century, but the collapse of the 'free trade' system was due rather to the refusal of the European countries and the United States, the emergent countries, to remain within and support the system. It was in these terms that Kindleberger criticized the United States for displaying world economic irresponsibility.

It is, perhaps, 'fortunate' that, unlike Germany and the United States under *pax britannica*, the countries that could potentially 'spoil' the liberal trading system today, Japan and West Germany, are closely linked to the hegemon through the NATO alliance and the US–Japan Security Treaty. This important distinction between *pax britannica* and *pax americana* is enough to rule out any simplistic comparative assessment of the implications of hegemonic decline. More importantly, the rise of West Germany and Japan, and the relative decline of the United States under *pax americana*, did not simply develop by chance but was consciously engineered to enhance, not under-cut, stability. Also, the different context of relative decline must be kept in mind. In the nineteenth century, relative British decline was potentially more destabilizing because free trade then was based, largely, on crude intersectoral notions of comparative advantage. In the post-war period, however, the composition of trade had altered significantly to include intrasectoral comparative advantage, meaning that relative decline itself had to be qualified in the context of trade sectors. This was possible because of increased industrial specialization and broadening of the domain of industrial activity.

Hegemonic power is usually defined as preponderence over other members of the regime but without any clear reference to the magnitude of preponderence. The reason for this is that discussions of magnitude or threshold levels can hardly be supported by objective criteria. It cannot simply be asserted that a hegemon be, at least, three or four times as large as its nearest rival for it to be able to exercise leadership. Likewise, it would be fallacious to argue that since the magnitude of preponderence had dropped to, say, a factor of two, the hegemon, therefore, had lost the ability to lead. We could, of course, accept such logic as a matter of faith or convenience, but we could neither justify nor defend them. Both Britain and the United States may have been in a similar position at the close of the Napoleonic Wars and the Second World War, respectively, but according to Ernest Bevin, Britain in the earlier period held only 30 per cent of the world's wealth compared to about 50 per cent for the United States in the late 1940s.[4]

Relative decline simply refers to a narrowing of the gap separating the hegemon and the second largest country without a reversal in their relative standing. In itself, this is not sufficient to deny the hegemon control over the system unless it is also accompanied by a secular economic decline. When that happens, the system must either be reconstituted under a new hegemon, which is unlikely under the present conditions, or generate supporters. A supporter, as we defined earlier, is a country with demonstrable interest in regime stability but lacking the leadership qualities. While the hegemon would continue to exercise its powers of veto, a joint hegemon–supporter leadership necessarily implies a greater level of bargaining and co-ordination within the system. Elements of such policy co-ordination can be discerned in the G-5 exchange-rates agreement of 1985. When Japan and the West European countries originally proposed curency revaluation, the United States, finding it less to its advantage, promptly vetoed such proposals. When, later, it finally agreed to devalue the dollar, it had to accept the condition, imposed by the others, to manage its fiscal affairs more prudently. This, however, was soon forgotten and only after the stock market crash of 1987 did the United States show any serious sign of coming to terms with its fiscal deficits.

Returning to the issue of regime maintenance, the costs to the United States of its leadership have been assessed by Sakamoto Masahiro, a senior researcher with the Japan Trade Association.[5] For comparative purposes, Sakamoto estimated the cost burdens for five developed countries: the United States, West Germany, Japan, France, and the United Kingdom. The indicators used by Sakamoto included defence expenditures, foreign aid, contribution to the United Nations, reserve currency role, and international trade, which were weighted for the GNP of each country. Not surprisingly, he reached the conclusion that the American costs of regime maintenance had been proportionately greater than that of the other countries. However, while Germany, France, and the United Kingdom were not too far behind the United States, except on some indicators, Japan was found lagging behind in all except in terms of contributions to the United Nations.

Based on his findings, Sakamoto argued that the American decline was due to the fact that the United States, had to shoulder a disproportionately larger share of the costs. He advocated a greater burden sharing by Japan since that would be in its own long-term interests. While there was nothing wrong with the findings, his logic was not convincing. First, in so far as the costs, as he identified them, were responsible for the American decline, it should be pointed out that all he demonstrated was that American costs were greater than costs to the other countries, and not that costs exceeded the benefits, tangible or otherwise. Second, of the various indicators used by Sakamoto, only three could be classified as true costs of regime maintenance: the reserve currency role, international trade, and defence expenditures.

With respect to foreign aid, it is by no means certain that it is a cost for the aid giver, since it also brings important benefits, perhaps more than offsetting the dollar costs. Foreign aid has been used, typically, to secure export markets for domestic producers and the origin of this motivation can be traced back to the Marshall Plan. At that time, the Undersecretary of State for Economic Affairs, Will Clayton, argued that the United States would need export markets for $14 billion worth of US goods a year to stave off the possibility of over capacity in the economy.[6] The Marshall Plan was partly a response to this American fear. Aid to the Third World, particularly in the early years of tied aid, served a similar purpose.

As legitimate costs, we might include the various concessions allowed to Japan and Western Europe, especially in the early post-war period. For these much weaker economies, there was a genuine fear that, under liberal trade, not only would it be difficult to develop their industrial potential, but also that the existing industries might be swamped and overrun by American capital. Obviously, the commitment to liberal trade could not have been what the United States may have hoped for. When faced with a similar situation in the nineteenth century, Britain resorted to colonial subjugation. This, however, was not possible for the United States. The only alternative was to make concessions to the needs of these countries in the hope that, once strong, they would become supporters of the system. Thus, after the war, the United States acquiesced to the pursuit of protectionist policies by Western Europe and Japan, while at the same time allowing relatively open access to its own market. Bhagwati and Irwin termed this an internationalized version of 'affirmative action',[7] which was, in general, more successful than its domestic counterpart in the United States. Other measures were also taken to enhance their export potential. For example, in the case of Japan, the General Headquarters of the Supreme Commander of the Allied Powers (SCAP) set the yen–dollar exchange rate at Y360=$1 as opposed to the pre-war rate of Y2.50=$1. Tristan E. Beplat, who was in charge of money and banking issues for the occupation forces, recalled that the SCAP did this because, 'We wanted the Japanese to be able to export . . .'. This was playing it safe since, as he put it, 90 per cent of Japanese exports could probably sell at the Y300 level.[8]

Robert Keohane identified three specific benefits that other regime members derived from the US-led liberal economic order.

1. A stable international monetary system with provision of sufficient liquidity.
2. An open market in the United States.
3. Access to oil at stables prices. The United States and American multinational corporations (MNCs) provided oil to Europe and Japan from the Middle East where the oil MNCs were dominant and, in emergencies, from the United States itself, as in 1956–7.[9]

The US policies were designed to provide temporary advantages to Western Europe and Japan and it is ironical that the success of these policies is often cited as evidence that costs exceeded the benefits to the United States. This is so, whenever we use statistics on the GNP ratios between these countries to suggest the decline of the United States. These results were intended as such, but what became problematic was that the process that was intended to be of a temporary nature, lasted longer than desirable. The Japanese economy remained relatively closed to foreign competitors while domestic manufacturers in Japan continued to take advantage of open markets elsewhere to boost productive capacity. This is, today, the most important factor aggravating protectionist sentiment in the United States. Amaya Naohiro, former Vice-minister for International Affairs, Ministry of International Trade and Industry (MITI), wrote that there was a need today to

> search for fair handicaps that will compensate for differing levels of ability and right the structural imbalance on international accounts. The first step is a new round of multilateral trade talks under GATT to review and revise GATT rules and standards and to breathe new life into a threatened but admirable institution.[10]

Rather than relative GNP figures, a more accurate measure of economic decline can be obtained by comparing productivity levels (table 3.1). Indeed, this testifies to the problems that the US economy has been faced with since the early 1960s.

Table 3.1 Productivity gains (%)

	1963–73	1973–9
United States	1.9	0.1
Japan	8.7	3.4
West Germany	4.6	3.2
France	4.6	2.7
United Kingdom	3.0	0.3

Source: Sakamoto, M. (1981) *Keizai Taikoku no Chosen*, Tokyo: Nihon Seisan-sei Honbu, p. 78.

Although 'industrial strength' is a difficult concept to measure, it is important to gain a perspective on it as the determinant of a country's outlook on liberal trade. As Harry Johnson concluded, it may be possible to arrange countries in order of increasing protectionism and decreasing industrial might.[11] Productivity trends may be used as one indicator of industrial might, or at least as a measure of future direction. As Table 3.1 shows, increases in American productivity levels have lagged well behind those of other advanced industrial countries since the early 1960s. Productivity losses could be due to a host of factors, but the one that appeals most to the American public is the burden of regime maintenance. Sluggish export growth, resulting from closed markets overseas, may bite into productivity gains by restricting the possibilities for economies of scale, but this should not normally be a source of serious concern in a large market economy. Alternatively, it could be argued that it was the rising level of imports that was driving American businesses out of their own domestic markets. But to restrict imports, however, would be only to treat the symptoms rather than the causes. These were an obsolescent production technology and poor labour–management relations etc. that made it difficult for American companies to compete with foreign manfuacturers in their own domestic markets. The trade imbalance is, to an extent, a reflection of these underlying forces. In turn, it eroded the earlier, even if shallow, consensus on liberal trade starting as early as the 1970s. Marina Whitman expressed these protectionist tendencies as

> pressures for the United States to forswear not only dominance but leadership as well, and for the reconstitution of the international economic system along strictly symmetrical lines, in which the United States would occupy no special roles, enjoy no unique privileges, and take no particular responsibility for the viability of the system as a whole.[12]

Some US administration officials, eager to help restore the earlier consensus on open trade, asserted that US export competitiveness had actually improved over the past decade. Testifying before a House Ways and Means Subcommittee, Bergsten, Assistant Secretary of Treasury for International Affairs in the Carter Administration, said,

> The US share of industrial country exports . . . ended the decade (1970s) slightly smaller than in 1970, when viewed in terms of nominal values. To get an accurate view of the market shares, however, it is necessary to look at these shares in real terms . . . the very strong export volume growth of 1978 and 1979 resulted in a market share at the end of decade of 20.4 per cent – a full percentage point higher

than the 1972 trough, and slightly higher than our share at the start of the decade.[13]

These findings, however, were based on a group of countries lumped together, which necessarily concealed movement of individual countries within the group.

The important fact is that the present crisis of the liberal trading order cannot be managed by assertions that the United States had actually not done too badly or that there was no cause for concern. The deterioration in the state of the American economy and the dislocations within the industrial structure caused by 'excessive' import penetration are legitimate grounds for disquietude. The only long-term solution would be to revitalize American industrial structure and greater support, from the other large economies, to regime stability.

THE POST-WAR LIBERAL TRADING SYSTEM

The post-war liberal international economic order was based on the two principles of open markets/liberal trade on the one hand and decentralized decision making on the other. The reality, it needs hardly be mentioned, only roughly approximated these two guiding principles.

Based on the above two principles of the regime, we would naturally exclude from its purview states that maintain a command economy – the Soviet Union, Eastern Europe, and the People's Republic of China. Although some of the East European countries – Poland, Romania, and Yugoslavia – do participate in the GATT, the underlying philosophy of GATT, as Sydney Golt wrote 'is precisely to limit, and subject to control and, where necessary, surveillance, the distortion of the market produced by state intervention'.[14] Even in some of the other countries, decentralized decision making is only partially realized. There exists a vast literature that demonstrates, for example, the high level of government intervention in the Japanese economy. Yet there remains a basic difference between government intervention, as in Japan, and other command economies, in so far as 'administrative guidance' in Japan was not 'mandatory but only indicative . . . whereas in a command economy, everyone's action is always potentially subject to discretionary, mandatory, and specific direction by government'.[15] The thesis of Japan Inc., too, was only partially realized in the 1950s. Still, we do not deny that the Japanese government plays a more intrusive role in its economy, than do other Western governments in theirs. Indeed, the 'indicative nature' of administrative guidance can, and at times in the past did, take on an authoritarian characteristic, as Chalmers Johnson illustrated with reference to MITI's plan to stabilize steel prices, in the 1960s, by forcing production cuts and the unsuccessful attempt by Sumitomo Metal to defy the 'recommendation'.[16] It would be unwise, however, to generalize from this. We could cite numerous instances to attest to the failure of the MITI to control the direction of specific industries. If the government had, at its disposal, the discretionary powers enjoyed in the centrally planned economies, there would today be fewer car manufacturers in Japan.

With respect to the second principle of free trade, no one is under the least bit of illusion that it has been realized. Rather, as Stein noted, the years of free trade were only 'periods of *freer* trade'.[17] From the very beginning, it was agreed that trade expansion would be controlled and managed. These controls were necessitated by the economic disparities between the members of the regime and the reluctance of states to accept limits to their economic sovereignty. Even so, there was a general commitment to strive for progressive liberalization in trade flows. The present protectionism, however, threatens to reverse the process of liberalization. The danger was that, unless controlled, it could ultimately weaken the political will in the United States to maintain an open economy and, thereby, lead to the dissolution of the international trading system. For stable liberal trade, it is important that the leading economy maintain open trade. According to Wolf:

The most important role of large market economies in world trade is as the major market on which all can rely and in which global supply and demand can be balanced relatively smoothly. If a major market is suddenly cut off from the rest of the world, especially by quantitative controls, the impact of global supply and demand fluctuations will be felt more sharply in the remaining open markets. Partly for this reason, such protectionism tends to spread rapidly.[18]

The hegemon in the liberal trade regime, by virtue of its large economy, serves as an important vent for releasing the possible tensions arising from periodic global supply and demand imbalances, which if left unresolved might create pressure for states to erect barriers around their domestic economy. How this 'vent' for surplus works was illustrated by Bernstein:

> In the past three years, producers (in Europe and Japan) found that the growth of their capacity far outstripped the growth of home demand, and in order to maintain output and employment they increased their exports. As the United States is a very large market for all types of manufactured goods, a deficiency in home demand could be offset by capturing a moderately larger share of the US market.[19]

In the absence of adjustment mechanisms within the system, it is possible that the Japanese government, for example, might have been tempted to raise trade barriers to protect domestic manufacturers. The problem, of course, is that the United States can no longer, by itself, continue to provide this adjustment mechanism for the rest of the world.

In the United States, protectionism was particularly strong in Congress. This was because Congressmen, like politicians everywhere, had to appear responsive and sensitive to demands from their constituents, if only for electoral purposes. In 1985, for example, the US Congress passed several protectionist trade resolutions against Japan and, as of late 1985, there were about 360 protectionist bills (300 in the House; 60 in the Senate) pending that sought to provide relief to various affected industries. The reason Japan became the target of Congressional wrath was due, in the main, to the following two factors.

1. The perception that Japanese imports into the United States were causing significant damage to American industries. Such concerns could be traced back to the days of the textiles dispute, but with trade conflicts involving the critical areas of US industrial structure, like steel and auto, the level of protectionist sentiment had increased dramatically.
2. The belief that the Japanese government unfairly kept out American products from its domestic market. This, too, is a long standing irritant in US–Japan trade relations centering around a number of agricultural products, tobacco, and telecommunications equipment. But, unlike in the past,

current US demands do not focus exclusively on any specific industry. Rather, American attention, in recent years, was centred on the inequities within the Japanese economic structure. The ballooning US trade deficit led to the belief that piecemeal efforts were no longer enough to eliminate the trade imbalance between the two countries.

On top of the objective conditions influencing the rise of protectionism, the immediate political considerations of the members of Congress played a catalytic role. Their protectionist demands, in 1985, could be partly attributed to the fact that 1986 was an election year and 32 Senators, including 22 Republicans, had to face the test of re-election. Of the 22 Republicans, 16 had won their first election in 1980, riding the crest of President's Reagan's popularity, and because their claim on incumbency was of recent vintage, there was a greater danger of losing office if they appeared to be insensitive to the popular mood. These considerations were enough to tip the balance in favour of protectionism.

Despite the highly volatile mood of Congress, the US administration remained firmly committed to the principles of liberal trade. It viewed liberal trade as being in the general interest of American economic revitalization. Noting that one out of every eight jobs in the manufacturing sector was export based, Bergsten argued that, 'Our future prosperity at home is closely tied to our success in boosting sales abroad . . . We must avoid protectionist trade policies, at home and abroad, which would shrink our export markets just when we need their maximum expansion'.[20] Nevertheless, Congress could not allow itself to be seen as having abandoned its electorate and various interest groups. It must be admitted, however, that the rhetoric flowing out of Congress did have some functional effect on US trading partners. Foreign governments could not ignore the passions being stirred in the United States and this, probably, made them more amenable to listen and respond to American demands. This may be as much as Congress had really hoped for.

To placate an irate Congress, President Reagan in early September 1985 promised to take action under Article 301 of the Trade Act of 1974 against Japan, the European Community (EC), and Brazil unless they ceased their 'unfair' trade practices with respect to certain items by 31 December 1985.[21] He also outlined a new trade policy to include granting of export subsidies of about $300 million. No one was under the slightest illusion that this token gesture would significantly boost US exports, but it was still good politics. Such measures, while contrary to the principles of liberal trade, could still be justified as necessary to counter the greater evil of large-scale protectionism.

JAPAN AS SYSTEM SUPPORTER

It is unlikely that Japan can, today or in the near future, take upon itself the leadership role. At the same time, as mentioned above, the US capacity to continue to provide a 'vent' for surplus management had weakened. Such conditions raise questions about the future stability of the LIEO unless supportive mechanisms are created to fill the void. In Japan, there is a clear understanding that its future prosperity will be determined by whether or not the existing trade regime remained intact. It is accepted that Japan's post-war growth and economic resurgence was due largely to easy access to foreign markets and that maintenance of a favourable regime required Japan to play a more active and supportive role. Prime Minister Nakasone, noting the importance of external factors in Japan's economic development, voiced the concern that, 'Today . . . we see that there is an unprecedented rise of protectionism caused by delays in structural adjustment, bringing high levels of unemployment and accompanying large imbalances in the current account, and which threatens to undermine the free trade system'. He went on to propose that, 'In order to strengthen the free trade system . . . Japan will need to play a role both important and commensurate with its status in the world economy'.[22] Foreign pressure, too, has helped to reinforce this perception.

Writing on the irony of post-war changes, James Morley suggested that by pressuring Japan to take on a greater burden for maintaining the LIEO, liberalize its economy to American and foreign imports, and show a greater sensitivity to the weakened sectors of the American economy, 'We [the US] are picking up the role Japan played in the post-war period and Japan is being thrust in ours'.[23] However, while we make a case for Japan as system supporter, we do not argue for role reversal, as the above quotation may imply.

To substantiate the argument that recent Japanese economic policies can be analysed under the framework of regime supporter, it is necessary to demonstrate a clear break from past policies of trade liberalization. The process of economic liberalization in Japan was begun in the mid-1960s, but it is only in the 1980s that we find evidence in the Japanese decision-making process that liberalization was not simply to be grudgingly accepted but had to be accelerated in the interest of stabilizing the trade regime. The early period, therefore, could be viewed in terms of Japanese response to American and foreign pressure whereas, in the 1980s, the same process has been rationalized essentially in terms of self-interest. This was particularly true of the Action Programme of 1985. The previous six market-opening measures had very little impact on the import side and Japan's import of manufactures, as a percentage of total imports, remained well below similar figures for the United States, EC, and other advanced countries. While the Action Programme, too, may not have an immediate impact on manufactured imports, it will be argued that it was sufficiently different from the past pattern to warrant recognition as a significant new departure. This, however, is not to deny the utility of foreign pressure, but its utility is in the somewhat different area of facilitating decision making, given the constraints of the consensual approach to decision making in Japan. Foreign pressure, in the earlier period of economic liberalization in Japan, was instrumental in achieving that objective, but its utility today is more of a tactical nature, useful in overcoming the narrow interests of disaffected groups and in securing consensus. This argument will be explored further in later chapters.

Returning now to the broader issue of leadership and support, we should make clear that we do not necessarily postulate an institutionalized framework. From the Japanese point of view, supportership has essentially been conceptualized as involving two separate lines of action. First, it was defined to mean that Japan had to co-operate with the United States in reversing its economic decline, a strategy designed to revitalize American leadership function. This aspect of supportership is particularly evident in the writings of Amaya Naohiro. Second, it meant that Japan had to accept a greater burden to ensure that regime costs did not weigh too heavily on one individual country. There was the recognition that Japan had not pulled its weight in the international system and that the costs had to be more evenly apportioned.

This reappraisal of Japanese role within the system benefited from the internationalization of one of the most conservative arms of the Japanese bureaucracy – the Ministry of International Trade and Industry (MITI). The process of change within MITI started in the mid-1970s. When it published its first 'long-term vision' on the industrial structure of the Japanese economy, on 1 November 1974, it explicitly pointed out that protectionist policies could no longer be continued as in the past and that internationalization of the Japanese economy could not be avoided.[24]

Throughout the post-war period, MITI's economic nationalism (to some extent necessary and desirable) had been responsible for the proliferation of protectionist measures that virtually barred imports of manufactured goods into the domestic market and provided a safe environment within which reindustrialization of the Japanese economy could be undertaken. Chalmers Johnson suggested that liberalization came not through the MITI initiative but as a result of prior 'realization on the part of the industry that it had to "internationalize" if it was to avoid isolation'.[25] Within MITI, the transformation became possible only after a new crop of more internationally minded bureaucrats had taken over the leadership from their more conservative counterparts. The internationalization of MITI does not mean that it is, therefore, less concerned about the interests of the industrial sector, but simply that, given Japan's dependence on foreign trade and the maturing of the economy, a new set of goals and objectives was needed.

Amaya Naohiro, Administrative Vice-minister of MITI, who played a key role in resolving the US–Japan auto dispute, later explained his motive saying that the single most important thing for Japan was to help in the rebuilding of American industry. Trade disputes with the United States have long been a part of Japan's post-war (as well as pre-war) history, but as Amaya noted, what had happened over time was that such disputes had gradually moved closer to the heart of US industrial structure.[26] Protectionism, he explained, only begins to assume a threatening shape when the core of the industrial structure loses its competitive edge. As we shall see below, the implementation of voluntary export restraint at the time of the US–Japan auto dispute was clearly motivated by a concern to provide a 'breathing space' to the American auto industry and not the result of American pressure on Japan.

Thus, although the internationalization of MITI may have started in the 1970s, its first concrete manifestation was in the auto dispute even though its resolution through voluntary export restraint (VER) by Japan was not, by itself, unique. Export restraint was used in the case of the first textile dispute in the early 1960s, the steel dispute of 1969, and again with respect to colour televisions in the late 1970s. However, in none of these earlier instances was there a clear-cut basis for exercising restraint in the interest of revitalizing the affected industry in the United States. Also, only in the case of colour televisions was the quota on Japanese exports significantly below actual export figures, but American television manufacturers had, by that time, already decided to relocate production outside.

At the time the steel dispute flared up again, in 1977, Amaya Naohiro was the Director General of the Basic Industries Bureau of MITI and may have contributed to an early resolution of the dispute. But, it may still be worthwhile to keep it separate from the management of the auto dispute.

In the case of the textile dispute of the late 1960s, Destler *et al.* wrote that by the time agreement was reached on 15 October 1971, Japanese textile exports to the United States were already on the decline as the result of competition from other Asian countries which had, ironically, placed Japanese manufacturers in much the same position as their American counterparts.[27] This made them interested in the same kind of trade restrictions that they had for long resisted. Likewise, the reason that the Japanese steel industry accepted, even welcomed, the trigger price mechanism (TPM) introduced by the United States in 1977, was because they really benefited from it since the TPM was based on Japanese CIF prices and effectively prevented the newly industrializing countries (NICs) from exploiting their cost advantages. In contrast to these two instances, the Japanese auto industry remained opposed to VER that would lower their export volume, but was forced by MITI to accept a lower sales quota in the interest of providing American manufacturers a breathing space to modernize their production facilities. That this was a new direction for MITI becomes clear when we compare it to MITI's position during the textile dispute of the late 1960s. At that time, some officials in the Ministry of

Foreign Affairs termed MITI bureaucrats as 'champions of economic nationalism' for their inability to make concessions in international negotiations arising from their commitment to protect domestic industry.[28]

In Japan, the concern with the future stability of the LIEO has been formulated around the question of leadership in the system. The starting points of such analyses have been the economic decline of the United States and its diminished leadership capability. Amaya wrote that, since a liberal trade regime had never been successfully maintained on the basis of co-operative arrangements, it was essential, therefore, 'for Japan to prevent the destruction of *pax americana*'.[29] For system stability, he argued, it was necessary to help build a second *pax americana*. Although he added the disclaimer that his views did not necessarily reflect those of MITI, to remains a fact that he was a powerful and influential member of the policy-making structure of MITI. The outcome of the auto dispute, in which he was the principal Japanese negotiator, was clear testimony of his influence. For the role that he played in the auto dispute, he acquired the reputation, in industry circles, of being 'Reagan's mistress'. We will look into this, in detail, in the next chapter, but we should point out that the basic thrust of Amaya's logic was maintained in the subsequent years as well, under Prime Minister Nakasone.

A final point that ought to be mentioned is that while the application of the concept of supporter to Japanese foreign economic policies is reasonably justified, we should not expect a perfect fit between the ideal and the reality. Some of the particular instances that we consider in this book do suggest the applicability of the concept of system supporter to Japan, but we do recognize that more will have to be done, particularly in the regional context, before Japan as a system supporter can become a force of stability in the international trading system. The process is still in an evolutionary stage and, as we would expect, there remain many groups within Japan that oppose the government's attempt to define a new role for Japan in the international system, on the grounds that the social costs are too high. For example, throughout much of the post-war period, the Japanese government pursued, successfully, 'full'-employment policies, but with industrial restructuring it is expected that Japan will, in future, have to deal with the 'Western' problem of structural unemployment. As that happens, domestic opposition will stiffen and whether the government will be able to overcome this will depend to a large extent on its ability to forge a new social consensus, much like Prime Minister Yoshida did in the early post-war period, emphasizing economic growth, low defence spending, and close ties with the United States.

In this transitional phase, the residual internal constraints may not always enable the government to act in a manner that it would like, forcing a compromise between competing objectives. These issues will be taken up in detail when we consider the issue of demand expansion and economic stimulation.

Part Two

Japan and system support

4

The US–Japan Auto Dispute

BACKGROUND TO THE AUTO DISPUTE

The auto dispute between Japan and the United States and its resolution provides the first real indication of Japan's growing role in the maintenance of the international trading system. Although the outcome of the crisis placed additional restrictions on the flow of goods, it will be argued that it is necessary to go beyond a mere symptomatic reading of the events. As such, while the auto dispute has been studied in some detail by Winham and Kabashima,[1] our focus will not only concern the negotiating strategy of the two parties, but will also seek to grasp the intentions behind the stand taken by the Japanese Government.

The theory of hegemonic stability suggests that the stability of a liberal trading regime will depend on the presence of hegemonic control in the system. In the late 1970s and early 1980s, the LIEO confronted a severe threat to its stability as the result of a growing tide of protectionism in the United States, the country that stood in the leadership position. This protectionism could be attributed to a general economic decline and gradual loss of international competitiveness. From the standpoint of the hegemonic-stability thesis, it was desirable, therefore, to reverse, if possible, the decline of the American economy and to rejuvenate the industrial structure. In the late 1970s, the protectionist mood within the United States found its major prop in the auto industry, which was seen as losing out to Japanese competition. The danger was that if the United States took steps to block out imports, as was being demanded by the auto industry and the United Auto Workers (UAW), other industries, even those on the periphery, could be tempted to escalate their own demands. On the other hand, if the auto industry could be strengthened without resort to overt-protectionism, it was felt that this would relieve pressure on the system. Even though the immediate crisis of the auto industry was precipitated by external factors, namely the oil crisis, its decline cannot be isolated from the decline of the American economy. We will present the argument here that the Japanese Government acted with due concern to facilitate the reorganization of the auto industry as part of a long-term strategy to maintain the liberal trading system.

The clearest signal of a looming crisis came when the UAW, in late 1979, demanded relief from the inroads being made by Japanese car manufacturers and which threatened to disrupt American car manufacturing. The issue was immediately taken up by Congressmen and Senators, especially from the Great Lakes region.

Senator Donald Riegle, irritated by the growing mass of literature that urged the United States to learn from the Japanese experience in respect to production technology, management practices, etc., wrote,

> but we might also want to follow their example in closing off their domestic market while they built their modern automobile industry. Perhaps it is time for us to copy that part of their experience and protect our own market.[2]

In January 1981, when Transportation Secretary Goldschmidt submitted a report to the outgoing President on the state of the US auto industry, he spelled out the need for a five-year import quota on Japanese cars so that Detroit had a 'breathing space' to complete the switchover to the production of small cars and the modernization of its production facilities. Senator Riegle was correct in noting that the Japanese auto industry had been built up behind a thick, impenetrable wall of tariff and non-tariff barriers, but there is a distinction to be made between infant-industry protection and stagnant-industry protection. For a late developing country, or for a country in the position Japan found itself in the early post-war period, industrial development could only occur if the fledgling and weak industries were protected from foreign competitors. This rationale could hardly apply to the case of the US auto industry, where decline was the direct result of shifts in demand patterns and consumer preference for small fuel-efficient cars as opposed to the 'gas guzzlers' being produced in Detroit. One of the main arguments against protecting a declining industry is that such protection, by providing a captive market, takes away the incentive to restore the ability to compete in a free and open market. It creates a dependence that is unhealthy and examples are not hard to find.

Yet, despite all the known ills, protection cannot always be avoided. Political leaders cannot ignore the demands of organized sectors of the economy and still hope to secure their political future. In the auto dispute, the US Congress from the beginning took a protectionist stance, largely because of the growing unemployment problems resulting from plant shut-downs and production cut-backs.

On top of the political imperative there may even, at times, be valid economic grounds for protection, if the industry can be expected to regain competitiveness. The economic consideration would be to avoid large-scale disruption in related industries and the economy in general. This, of course, depends largely on the nature of the industry in question. In the midst of the auto dispute, the US Congress passed concurrent resolutions declaring it to be a strategic national industry, considering the fact that one in twelve manufacturing jobs was related to the auto industry and because the automotive sector provided a 'market for 24 per cent of the US steel output, 17 per cent of aluminium, 54 per cent of iron, and 59 per cent of synthetic rubber'.[3]

Throughout the dispute, the Japanese auto industry remained opposed to restraints on their export of passenger cars to the United States. It denied that the American auto industry was an industry in decline and instead viewed its plight as only a transitory, although painful, phenomenon. Even Douglas Fraser, president of the UAW, admitted as much, but what he objected to was the 'continued unfair exploitation [by the Japanese] of their current, temporary advantage', whatever that may mean. He went on to note that if this practice was continued, it could lead to an overreaction of protectionism in the United States.[4]

In any case, whether it was a temporary or a secular decline, it was clearly adding to protectionist demand. Unless steps were taken to ensure the long-term survival of US auto manufacturing, the task of maintaining a liberal trading regime would become all the more difficult. As Kamijo wrote, 'To prevent the possibility of the United States taking the protectionist road, it is necessary for Japan to . . . contribute to strengthening of the international competitiveness of US industry and to the further growth of its export structure'.[5]

In the early post-war period and through to the 1970s, both Detroit's auto manufacturers and the UAW had been strong exponents of the liberal trading order – not surprisingly, since the industry stood as the world leader. In the late 1970s, however, they formed the core of the protectionist forces. For Japan, the problem of how to contain protectionism and strengthen the LIEO seemed to focus on its response to the distress of the American auto industry. This would explain why the Japanese government and the MITI were eager to avoid causing excessive damage to the US auto industry, allegedly being caused by Japanese exports. This is not to suggest that this was the only factor that figured in the Japanese decision-making process. There were other factors as well, but most of these could be seen as constant parameters that have always been a part of US–Japan trade conflicts.

The thesis that Japan was cognizant of its new world role can only be supported if it can be demonstrated that the management of the auto dispute was fundamentally different from previous trade conflicts. It is true that Japan had, on several occasions in the past, agreed to exercise voluntary export restraint and so the outcome of the auto dispute itself was no novelty. The difference can be found in the underlying rationale behind the actions of the Japanese government. This, however, raises the question of why the dispute festered for over a year and a half if the Japanese government was, from the beginning, in support of voluntary export restraint (VER). The duration of the crisis would appear to make the traditional explanations of linkage politics and foreign pressure more attractive, but these, it will be argued, provide only a partial explanation and should, more appropriately, be seen as constant parameters.

One constant feature of US–Japan trade disputes has been the inevitable linkage with defence issues and Japan's alleged 'free-ride' on American security commitments. The belief that Japan was taking a free-ride on US defence efforts troubles many Americans, who see in this a distinct advantage for Japan because it frees resources that could then be diverted to achieve economic ends. Former US Senator Paul Fannin expressed this sentiment when he testified in front of the Senate Committee on Finance in March 1981, in favour of a bill sponsored by Senator Danforth, to restrict car imports from Japan. In his written statement, he said, 'If we had subsidized Chrysler to the extent of 15 to 20 per cent of their budget, as we have subsidized Japan and its industries, Chrysler would be prosperous today'.[6] In Japan, the defence-trade linkage has almost become a fact of life, under which trade concessions are regarded as inevitable. Thus, only a day after the Japanese voluntary export restraint on autos was announced, the *Nihon Keizai Shinbun* (*Japan Economic Daily*) observed that, because of the inevitable defence-trade linkage, the argument proffered by MITI that the agreement was necessary in the interest of the long-term stability of the LIEO was only the superficial explanation (*tatemae*).[7] It concluded that MITI had been forced to accept the VER only during the latter part of the dispute. The paper reported that as late as November 1980 MITI officials were of the view that there was no reason for Japan to exercise a VER. In reality, however, as we shall see below, MITI had been urging Japanese car manufacturers to exercise 'self-control' (though not export restraint) on their exports to the United States as early as June 1980.

External pressure is another constant element in United States–Japan trade relations, but a helpful one given the nature of the decision-making process in Japan and its effectiveness in forcing a solution to the problem of *so-ron sansei kaku-ron hantai* or agreement in principle, disagreement on specific. Thus, pressure, at times, has even been welcomed by the Japanese government. This suggests that pressure has not become altogether redundant. Pressure will continue to be important in resolving trade disputes and for breaking the stalemate emerging from the nature of bureaucratic and organizational politics. Decision making in Japan is based on the prior achievement of consensus, but reaching consensus is not easy and, as is well known, decision making, in Japan, can be an exceptionally time-consuming process. The advantage of the consensual approach, on the other hand, is that once a decision is finalized, implementation is free of the many problems that are encountered in the West. The difficulty of reaching consensus would be considerably eased if, for example, in trade disputes, the scope of the issue did not transcend ministerial boundaries, but this is rarely the case. Thus, with each ministry trying its utmost to preserve its domain, building a level of consensus is not an easy task. It is in this respect that external pressure can play a functional role. Commenting on the nature of the decision-making process in Japan, Deputy US Trade Representative Hormats states that

> one reason why Japan, despite major import liberalization, is perceived to be so protective of its market . . . is its style of negotiating – its seeming inability to act unless faced with major pressures to do so and then, seemingly, only with the greatest reluctance.[8]

Decisions usually entail a redistribution of costs and benefits, not always on an equitable basis. Therefore, opposition can be expected from those who stand to lose as a result of the decision, even though there may be total agreement with the principle underlying the issue at hand. A key characteristic of the Japanese decision-making process, as Albert Craig writes, is the careful avoidance of a situation 'in which one man wins and another, who has openly declared his position, is marked as a loser when the decision goes against him'.[9] In disputes that span the jurisdiction of two or more ministries or organizations, it is easier to rationalize concession and 'defeat' if there is outside pressure, thereby preserving the facade, however superficial, of no organizational winners and losers. As such the utility of foreign pressure is in breaking out of the dilemma caused by *so-ron sansei kaku-ron hantai*.

Voluntary export restraints had been used in the past, but only in the case of the auto VER was MITI favourably predisposed. In the case of Japanese colour televison (TV) exports to the United States, an orderly marketing agreement (OMA) was reached in May 1977. Both the colour TV and auto industries are high-technology industries, and the agreement reached on both issues brought about an absolute reduction in the volume of exports to the United States. This is, however, where the similarity ends. For instance, the American TV industry was not particularly concerned about rebuilding its production base in the United States. Most American TV manufacturers, with the sole exception of RCA, were small-scale operators and their strategy was to seek cost advantages by relocating outside the United States.

In 1967, Japan's TV exports to the United States totalled only about 320,000 units, but in the following year this more than doubled to 680,000 units. In June of the same year, an anti-dumping suit was filed with the Commerce Department which launched an investigation lasting for several years but then was abruptly terminated. In the meantime, Japanese exports continued to grow steadily, reaching 1.21 million units in 1975. This suddenly doubled again to 2.96 million units in 1976. In September 1976, the domestic manufacturers filed for protection under Article 201 (escape clause) of the 1974 Trade Act.[10] Negotiations started with Japan even while the International Trade Commission (ITC) was investigating the case of damage to the US industry and an agreement was reached in 1977 to limit Japanese exports to 1.75 million units a year. Despite the agreement, however, TV manufacturers in the United States continued to shift production overseas. Zenith, in the early 1970s, had started production cut-backs in its main factory in Illinois and set up new facilities in Taiwan and Mexico. Most of RCA's colour TV production had also been moved out to Canada. Thus, as Ogura Kazuo wrote, 'by relocating their production abroad, they (the US manufacturers) had clearly indicated that they had given up, from the very beginning, trying to compete with imports through a rationalization of their management and manufacturing processes'.[11] Ironically, while American manufacturers shifted production to other countries, Japanese manufacturers started production in the United States. In 1979, for example, export of colour TV sets from Japan to the United States totalled only 700,000 units, while their production in the United States was about 3.5 million units. As a result, by the time the OMA expired in June 1980, it no longer had any trade restrictive effects.

In the case of the steel dispute, as mentioned earlier, the Japanese steel industry was very receptive to US demands for export restraint. In 1978, three years after the 1969 VER had lapsed, steel exports became, once more, a source of friction between the two countries. At that time, the President of Nippon Steel, Saito Eishiro, and other industry representatives, themselves proposed to MITI that it arrange an OMA with the United States. Patrick and Sato wrote that there were four reasons why the steel industry was so favourably inclined to export restraint:

1. the interdependent nature of the industry;

2. sense of indebtedness to the United States for assistance in the early developmental stage;
3. profitability of VER;
4. fear of losing a large and stable market in the United States.[22]

Since the steel industry itself wanted export restraint, MITI went along and as a result of negotiations with the United States a trigger price mechanism (TPM) was agreed upon, which ultimately proved highly beneficial to the Japanese steel industry, since it took away the competitive edge of South Korean steel manufacturers and secured for Japan a stable market share in the United States.

The export restraint agreement on autos was different from all earlier export restraint agreements, although, as with steel and textiles before, it could be argued that the auto VER agreement was possible only because it resulted in increased profitability for the Japanese car manufacturers. This, however, ignores the fact that the auto industry in Japan was strongly opposed to formal export restrictions. Their opposition was due to the belief that the difficulties of the American car manufacturers were of a temporary nature and that a general recovery of the car market in the United States, expected even by American sources (see table 4.5), would improve the sales position of Detroit. Thus, they argued, there was no real justification for restricting Japanese imports. Also, they did not want to be saddled with restrictions in a market that was likely to recover in the near future. The position taken by MITI, on the other hand, stressed the importance of a respite for American car manufacturers from Japanese imports, allowing them reasonable certainty regarding market standing at a time when additional, yet necessary, investment appeared too risky. Before we look into the specifics of the VER, we will, in the next section, present a discussion of the problems that confronted the American auto industry and how they grew to crisis proportions.

THE POST-WAR DEVELOPMENT OF THE JAPANESE AND AMERICAN AUTO INDUSTRIES

The auto industry is the largest single export earner for Japan, earning $36.93 billion in 1984 (FOB basis) and accounting for 21.7 per cent of total Japanese exports. Toyota and Nissan have both become synonymous with Japan's industrial strength and a significant landmark was reached in the late 1970s when total Japanese auto production exceeded that of the United States for the first time, though largely due to a steep decline in American auto production. Few, including MITI, which strongly supported the building of an auto industry early in the post-war period, could have foreseen the dramatic growth of the auto industry in Japan.

MITI's position, at that time, was simply that comparative advantage was not simply a natural order but could be artificially created. Against the proponents of instituting an international division of labour, it argued that a domestic auto industry was indispensable for broad-based industrial development because other related industries would spring up around it. The biggest handicap at the time was the size of the domestic market, considered too small to support an efficient auto industry. However, the outbreak of the Korean War in 1950 provided a welcome surge in demand through the special procurement programme of the US military. In the early 1950s production in Japan reached an average annual figure of 40 to 50,000 units, centering around trucks. American production around this time was well over 8 million units.

During the 1960s, liberalization of the Japanese economy was the main task confronting the Japanese government. The government had already announced, in June 1960, that it would take greater steps toward free trade and foreign exchange liberalization. With the pending issue of economic liberalization, MITI's main concern was to provide effective production to the nascent auto industry, composed of about a dozen companies. MITI particularly feared capital liberalization which, when it did happen, would leave the Japanese industry vulnerable to foreign take-over bids. This was considered a serious threat given the low-equity position of Japanese firms. In an interview, Kawamata Katsuji, Chairman of the Japan Automobile Industry Association, claimed that the inevitable effect of capital liberalization, if it went ahead as planned, would be the 'industrial colonization' of Japan. However, capital liberalization was the promise under which Japan had joined the OECD in the mid-1960s, and when the interviewer suggested that it made no practical difference if a few people at the top had 'blue eyes' since all the others would still have 'black eyes', and the government would still collect taxes on profits, Kawamata very indignantly brushed aside the notion of obligation and said, 'Every country has the right to formulate its own economic policies. We will liberalize what we can, but not what we cannot. The automobile industry cannot be liberalized'.[13] Toyota, the industry leader, most fearful of a take-over bid, took the precautionary measure of barring foreign directors from participating in the management of the company.[14]

MITI's response to the impending liberalization of the economy was to encourage mergers so as to strengthen the viability of each individual auto manufacturer. The policy, however, had little success and the only merger achieved by MITI was that between Nissan and Prince Motors Company in 1966. Although MITI tried to forge what it believed to be an 'appropriate level of competition' and economies of scale, one cannot help but feel that the auto industry did not lose much and may even have benefited from MITI's failure to achieve rationalization. This was because the typical feature of vertically integrated industries in Japan more than offset the gains to be had from horizontal integration. As Bain wrote,

> some such integration [i.e. vertical integration] may give rise to economies in production, reflected in the fact that the integrated firm can perform a series of successive productive functions more efficiently than they would be performed by a number of individual firms, each of which performed only one function.[15]

More importantly, vertical integration, by giving control over supply of parts, enabled the Japanese manufacturers to operate with low levels of in-process inventory compared to their American counterparts, thereby improving their cost competitiveness. The level of vertical integration in American and Japanese auto industries is markedly different. When measured by adding manufacturing costs paid to subsidiaries to in-house costs, the vertical integration at Nissan and Toyota was 78 and 73 per cent respectively, in 1983, compared to 28 per cent for General Motors (GM), the most integrated American car manufacturer.[16]

In contrast to the gains that were made in the Japanese car industry, the American auto industry confronted a crisis of major proportions in the late 1970s. The immediate cause of the crisis was the hike in oil prices in 1979, but the process of decline had begun well before that. For example, labour productivity in the American industry consistently lagged behind wage increases. During the period 1968–77, wages rose by 124 per cent, but annual productivity increase averaged only 3 per cent a year. Wages in the auto industry were above the average for the manufacturing sector in general. The appropriate response to wage increase would have been to try and raise the level of productivity through new investment. Instead, the management responded by building bigger cars which allowed for large price mark-ups. As the size of the car got bigger, there was also a proliferation of models being produced. The trend toward product differentiation had been set in motion in the 1920s. At that time Ford produced only the Model T and the Lincoln, but GM started out with a strategy that offered a wide range, from Chevrolet, Pontiac, Buick, Oldsmobile, and Cadillac. As a result, 'after a while, the auto industry was forced to convert to the GM-type strategy'.[17] As the number of models produced by each maker increased, it necessarily meant a smaller production run for each model type. The result was a deterioration of the cost structure as smaller production runs meant costly retooling. In terms of the top ten cars produced, in 1982 GM came in tenth with its Cierra Supreme (production run of 321,000) while the Toyota Corolla was first (production run of 574,000). By 1984, however, the situation had improved somewhat: GM's Cavalier came in fifth (400,000 units) and Ford's Escort was tenth (342,000 units).[18]

As far as profitability of the American car manufacturers was concerned, there was no immediate cause for worry given consistently high demand for big cars. Fuel prices were relatively low by international standards, which meant that operating cost, despite poor fuel efficiency, was low. Even after the first oil crisis of 1973, there was little change in demand patterns, but the second oil crisis, following the Iranian Revolution and oil-production halt in 1978, resulted in a dramatic shift in market demand. We can estimate the difference between the two oil crises, in terms of the impact on the average consumer. After the 1973 oil crisis gasoline prices went up only 6 cents but posted an increase of almost 40 cents after the 1979 oil crisis.[19] As a result, sales of big cars plummeted and inventories soared.

The quadrupling of oil prices in 1973 by OPEC had led to a worldwide energy-conservation campaign, except in the United States, where extravagant use of gasoline, 40 per cent of total US oil imports, continued as in the past. This inevitably became the Achilles heel for effective Western response to OPEC and there was considerable criticism of extravagant consumption patterns being continued in the United States. The US government eventually realized that it could not continue with its domestic energy policies and on 22 December 1975 the Energy Policy and Conservation Act was announced, which set the target of raising the average fuel efficiency of domestic cars to 27.5 miles per gallon, by 1985, in stages, beginning in 1978, or about double the existing level of 13 miles per gallon. The lead time was essential to allow Detroit the leeway to complete the switchover to the production of more fuel-efficient cars. Unfortunately, however, events moved faster than Detroit's transition.

Forced by the requirements imposed by the Energy Conservation Act, Detroit adopted the strategy of gradually reducing the size and body weight of cars. Only a month before the Act was announced, the President of GM, Elliot Estes, had denounced all efforts to restrict the size of cars for conservation purposes, saying that it was a 'badly mistaken notion that America can save its way to energy prosperity starting with automobiles'.[20] Detroit's strategy of increasing fuel efficiency was necessarily long term because of the massive investment requirements. It was estimated that the American car manufacturers would have to invest about $80 billion over a six-year period, and the original plan was to redirect profit from the sale of big cars to small-car production technology. There was, as Shimokawa Koichi wrote, a need to make as much profit as possible from the large cars, which ruled out a faster transition pace.[21] The 1979 oil crisis caught them totally unprepared to meet the sudden change in consumer demand. Perhaps they would have fared better if the government, between the two oil crises, had not been sending out mixed and conflicting signals, for example, imposing fuel-efficiency requirements while at the same time continuing oil price controls. In any case, Detroit was now in serious trouble, and domestic sales of the 'big three' declined from 9.3 million units in 1978 to 6.58 million units in 1980, a decline of about 39 per cent (see table 4.1).

If we break down the above sales figure by size of car;

Table 4.1 US Car sales (million units)

	1975	1978	1979	1980	1981
GM	3.75	5.38	4.92	4.12	3.80
Ford	1.98	2.58	2.14	1.47	1.38
Chrysler	1.00	1.15	0.94	0.66	0.73
Total	7.05	9.31	8.33	6.58	6.20

Source: *Jidosha Sangyo Handbook*, Nissan Motor Co. Ltd, 1985 edn, pp. 278–9.
Note: The total includes sales of AMC and VW (USA).

subcompacts and compacts; intermediate; and full size, the results are even more dramatic. This breakdown is given in table 4.2, below.

Table 4.2 Sales breakdown by size (single units)

	1977	1980	Change %
Subcompacts and compacts	3,179,402	3,345,476	+5
Intermediates and full size	5,227,897	2,911,066	−44

Source: *Jidosha Sangyo Handbook*, Nissan Motor Co. Ltd, 1985 edn, pp. 282–3.
Note: Excludes sales of luxury cars.

As can be seen, in just three years sales of big cars had declined markedly, and while sales of small cars did increase, it did not offset the decline in big cars. The reason that sales of US-produced small cars did not show a larger increase was due largely to competition from Japanese imports, which, besides their superior quality, had a definite cost advantage. We will look at this further below. Table 4.3 shows the annual sales and profit–loss picture of the American 'big three'.

Table 4.3 Total sales and profit of US 'big three' ($ billion)

		1975	1978	1979	1980	1981
GM	Sales	35.725	63.226	66.311	57.728	62.699
	Profit	1.253	3.508	2.893	−0.762	0.333
Ford	Sales	24.009	42.784	43.514	37.085	38.247
	Profit	0.323	1.589	1.169	−1.543	−1.060
Chrysler	Sales	8.572	13.618	12.002	9.225	10.822
	Profit	−0.260	−0.205	−1.097	−1.710	−0.476

Source: Nissan Motor Co. Ltd.

Chrysler, the smallest of the 'big three' was in trouble even before the oil crisis of 1979, having shown a net loss for 1975. The following two years it made a recovery, turning in a profit of around $500 million for 1976 and a more modest $160 million for 1977, before going back in the red. Both GM and Ford showed a net loss for 1980, the year following the oil crisis, although GM did recover in 1981. In 1982, only Ford showed an annual loss, with both GM and Chrysler well along in their recovery.

While the American auto manufacturers were concerned about their profitability, the UAW was more concerned with job security and the depletion of its rank-and-file membership, as a result of plant closure and industry-wide lay-offs. In the period 1978–80, the employment figure for the 'big three' declined from about 1,000,000 to 774,000 and there was little hope for any improvement in the near future. The first salvo in the auto dispute was fired by the UAW and it subsequently maintained a consistent pressure in the interest of securing employment in the industry. In the early phase of the dispute, emphasis was on getting the Japanese manufacturers to set up assembly plants in the United States just as they had done in the European countries.

Having looked at the developments in the auto industry in both Japan and the United States and the nature of the problem faced by the American car manufacturers, we will, in the next section, trace the major developments in the auto dispute. This will be done in chronological order in order to understand better how the dispute evolved over the period of the two administrations of Jimmy Carter and Ronald Reagan.

THE AUTO DISPUTE AND ITS RESOLUTION: AN ACCOUNT

Japanese car exports had a lowly beginning with only two units exported in 1955, but the growth since then has been remarkable, though not without the usual early jitters. Toyota, for example, had major problems trying to penetrate the American car market with its top of the line Toyopet Crown. Later, with a revised strategy of concentrating on the lower end of the market, it had considerable success. In 1970, a strike at General Motors, lasting over two months, disrupted the production of the small Vega cars and this had the important effect of allowing the Japanese car manufacturers to establish a firm foothold in the US market. However, as long as the total US car market was increasing, Japanese exports could be painlessly tolerated, but problems began to surface when exports from Japan showed no signs of slowing down, even as the market was on a decline.

For auto manufacturers in Japan, increasing export sales had become an important goal since the 1973 oil crisis which had resulted in a decline in domestic car sales in 1974 and relative stagnation thereafter. The 1979 oil crisis further reduced market demand in Japan and there was also a shift in demand patterns. Demand for small cars, with engine capacity of between 551 cc to 2000 cc, declined in 1980 by 6.9 per cent, but there was some increase in demand for light cars with engine capacity of under 551 cc, such that total car sales declined by only 2.7 per cent in 1980.[22] In the United States as well, as we saw, car sales declined from 8.33 million in 1979 to 6.58 million in 1980 and down to 6.20 million in 1981. On the other hand, auto exports from Japan increased from 1.41 million in 1978 to 1.55 million in 1979 (an increase of 9.8 per cent), to 1.82 million in 1980 (an increase of 17.6 per cent over 1979). Thus, imports were taking up a larger share of a shrinking US market. In 1975, Japan's share of the US car market was about 9 per cent, but this increased to around 21 per cent in 1980. The market-share figure represents the share of Japanese cars in the total US car market, including full-size and luxury cars. When one considers Japan's car sales as a percentage of only subcompact and compact cars, their market share had increased from 29 per cent in 1977 to 36 per cent in 1980.[23]

Understandably, this was a worrisome development for American car manufacturers who feared that if the Japanese inroad remained unchecked, their own share of the market would decline even further making new, and necessary, investment for the production of small cars a very risky proposition. They felt that the profitability conditions of their investment programme required not only some assurances against further deterioration in their market share but preferably some improvement. Otherwise, it was feared that they would simply be adding on excess and redundant capacity.

The US–Japan auto dispute, in its initial phase, proceeded along two interrelated but somewhat separate tracks. The first was Japanese investment in the United States and the second, import restrictions on Japanese cars. When the issue was first raised in October 1979, Douglas Fraser of the UAW called for either Japanese production in the United States or restrictions on car imports. At that time, none of the Japanese manufacturers had any plans for setting up production facilities in the United States, even though they had set up production facilities in European countries. Japan's reliance on exports for car sales in the US market was seen as costing American jobs. Of course, by relying on exports, the Japanese manufacturers could benefit from the lower production costs in Japan, but more importantly, there were few, if any, positive incentives to locate plants in the United States, purely from an economic point of view. A manufacturer decides to invest abroad on the basis of perceived gains from such factors as worker productivity, labour costs, tax benefits, worker–management relations, etc., and no matter how one looks at it, there was no major incentive to locate production in the United States. Of course, the United States represented a growing and important market, but there is no economic argument to suggest that a large market is reason enough for investment, since demand can just as easily be met through exports. Lacking positive incentives, the UAW pressed for negative sanctions in the hope of attracting Japanese car manufacturers in to the United States just as the Europeans had done. In additon, Fraser raised what could be called the 'moral imperative' when he blamed Japanese imports for unemployment in the United States. He argued that annual sales of about 200,000 units was sufficient economic reasoning to justify setting up production facilities in the United States.[24]

Up until June 1980, the main thrust of American demand was to pressure the Japanese manufacturers into local production. This point was raised by Fraser when he visited Japan in February, by President Carter when he met with Prime Minister Ohira in May 1980, and again by USTR Askew during his visit to Japan, also in May 1980.

On the occasion of his first summit meeting with Prime Minsiter Ohira in Tokyo, President Carter pointed out that unemployment in the United States was becoming a political issue, but he also assured the Japanese government that he would not impose any restrictions on Japanese car imports. Instead, he urged that Japan take the following steps to prevent the politicization of the dispute:

1. boost car imports from the United States;
2. undertake investment in the United States;
3. produce in the United States on joint-venture basis.[25]

It was agreed that negotiations between the two countries on the above points would be undertaken when Askew visited Japan later in the month. As a result of talks with Askew, the Japanese government agreed to adopt the following measures:

1. encourage capital investment in the United States;
2. conduct a survey of the US market for production in the United States;
3. improve standards and simplify procedures for US car imports;
4. remove tariffs on auto parts;
5. help increase imports of auto parts from the United States.[26]

The final two points were part of President Carter's specific request, but it is hard to see the Japanese firms significantly increasing their sourcing from the United States. This is largely because of the structure of the Japanese industry, described above, and the just-in-time inventory system. The Japanese manufacturing system is geared to maintaining a minimum level of in-process inventory, which is one factor behind their cost advantage, and if they were to do more sourcing from overseas, it would mean a significant revamping of their production processes.[27]

In time, demands for import restrictions on Japanese cars began to gain strength and Fraser called this a short-term necessity. The Japanese view, both official and of the industry, was that it was inappropriate to blame Japan for the misfortune of Detroit. In March 1980, the Joint Economic Committee of the US Congress convened an open hearing on the state of the US auto industry. Testifying before it, Suzuki Yasuhiko, Vice-president, External Relations, Nissan Motor Corporation of USA, stated that, "The current automobile problem is not an issue of imports versus domestics, but large cars versus small cars'.[28] In his testimony, he listed the following factors as reasons why import restriction was not the answer to the problem:

1. it would not put workers back on the job;

2. it would penalize consumers;
3. it would help fuel inflation;
4. it would deny consumers freedom of choice;
5. it would increase fuel consumption and dependence on OPEC.

Articulating the official view, Amaya Naohiro wrote that Detroit's misfortune was simply the result of poor demand for big cars and that Japanese exports only helped fill the gap between domestic demand and supply, which worked to the advantage of American consumers.[29]

With respect to the five factors listed above, few would deny the validity of the first three factors. On the issue of restoring employment levels in the US auto industry, the Managing Director of Nissan in a round-table discussion published in the MITI publication *Tsusan Journal* said that, regardless of the decision taken by the United States on the question of import restrictions, it was unlikely, first, that the demand trend could be reversed to favour big cars, and second, since small cars embodied a lower labour content, the unemployment would continue for some time.[30] Also, one of the tasks confronting the US car manufacturers was modernization of their production facilities, and this implied a higher level of automation; not the typical Detroit automation of 'conveyor belts', but robotics and other labour-saving technology. As experience since then has shown, despite recovery in the US auto industry, employment fell from 793,000 (total for GM, Ford, Chrysler, AMC, and VW of USA) in 1981, when the VER went into effect, to 723,000 in 1983. During this period, production had increased by 1.2 million units, including both passenger and commercial vehicles. On the final point mentioned by Suzuki, Fraser asserted that American cars were not necessarily less fuel efficient, adding that 'the Ford Fairmont [Tempo] and Mercury Zephyr [Topaz] have 1980 EPA ratings of 23 mpg in city driving and 38 in highway driving. Toyota's Corona, Celica, Supra and Cressida models were rated at 20 city and 28 highway'. Still, even allowing for this exception, it cannot be denied that average fuel efficiency was above that for American cars, but, moreover, it must not be forgotten that what sustained the demand for Japanese cars in the United States was not only fuel efficiency but also their perceived superior quality and competitive prices. The difference in quality can be gauged from the number of recalls. In 1979, GM recalled 4.81 million units, Ford recalled 1.4 million units, and Nissan only 290,000 as its first recall in the United States.[31]

The American consumer seemed to prefer Japanese cars to domestic makes and this can be observed from the sales statistics given in table 4.4 which shows sales to production capacity ratios of US manufacturers.

Table 4.4 Production capacity of selected US cars, 1981

Make	Maximum with overtime	Straight time	Sales	Capacity utilization of straight time (with overtime)	
GM Chevette	500,000	415,000	402,000	97%	(80%)
GM 'J' cars	330,000	270,000	164,000	60%	(49%)
Ford Escort/ Lynx	560,000	435,000	390,000	89%	(49%)
Ford Exp/L N-7	190,000	160,000	73,000	45%	(38%)
Ford Fairmont/ Zephyr	440,000	350,000	234,000	67%	(53%)
Chrysler Omni/ Horizon	330,000	270,000	131,000	48%	(39%)
Chrysler 'K' cars	650,000	540,000	347,000	64%	(53%)

Source: 'Issues Relating to the Domestic Auto Industry', Hearings before the Subcommittee on International Trade of the Committee of Finance, US Senate, 97th Congress, 1st Session on S–396, 9 March 1981, and *Jidosha Sangyo Handbook*, Nissan Motor Co. Ltd, 1985 edn. p. 281.

However, US car manufacturers argued that if Japanese imports were restricted, they would be in a position to move in quickly to fill the shortfall in supply since they already had excess capacity. As table 4.4 shows, there were many production lines that were relatively idle.

During the summer of 1980, the emphasis of US demands shifted to import restriction. On 12 June 1980, the UAW filed a petition with the International Trade Commission (ITC) for protection for the auto industry on the grounds of damage from Japanese imports. The UAW petition recommended that, as relief measures, the tariff on passenger-car imports be raised from 2.9 to 20 per cent and that an import quota be adopted using either 1975 or 1976 as the base year. On 4 August, the

Ford Motor Company filed a similar petition for relief, suggesting the following concrete steps.

1. Import quotas using 1976 as the base year:

   – passenger cars   1.7 million units per year.
   – small trucks   260,000 units per year.

2. A 25% tariff on small-truck imports.

In the interim, the Japanese Prime Minister, Ohira, suddenly died in office and Carter took the opportunity to go to Japan in early July to attend the memorial service. About a week before his departure for Tokyo, a task force set up in mid-May and headed by Transportation Secretary Neil E. Goldschmidt submitted a report to the President on the plight of the American auto industry and on relief measures. The report reflected both President Carter's preferred style of decision making and the divisions within the administration. The President had already established the practice that all reports to him list all the possible options available, including the advantages and disadvantages of each, but refrain from making a specific recommendation, leaving the final decision with him. In keeping with this tradition, the Goldschmidt report simply noted the options but did not recommend any specific relief measures. The report also reflected the divisions within the administration, for example, USTR Askew and Chairman of the Council of Economic Advisors, Charles Schultze, were both proponents of free trade, while Secretary Goldschmidt himself favoured import controls.[32] The options listed covered the spectrum, including sending a 'purposefully indirect' signal to the Japanese that the President was 'very concerned', and at the other end, a negotiated VER which, the report noted, ran the risk of litigation under the US anti-trust laws. The President chose the milder option, and to demonstrate his concern he made a brief stop-over in Detroit on his way to Toyko. Later, GM Chairman and Chief Executive, Thomas A. Murphy, observed, 'This is a very good first step. The fact that the President was here is a demonstration of the importance with which he views the situation'.[33] While in Detroit, the President announced an aid package easing regulatory standards on auto emissions and safety, and easier credit for auto dealers, promising total savings of $500 million over a three-year period.

The plan also promised to set up a tripartite structure between the government, labour, and management, to study appropriate policy responses on each of the five issues of environment, research and development, tax structure, employment, and trade. The President also expressed the hope that the ITC would expedite its investigation of the UAW/Ford petition and hand down its decision ahead of the stipulated time limit. For Detroit, this was perhaps the most encouraging feature of Carter's visit since it could conceivably lead to early negotiations with Japan. Carter himself, however, was totally opposed to import restriction because it would undercut his goal of controlling inflation and increasing fuel efficiency. The *New York Times* observed that requesting an early ITC decision did 'not imply that the President ha[d] made up his mind, merely that he want[ed] to get the case resolved quickly'.[34] Carter knew that he would have to negotiate with the Japanese should the ITC rule in favour of the petition, but it seems that he also expected the problem to disappear if the ITC found no evidence of damage from Japanese imports.

Interestingly, in the period following the UAW/Ford petition, both the US Congress and the Japanese government were working on the basis of their respective worst-case scenario. For the Congress this was the rejection of the petition, and for the Japanese government if the ITC upheld the petition. Fearing an unfavourable ITC decision, Senators Riegle and Metzenbaum, and twenty-one others, introduced a resolution in the Senate on 5 August 1980 to provide specific authority to the President to begin negotiations with the Japanese government on restricting car imports. Passage of the resolution would have enabled the President to begin negotiations without having to wait for the ITC decision. Carter, however, was not keen on this. The following month, testifying before the House Foreign Relations Committee, Subcommittee for Asia and Pacific Affairs, senior administration officials stated quite clearly that the government would only proceed on the basis of an ITC ruling, whatever that might be, and that it would not abide by any resolution passed by the Congress giving the President authority to begin negotiations.[35]

The Japanese government, likewise, was preparing for its worst-case scenario. It felt it prudent to do so for a number of reasons. First, the Japanese car manufacturers were doing very well in the United States at a time when the American manufacturers themselves were faced with hard times ahead. The UAW was also very successful in portraying Japan as preying unfairly on the misfortune of American car makers. It was also not very reassuring to know that Carter, in May, had been forced to withdraw his nomination of Robert E. Baldwin to fill a vacant ITC seat on the grounds of stiff congressional oppositon that Baldwin was too much of a 'free trader'.[36] In the past, presidential nominations to the ITC had never been opposed by the Congress and this rare incident was just another indication of the mood of the moment and one that could have been imputed to have some bearing on the ITC decision.

MITI's immediate concern was to avoid exacerbating the situation. However, its options were rather restricted because, even though it favoured export controls (but not import controls imposed by the United States), the US administration was opposed to any form of trade restraint. Under the circumstances, it did the best it could, which was to encourage the Japanese manufacturers to control their exports to the United States voluntarily. The Japanese press reported that MITI began urging the major Japanese producers, Toyota, Nissan, and Honda, from June 1980, to restrain their exports.[37] MITI could not unilaterally impose export restraint because that required some form of inter-governmental agreement.

The Japanese Government wished to avoid a repeat of the situation in 1972 when the Consumers Union had filed a suit against the State Department claiming that the VER on steel with Japanese and European exporters was in violation of the anti-trust laws. Although the suit itself was rejected, Patrick and Sato wrote that the aftershock of the dispute was part of the reason why the steel VER was allowed to lapse in 1975.[38] The problem of unilateral action in autos became all too obvious when the Department of Justice in the United States and the Federal Trade Commission promptly launched an anti-trust investigation on suspicions that Japanese manufacturers, under the direction of their government, had formed a cartel to restrict supply in the United States.[39] Later, and when the auto VER was finally implemented, the Japanese governemnt sought, and obtained, formal assurances from the Office of the Attorney General that the restraint agreement would not be regarded as a violation of the US laws.

Throughout the duration of the auto dispute, President Carter's oppositon to quantity restrictions was consistent and unfailing. In September 1980, Japanese Foreign Minister Ito went to Washington and following his meetings with senior administration officials, including President Carter, he held a news conference where he confirmed that he had received no request for Japan to restrict export of cars to the United States. Still, he volunteered that, 'Japan would continue to make efforts on its own to help maintain the free trade regime'.[40]

The ITC, as it turned out, and despite President Carter's wish for an early decision, stuck to its original timetable.[41] Accordingly, on 10 November, the ITC handed down its decision and by a vote of three to two rejected the UAW/Ford petition and absolved Japan of any guilt in the decline of the American auto industry. This closed the door for the administration to negotiate import restriction with Japan. Congressional action, however, was still possible. Naturally enough, the ITC decision was greeted with relief by both the Japanese manufacturers and US auto importers, but the US auto industry expressed bitter disappointment and vowed to take the fight to Congress. Had the ITC decision been a unanimous one, it would probably have had some restraining effect on the demand for import restriction, but it was very close and instead of resolving the issue, left it open for further consideration. Also, it is well within the American tradition, just as the founders of American democracy had intended, not to accept passively rule/tyranny of the majority, but to demand protection of minority rights, and the American auto industry must have been heartened by the close decision which enabled it to continue the fight. Moreover, even those ITC members who had voted to reject the petition lashed out against imports, either directly or indirectly. Michael J. Calhoun, Vice-chairman of the Commission, stated that the 'integrity of the international trading system' required a 'certain sensitivity' on the part of overseas suppliers 'to avoid achieving their success at too high a cost to the host society'. He did not specifically point to the Japanese car industry nor, indeed, did he have to when he continued saying, 'I have found a disturbing absence of such regard and sensitivity on the part of particular foreign automobile manufacturers'.[42]

The presidential election of November 1980 resulted in a defeat for President Carter, partly an indictment of his un-Democratic policies of pursuing the goal of low inflation even at the cost of high unemployment.

The new Republican administration could not have been

oblivious either to the distress in the auto industry or to the mood in the Congress, and one of Reagan's earliest decisions was to appoint a special task force to study the auto problem and make its recommendations to him. The task force was headed by Secretary of Transportation Lewis, and the other members included USTR Brock, Commerce Secretary Baldridge, Labor Secretary Donovan, and Weidenbaum of the Council of Economic Advisors (CEA). Like the earlier Goldschmidt task force, the present task force also seemed divided on the policy response. Because of this division and because the composition of the cabinet seemed to favour 'free traders', some like Obi Toshio considered it unlikely that Reagan would take any protectionist steps, considering, for example, that ten of the fourteen cabinet members, including Haig, Stockman, Weidenbaum, and Regan, all opposed import restraint.[43] Donald Regan, for instance, had strongly criticized President Carter's aid package announced in Detroit in July 1980, saying to the effect that the cause of the present problem confronting the auto industry lay neither in Japan nor in Europe, but in Washington, implying the policies of the administration to sustain high interest rates and the emphasis on fighting inflation first. Interestingly, the Reagan administration continued these same policies, even retaining Paul Volcker at the Federal Reserve Bureau. On the other hand, those who favoured import restrictions on Japanese cars included Lewis, Baldridge, and Brock. The Lewis task force, set up on 28 January, was charged with the mission of submitting a final recommendation within two months. The task force sought to present a unified position favouring VER, but opposition from Regan made it difficult to reach a consensus. Finally, in mid-March, a spokesman announced that agreement had been reached within the task force, as the result of concessions on both sides, particularly Regan.

It is perhaps significant that consensus was finally reached at the second meeting of the task force called by President Reagan on the 17th and only a few days after a Reagan interview was published in the *New York Daily News*, where he stated that he was in favour of voluntary export restraint by Japan, as had been advised by both the Commerce and Transportation Secretaries. Donald Regan may have had no choice but to 'soften' his opposition.

On the 19th, when the report of the task force was formally

submitted, President Reagan attended an expanded ministerial meeting where he stressed the following points:

1. support for the liberal trading system;
2. belief that government should not get too involved in the aid of particular industries;
3. the view that the prevailing poor conditions in the auto industry *was not entirely its own fault*; and
4. therefore, the government had the responsibility to aid the auto industry.[44]

The President thus very nearly overturned the earlier ITC ruling. In late March, Foreign Minister Ito revisited Washington to finalize preparations for Prime Minister Suzuki's visit in May and met with President Reagan on the 24th. The President reiterated his commitment toward preserving the liberal trading order but, pointing to the fever-pitch protectionism in the Congress, signalled strongly that it might be necessary for Japan to exercise VER.[45]

The Japanese auto industry itself remained completely unconvinced on the need to exercise export restraint. They point to forecasts made by US car makers themselves indicating that domestic sales were likely to exceed 1 million units (passenger cars) in 1981. It was advantageous for them, therefore, to await the market trend since they could then hope for a better bargain. Accordingly, they strongly opposed the government's resolve to settle the dispute before Prime Minister Suzuki's pending visit to Washington.

However, after a meeting between Ishihara, Chairman of the Japanese Automobile Industry Association (also President of Nissan Motor Co. Ltd) and MITI Minister Tanaka Rokusuke in April, it was confirmed that the two men had reached an agreement recognizing that Congress would otherwise take the legislative route if Japan failed to exercise VER.[46] The agreement was only on the principle of VER and the specifics were still to be worked out. MITI knew there was a considerable gap between US demands and what the industry was willing to concede at the time.

MITI entered into a final round of negotiations with leaders of the auto industry on 21 April, and while the industry sources had been insisting upon restraining not below the level of exports for 1980, that is, around 1.82 million units, a MITI

73

official revealed after the first day of talks that consensus could probably be reached at a level of 1.7 million units.[47] The official US request, according to some sources, was around the level of exports in 1979, or 1.52 million units, but at various meetings earlier in March between Brock and Ito, Brock and Amaya, and Brock and Okita (former Foreign Minister) a tentative agreement was reported to have been reached at the level of 1.6 million units, although this was considered very demanding on the Japanese auto industry.[48] Another unresolved issue was the duration of the VER. The Americans wanted the VER to apply for a period of three years, which was considered an adequate 'breathing space' for Detroit to recover and complete the necessary retooling for transition to small-car production. The Japanese auto industry, however, insisted that restraints apply for only a year since they did not want to be saddled with quantitative restrictions in a market that most predicted was likely to improve in 1981 and thereafter. The US government forecast, though less optimistic than the industry forecast, still pointed to a steady recovery of sales, as suggested in table 4.5 below.

Table 4.5 US government estimate of auto sales (million units)

Year	Passenger cars	Trucks	Total
1981	9.1	2.4	11.5
1982	11.0	2.8	13.8
1983	12.0	3.0	15.0
1984	12.0	3.0	15.0
1985	11.5	2.9	14.4

Source: *Nihon Keizai Shinbun* (Chokan), 9 April 1981, p. 1.

As had been recommended by the presidential task force, USTR Brock left for Tokyo in late April to negotiate the VER. The final round of negotiations between Brock and MITI began in the early evening of 30 April 1981, which was later described in some detail by Amaya Naohiro, the principal negotiator on the Japanese side. The talks began at 6.30 p.m. with the Japanese side outlining its proposals, as below:

1. The VER would be for a duration of three years.
2. Japan would exercise VER in the first year of the agreement,

with total permitted exports not to exceed 1.7 million units (April 1981 – March 1982).

3. At the end of the first year, there would be fresh negotiations on whether or not to continue the VER.

4. MITI would be responsible for the allocation of quotas to the Japanese manufacturers.

5. MITI would oversee the implementation of the VER and take steps to ensure compliance under the Export Trade Control Act should it appear that the quotas would be exceeded.[49]

Amaya noted that the Japanese offer represented the maximum possible concession and that there was no fall-back position. Brock, however, maintained that the package was still insufficient to block the passage of the Danforth Bill to restrict Japanese car imports.[50] The United States instead proposed a three-year VER at the level of 1.6 million units. The proposed US figure included, besides passenger cars, station wagons and light vans and also included sales in Puerto Rico, all of which had been excluded from the Japanese figure of 1.7 million. Converting the US figure to the Japanese equivalent produced a figure of between 1.45 and 1.5 million, a level that the Japanese industry sources regarded as too low and unacceptable. The talks had reached a deadlock and there was a total silence in the room as each side contemplated its next move. Amaya wrote that the few minutes of silence seemed like a few hours. After a while they agreed that a change in environment and a more relaxed atmosphere might provide fresh ideas. The negotiators adjourned for dinner and drinks, an important phase in official and private negotiations in Japan, where many deals are successfully negotiated and concluded during a night out on the town. Away from the formal setting of the negotiating table and after everyone had settled down with a drink, Amaya took it upon himself to explain to Brock something of the Japanese psyche. The Japanese people, he observed, had both an emotional streak as well as a utilitarian attitude. In the pre-war period and during the war, emotions and petty nationalism were the dominant driving force, but the disastrous wartime failure brought about a major shift in attitude, away from emotionalism to utilitarianism. Given the delicate balance between the two distinct impulses, it was possible, he argued, that should the United States continue to be insensitive and put too much pressure on Japan, the latent emotionalism would be reactivated, to the advantage of neither of the two countries.[51] Amaya hoped that this would have the desired effect of softening the American position. Later that same night, Minister Tanaka held meetings with leaders of the auto industry to brief them on the result of the day's talks and to prepare a new position for the morning's meeting with Brock. The Minister pleaded with leaders of the industry to make some additional concessions but, according to Amaya, was met with stiff opposition. Amaya took Ishihara aside to make a personal effort and began by suggesting that while it may have inspired 'popular admiration' when Japan, before the war, had walked out of the League of Nations, Japan could not afford a rupture in the auto talks since it would lead to the worst possible outcome – a trade war that could not possibly be won by Japan. If the auto industry, therefore, persisted with its hardline position, all would suffer. Amaya went on to observe that Ishihara made no outwardly visible concession, but by what was left unsaid he knew that his efforts had not been in vain.[52]

Amaya's negotiating tactic in this final phase was a tried and tested tool of mediation, of threatening each side with dire consequences if agreement could not be reached and presenting to each a picture of the other as totally intransigent, hoping that this would bring forth concessions on both sides.

The next morning agreement was reached with Brock on the following main points:

1. that the VER would be for a three-year period, ending 31 March 1984;
2. the first-year quota would be set at 1.68 million units;
3. the second-year quota would be at 1.68 million units plus a 16.5 per cent share of whatever growth took place in the American market in 1981; and
4. discussion on VER for the third year.

The quota of 1.68 million units was the average level of Japanese exports to the United States in the preceding two years and the figure of 16.5 per cent represented Japan's share of the US market in 1979, also the average market share for the three years 1978–80. This was intended to reserve for Japan a certain market share, given forecasts of growth in sales in 1981.

76

ANALYSIS OF JAPANESE MOTIVATIONS

In the preceding section we provided a chronological account of the auto dispute without attempting to explain the motivations of the chief actors. This, however, as stated at the outset, is crucial for our purposes. In this section we will try and explore the motivations of MITI that led it to support VER, unlike in past disputes which had also resulted in quantitative restrictions on Japanese exports. It is true that MITI bargained hard during the final phase of negotiations, but a supportership does not imply acceptance of the other side's position in its entirety. Bargaining on the specifics does not, therefore, negate the basic thrust of our argument.

The auto dispute lasted approximately a year and a half and requires an explanation why, if the Japanese positon was not the major stumbling block, a solution could not be reached much earlier. In past trade disputes, Japanese resistance was often blamed for delays in reaching a settlement. In the case under study here, the answer lies in the lack of political clarity and direction of the Carter administration. In order to demonstrate this, we will compare and contrast the policies of the Carter and Reagan administrations, and we are 'fortunate' that the dispute spanned two different American administrations. Also, as the detail in the preceding section showed, there were two very different approaches to the problem. Patrick and Sato, in their analysis of the steel dispute, touched briefly on the contrasts between the resolution of the steel and auto disputes and observed that in the latter instance, 'while the Japanese government (particularly MITI) was prepared to make necessary adjustments, the US government remained indecisive, thus contributing to the prolongation and escalation of the issue'.[53] It is unfair, however, to lump the two administrations together, because the indecisiveness was really only visible in the policies of President Carter. Carter, no doubt, would have liked Japan to initiate VER on its own initiative, but obviously could not bring himself to act in a manner that would compromise the consistency of his domestic programmes. An indication of the difference between the two administrations was evidenced from the gist of the meetings Foreign Minister Ito held with President Carter in September 1980 and with President Reagan in March 1981 (see pp. 71 and 73).

While MITI was unable to impose VER because of President

Carter's refusal formally to indicate its desirability, MITI did the best it could to contain the flood of exports to the United States. As mentioned above, MITI had been urging self-control on the part of auto manufacturers and this did have some effect in reducing exports in the fourth quarter of 1980. In the period January–March 1980, car exports to the United States had increased by a hefty 25.4 per cent over the same period in 1979, but under MITI's urging exports in the October–December quarter declined by 1.8 per cent over the same period in 1979. Total exports for 1980 were 1.82 million units and according to MITI sources, without the self-control, the total would have topped 1.9 million units.[54] It is true, however, that the decline in exports in late 1980 came too late and was rather too modest to have much impact on protectionism in the United States, but there was not much more that MITI could have done. The action MITI took was to call for 'self-control' (*Jishuku*) which had no formal binding powers because it did not specify anything in particular. It could not impose VER (*Jishu Kisei*) because such an action had to be based on some prior government-level understanding to avoid the problem of American anti-trust legislations. Thus, even if the Japanese auto industry had been favourably disposed to VER like the steel industry before it, MITI might still not have been able to do much. But the opposition of the auto industry made it all the more important for the United States to make a formal request so that MITI could use it to force compliance by the domestic industry. President Carter, however, could not bring himself to do so.

Instead, MITI was caught between a barrage of unofficial pressure and official complacency. President Carter seemed primarily interested in containing inflation. The Goldschmidt Report of 2 July 1980 had noted that import restrictions at the level of imports in 1979 would cost American consumers an additional $1 billion in higher prices for imported and domestic cars. Still, it was bewildering that President Carter, in an election year, went against the UAW, an natural ally of the Democratic Party. This may have cost him dearly, but it was also not an isolated instance. Why was it, asked Charles Schultze, Chairman of the CEA, that Carter did not significantly expand the budget to approve any tax cut, 'in the middle of a recession, in the middle of an election year . . . It was a very conservative non-constituency oriented campaign'. Poor Jimmy Carter, he wrote, 'was not the world's greatest politician'.[55] The second

Goldschmidt Report, submitted to President Carter in early January 1981 did not, unlike the first one, simply list the various options but strongly urged the President to seek export restraint from Japan for a five-year period. It argued that the

> Government should negotiate an import restraint agreement with the Japanese which reflects the real time period it will take for US automakers to accomplish the transition. This would define a réasonable period of time for our domestic industry to retool without facing the permanent loss of additional market share to Japanese producers.[56]

However, the recommendation came too late. Carter, having lost the election, had made it quite plain that he would allow President-elect Reagan to seek his own solution to the dispute, rather than negotiate with the weakened powers of a lame-duck presidency.

An interesting article by Kusano Atsushi on the early phase of the auto dispute suggested that Carter really wanted Japan to exercise VER on its own, despite his own opposition to any restictions in the flow of goods. He wrote that, in May 1980, responsible MITI officials approached the White House through private channels with a proposal to undertake VER if the United States so wished and in exchange for assurances that the United States would not implement import restrictions.[57] President Carter was informed of this offer in a memo by Stuart Eizenstat, White House Domestic Policy Advisor. The President sent back the reply that if Japan wished to undertake VER on its own, the US government would neither formally endorse it, nor oppose it. This was taken to mean that he had accepted the MITI offer. The deal, however, fell through when a staff member under Eizenstat, intentionally or otherwise, reported the incident to the American Embassy in Tokyo, where objection was raised about why the White House and not the State Department was dealing with the issue. If the incident did take place it would add support for the thesis presented here, but even so there are certain problems, which lead this author to doubt if the incident did take place exactly as reported by Kusano. We can understand why the proposal was transmitted through private channels since the Ministry of Foreign Affairs opposed VER, and the authors of the plan, a small group within the MITI, needed time and US approval to build their argument and have it officially accepted. What is difficult to understand is why MITI officials should have been concerned enough to seek assurances that the United States would not impose import restrictions. The chances of Carter supporting import restrictions were not very high since his own opposition to VER was well known and if Congress did pass such protectionist legislation (not likely at that early stage) Carter would certainly have exercised his veto.

We have argued that MITI favoured export restraint, and it is necessary now to demonstrate the extent to which its motivations support the thesis of Japan as a regime supporter. In reading Amaya's writings on the subject, one can be impressed with his concern for restoring the *pax americana*, but is that really what motivated him? Within the Japanese culture and society there is a strong emphasis in differentiating between *honne* (real intentions, often beneath the surface) and *tatemae* (up-front intentions). While we argue that his writings essentially reflect his *honne* it cannot be denied that there are others who hold a different view.

For example, Nukazawa Kazuo, Director of the Keidanren (Japan Federation of Economic Associations), remarked, in an interview with this author, that both Keidanren Chairman of the time, Inayama, and Amaya harboured a strong disdain for GATT and did not see much of a future for a multilateral trade regime, preferring instead to emphasize bilateralism that would at least secure access to important markets, even if outside the GATT agreement. As to the interpretation presented in this thesis, Nukazawa simply added that it was more 'kind' to Amaya than his own reading of Amaya's real intentions, but agreed that it was a matter of opinion. Where opinions diverge, it is necessary to try and fathom the reason behind the divergence, and this will be attempted here.

Nukazawa's interpretation, as well as the opinion expressed in the *Nihon Keizai Shinbun* of 2 May, 1981 (see p. 53), are deduced from the actual outcome of the auto dispute, and the outcome itself is analysed as a single discrete event. The result, it cannot be denied, restricted the flow of goods across countries and may also be argued to have violated GATT, although not formally. However, if we view the outcome as not just a discrete event, but rather as part of a process, we think it is possible to assert that Amaya was, indeed, concerned with strengthening the liberal economic order. In his writings,

Amaya distinguished between the short term and the long term and wrote that insistence on strict adherence to the GATT principles might safeguard that institution in the short term but would certainly undermine it in the long run. According to him, it was necessary to be flexible and adapt to reality and that the reality of the American industrial decline necessitated a tactical retreat until the foundation had been fortified. Elements within the Ministry of Foreign Affairs, in particular the former Ambassador to the United States, Ushiba, assumed this to be a dangerous strategy, bound to lead to further retreats and eventual collapse of the LIEO. Amaya, later, was to brand all those who had opposed MITI's policy of implementing VER as short-sighted 'soap-nationalists'.[58]

As Amaya saw it, the liberal trading system could not be maintained without strong and effective leadership in the system, a role that only the United States was capable of playing, despite its predicament at that time. He also discounted a co-operative arrangement which, while desirable, was also unrealistic. His notion of stability and order was based on an analysis of the social structure of Japan during the Tokugawa period, from 1603 to 1867–8. From this period of Japanese history he derived certain lessons for Japan today, which he expounded under the rubric of *Chonin no Kokkaron* – the theory of the merchant state.[59] Given Amaya's known penchant for finding solutions to modern-day problems in history, this is not at all surprising. David Halberstam related this well. It was typical of Amaya, he wrote, that when going to attend a summit conference in Washington, while his colleagues would be reading briefing papers, Amaya would almost surely be 'reading instead some esoteric book on twelfth-century China. The implication was clear: the answers were not in those briefing papers, the answers were in the distant past'.[60]

During the Tokugawa period, the Shogun, the effective ruler of Japan, pursued a policy of strict isolation from world affairs barring all but very modest levels of trade through the Dutch intermediaries based on the island of Deshima, off Nagasaki. This policy of *sakoku* was designed to protect and immunize Japan from the international forces of change, in the interest of the assumed higher objective of social order and stability. The policy, helped also by the establishment of a hierarchical society, was quite successful in achieving its objective. The social order was composed of four separate classes: the *samurai* who held the reins of political power and ensured peace and harmony internally; the farmers, who with their tax payment propped up the political order; the artisans; and the lowly merchants – the *chonin* – who increasingly gained in influence despite being on the lowest rung of the social order. The rise of the merchant class was due to a complex set of causes including the spread of money economy as the result of the *sankin-kotai* system, which required the local feudal lords (*daimyo*) to stay for a fixed length of time, periodically, in the capital city of Edo (Tokyo), and the inability of the *samurai* to meet their growing needs from the declining tax revenues. The *samurai* were forced to look to the merchants for loans to sustain their living conditions. The merchants had wealth but little else, since the *samurai* held exclusive rights to military, police, and political power. Because the merchants valued social stability and order they, in turn, depended on the *samurai* to provide this stability and learned to align their relationship with them very carefully and closely.

Thus, when the *samurai* were no longer able to sustain their extravagant lifestyle solely on the rice tax collected from the farmers, they turned to the merchants, who willingly made generous loans even with the prior knowledge that the loans might never be repaid. These were costs that had to be borne in the interest of preserving a favourable social structure. For Amaya, there were similarities in the contemporary inter-national system to the Tokugawa social order. Although the United States and the Soviet Union combined all four social classes, since the end of the Second World War Japan had travelled the road of the merchants, but today was at the crossroads where it had to ponder its future direction: whether to acquire political power as well or to continue on the present path. If the decision was to shun the road to political power, then Japan had to be willing to apply lessons learnt from past experience, where and when applicable. Even if it was to give priority to the acquisition of political power, it was unlikely to come close to the status of the superpowers. Just as the *samurai*, in the past, created and sustained a stable social order conducive to the growth of internal commerce, the existing liberal trading regime also depended, for its stability, on the United States. When the *samurai* fell upon bad times, they turned to the merchants; today, the United States suffered from the pains of industrial decline and Japan had to be ready and willing to help. For Amaya, the auto VER was just one such sacrifice Japan had to make for the greater good of the international system. Its immediate effect was to remove a thorn in US–Japan relations, but if it also aided the revival of the auto industry in the United States, it would also lead to the long-term stability of the system. It is in this sense that Amaya's approach can be seen as a long-term approach to maintaining the liberal trading system. In elucidating Amaya's view, the purpose has not been to endorse its built-in conservatism in favour of the status quo and against change, but rather to understand the motives behind his actions. We should not overlook, for example, that while the Tokugawa regime was indeed very stable, it was not a very just system.

The Ministry of Foreign Affairs (MFA), which had traditionally been very forthright in promoting good US–Japan relations, surprisingly took a position that was not favourable towards VER. The MFA argued that the GATT rules should be strictly adhered to and that deviance would invite further departures from the GATT-prescribed framework for the settlement of trade disputes. It took exception to the fact that VER was a 'grey-area' measure, not having a clear status under international law, and that it was much better to use the available safeguard measures. It was not necessarily against restricting Japanese exports but it preferred to employ other measures besides VER, in the interest of staying within the bounds of GATT. The problem with this was that since all GATT measures are non-discriminatory in nature, it was not possible to stay within GATT and at the same time take selective steps against Japanese exports. It is not necessarily true, therefore, as Amaya wrote, that 'The views of the Ministry of Foreign Affairs concerning the automobile dispute, can be likened to the MITI views in the earlier textiles dispute'.[61] In any case, the views of the MFA did not have much impact on the outcome of the auto dispute because, from start to finish, MITI represented the Japanese side. For example, a day before Foreign Minister Ito was due to leave for Washington, on 20 March 1981 he met with MITI Minister Tanaka Rokusuke at a city hotel where Tanaka is reported to have told him that since MITI had the ultimate authority to negotiate and settle the dispute, the Foreign Minister should not make any commitments and simply 'acknowledge' any proposal that the United States might make. The Foreign Minister, reportedly, agreed to this.[62]

The objection might be raised that the interpretation given here, of MITI's intention, was excessively favourable to Japan and ignored other possible explanations. As an alternative, it could be argued that MITI favoured VER only because that would allow it to extend its influence to the domestic auto industry. It is true that the Japanese auto industry was jealously protective of its interests and resentful of past attempts by MITI to restructure it. This commitment to preserve independence from MITI became evident, in the 1960s, when MITI tried to encourage mergers with the expectation that the consolidated manufacturers would be better able to withstand foreign domination and control. Part of the reason why MITI was relatively ineffectual in shaping the development of the domestic auto industry was due to inadequately developed *Amakudari* ties, given the 'newness' of the auto industry, as opposed to the steel industry. However, to argue that MITI was only interested in VER as a convenient mechanism to influence the auto industry, since it would control the allocation of export quotas, is problematic. We do not deny that MITI was unmindful of the potential for increased influence over the domestic auto industry, but it would be unreasonable to suggest that this was the main reason behind its support for VER. If anything, it was simply an additional bonus. MITI could not have been unaware that sectoral control without continued maintenance of the liberal trading regime would have had a seriously detrimental effect on the Japanese economy as a whole, and that was its primary concern.

In the period after the VER went into effect, the American auto industry made a remarkable recovery. Although production of passenger cars in 1981 (the VER period ran from April to March, beginning April 1981) was down by 2 per cent over 1980, and production in 1982 declined by a further 19 per cent over 1981, there was steady improvement after that. In 1983 production increased by about 34 per cent and in 1984 the increase was about 15 per cent. With the upward trend in production statistics, profitability also returned, in scandalous proportions according to some. The steep bonuses that the management of the American auto industry gave itself in 1985 raised eyebrows not only in Japan but also within the UAW, whose members had to take wage cuts to help companies through the crisis period. The recovery of the American auto industry, at least temporarily, contained and subdued the voices of protectionism, at least within the industry. However, there continued to be some support for the Local Content Bill, although it is unlikely to emerge as a main issue because the auto industry itself opposes the Bill, which might constrict its ability to procure internationally, and also because all the major Japanese car manufacturers now have firm plans to manufacture in the United States or are already doing so.

CONCLUSION

Finally, in this concluding section we will briefly review the effect that the VER had on US car manufacturers in terms of their recovery from the economic recession.

The auto VER was designed to restrict Japanese exports for a maximum of three years from April 1981, but has already been extended three times. In the first two years of the agreement, it appeared not to have any significant beneficial effect for Detroit. This was due to an absolute decline in market demand and sales. Total sales, including imports, declined from about 8.9 million units in 1980 to 8.53 million units in 1981 and to 7.98 million units in 1982. As a result, it was argued that the Japanese VER was not having much effect because the market would not have absorbed much more in any event. However, the fact that Japanese exporters were able to increase prices and still ship the maximum number of cars, under the MITI allocated quotas, suggests that they would have improved their market-share position without a VER. Table 4.6 below shows how the market-share position changed in the period following the VER agreement.

Table 4.6 Share of US car market (%)

Year	United States	Japan
1980	73.3	21.2
1981	72.7	21.8
1982	72.1	22.6
1983	74.0	20.9
1984	76.0	18.3

Source: *Jidosha Sangyo Handbook*, Nissan Motor Co. Ltd, 1985 edn, p. 279.
Note: US figures include VW (USA) and Honda (USA) production in the United States. Honda (USA) went into production in 1983.

On the investment side of the picture, in the period 1979–83, the American car manufacturers invested a total of over $51 billion worldwide to build better and more fuel-efficient cars. This was almost twice the total investment for the previous five years.[63] It is difficult to make accurate assessments of the effectiveness of the new investment, but according to Japanese industry sources the cost disadvantages of American manufacturers declined to about half the earlier levels.[64]

The VER was, by all accounts, important in the rebuilding of the US auto industry and the ITC recently published a report assessing the impact of the Japanese VER on US car manufacturers. This is shown in table 4.7 below.

Table 4.7 Impact of VER on US auto industry

		1980	1981	1982	1983	1984
Japanese car sales ('000)	Actual	1,822	1,845	1,774	1,861	1,950
	without VER	–	1,948	1,969	2,435	2,948
	Diff. (%)	–	−5.6	−11.0	−30.8	−51.2
American car sales ('000)	Actual	6,578	6,203	5,757	6,795	7,960
	without VER	–	6,128	5,629	6,436	7,342
	Diff. (%)	–	1.2	2.2	5.3	7.8
Total US car sales ('000)	Actual	8,975	8,529	7,978	9,181	10,400
	without VER	–	8,551	8,035	9,372	10,743
	Diff. (%)	–	−0.3	−0.7	−2.1	−3.3
Retail price of Japanese cars ($)	Actual	6,709	7,292	7,539	8,317	9,300
	without VER	–	7,107	7,180	7,486	7,962
	Diff. (%)	–	2.5	4.8	10.0	14.4

Source: Kawaharada, S. (1985) 'Shin Jidai o Mukaeru Jidosha Kaigai Jigyo', *Tekko Kai* 35: no. 9, p. 13.

The VER also brought about significant changes in the structure of the US auto industry. All of the major Japanese car manufacturers started production in the United States by 1988. Japanese auto-parts manufacturers also followed the lead of car markets and started setting up production facilities in the United States. There is no doubt that the stimulating factor was the VER. The most aggressive and forward-looking Japanese manufacturer was Honda (fifth in Japan in terms of total output, third in passenger-car output) which was the first to invest in the United States. Its aggressiveness appeared to have paid off handsomely. In 1985, Honda overtook Nissan to become second in the United States in total sales, including domestic production. Toyota, the largest of the Japanese car manufacturers, was the last to join the pack and planned to begin production in the United States in 1988, at the annual rate of 200,000 units. As a result of the investment already in place and that which is projected, direct exports from Japan will constitute a smaller share of total Japanese car sales in the United States (see table 4.8).

Table 4.8 Export from Japan and local production in the United States

	1984	1985	1986	1987	1988
Japanese production in the United States					
Nissan	–	5	12	12	12
GM + Toyoto (Nummi)	–	6	25	25	25
Toyota	–	–	–	–	20
Honda	13	14	30	30	30
Mitsubishi	–	–	–	–	18
Mazda	–	–	–	24	24
Total (A)	13	25	67	91	129
Exports from Japan	191	230	230	230	230
Total Japanese car sales (B)	204	255	297	321	359
US production as % of Japanese car sales (A/B)	6.3	10.0	22.5	28.0	36.0

Source: Kawaharada, S. (1985) 'Shin Jidai o Mukaeru Jidosha Kaigai Jigyo', *Tekko Kai* 35: no. 9, p. 13.
Note: Unit of car sales is 10,000.

As a result of these structural changes in the US auto industry, it is unlikely to confront challenges in the future in the shape of imports versus domestics, despite the Hyundai phenomenon. If problems do arise, these will likely be of a micro-level nature, of interfirm competition, for example Ford versus Honda (USA). What it means is that although the US manufacturers have survived their first major crisis, their future viability will depend on their capacity to compete with Japanese cars produced in the United States.

On the basis of our discussion in this chapter, it would appear that the auto VER did have the desired effects. It provided Japanese firms an incentive to invest in the United States and, more importantly, created the conditions necessary for the revitalization of the US auto industry. The latter, of course, was the main factor behind the stand taken by the Japanese government in favour of VER. This was premised on the belief that protectionism within the US auto industry had to be contained in the interest of maintaining the liberal trading order. In so far as this was true, it would support our argument that the Japanese government displayed a clear sense of responsibility toward the international system, even though it confronted stiff opposition from sources within Japan, particularly the domestic auto industry. Thus, only by recognizing the intentions behind the VER can we explain why, in the auto dispute, the position of the Japanese government was so different from that in the earlier trade disputes with the United States.

5

Trade Imbalance
and Import Promotion

THE US–JAPAN TRADE IMBALANCE AND
REGIME INSTABILITY

The auto dispute was the last of the major sectoral trade problems between the United States and Japan. Since then the arena of American concern has shifted from the particular to the general. The phenomenal growth of the Japanese trade surplus with the United States in the 1980s created a new set of conditions, fuelling the growth of protectionism. However, it must be recognized that the ballooning of the Japanese trade surplus did not result from the proliferation of import restrictive policies, but that did not prevent the rise in demand for retaliatory protection. It was also unfortunate that bilateral trade imbalances had become the focus of concern, but that was, perhaps, understandable since the US–Japan trade imbalance appeared to be representative of their general trading positions. Japan's surplus was not restricted only to the United States, and the US deficit with Japan, too, was part of the general picture. Furthermore, it was this bilateral nexus which accounted for a large portion of the overall surplus and deficit of Japan and the United States respectively. This led to a widely held belief in such impressionistic solutions that correcting the bilateral imbalance would resolve the overall problem. The pressure came from the United States, but Japanese policies too reflected an appreciation of the problems that their trade surpluses were creating for the stability of the system.

In this and the following chapter, we will look at macroeconomic issues in the relations between Japan and the United States, in particular the trade imbalance. The imputed causal variables that had led to the increase in the US trade deficit with Japan, from around $7 billion in 1980 to $40 billion in 1985, had become the primary stimulant to American protectionism. These imputed causal variables included trade barriers in Japan, the Japanese distribution system, Japanese government procurement policies, and low levels of domestic demand in Japan. It needs to be emphasized that, however true these causes may be, they had not been recently introduced. Nevertheless, in so far as the trade surplus had emerged as a destabilizing force in the system, Japan did recognize its responsibility to do something about it. Our focus will, accordingly, be on measures taken by the Japanese governemnt to remedy the trade imbalance. It should be pointed out, however, that absolute balance in trade relations between Japan and the United States is neither feasible nor should it be the objective. Ideally, we should not even have to consider bilateral balances, but unfortunately political realities are not such that we can ignore them.

Most experts agree that US–Japan trade was structurally impossible to balance and that Japan was likely to enjoy a surplus for quite some time. The magnitude of the present surplus, however, had to be reduced and this is what Japanese government measures hoped to achieve. Aside from the specific measures, to be discussed further (see p. 102), we can understand why the Japanese government, given its objective as defined above, continued to exercise voluntary export restraint on autos beyond the timeframe originally envisaged and considered necessary for the revitalization of the American auto industry.

The auto VER, as initially agreed upon, was to last for a period of three years and provide a 'breathing space' to the American car manufacturers, giving them time to adjust and adapt to the changed demand patterns. However, as we saw in the previous chapter, it did not begin to have a significant effect on the sales position of the American car manufacturers until after the second year. Only then did things slowly start to pick up for Detroit. Becuase of the late recovery, both countries agreed to extend the VER for an additional year. The situation continued to improve through 1984 and President Reagan openly stated that the US government would not seek another extension when the agreement expired in April 1985. Yet, when the Japanese government announced that it would extend the VER for another year at the expanded quota of 2.3 million units, it immediately created an uproar in the United States. There was displeasure that the Japanese government had boosted the export quota by a hefty 24 per cent and it became obvious that what the US government had really intended to mean was that, while formal restraints were no longer necessary, any increase should be kept within 'reasonable' limits. Perhaps it had not seriously considered the possibility that imports from Japan could rise drastically after the restraints had been removed. From the Japanese standpoint, MITI issued the justification that, without restraints, total exports for the year could reach 2.7 million units, implying therefore that the new quota was, in fact, a meaningful restraint. The Japanese government was genuinely taken aback by the American reaction and Prime Minister Nakasone went so far as to admit that the decision had been a mistake.[1] The following year the Japanese government decided to play safe, and in January 1986 MITI announced that the VER would remain in place, until 1987, at the previous year's level.

The new significance of the VER was as a mechanism to contain the more general nature of the trading imbalance. For Japan the auto VER, once in place, became a convenient tool for controlling the growth of Japanese trade surpluses. The restraint agreement was extended because, without such an extension, exports would probably have risen much faster. In 1985, total Japanese car exports to the United States amounted to $19.2 billion, about 30 per cent of total exports, and was also the main factor behind the increase in the Japanese surplus.[2] In 1986, the MITI Minister Watanabe suggested that, without the controls, auto exports would go up by a further 20 per cent to add a further $5 billion to the Japanese surplus.[3] Thus, the VER had become attractive of its own merits. One may wonder then as to why the Japanese government decided to raise the quota by 24 per cent in 1985, instead of continuing with the existing levels. An important consideration in this was the strong pressure from Japanese manufacturers for total elimination of controls, particularly from the smaller companies which had a small quota allocation and wished to improve their market position in the United States. At the same time, GM also wanted the restraints abolished so that it could increase its 'Original Equipment Manufacturer' (OEM) imports from Japan under the GM–Isuzu tie-up. GM had become an importer as well as a manufacturer. Confronted with cross-pressures, MITI chose what was, by its calculations, a middle road.

After the auto dispute, the US–Japan trade problem became focused on the general trade picture, although there were some negotiations on specific issues. One of the most prominent was the 'Market Oriented Sector Specific' (MOSS) talks, centering on leather, medical instruments, forestry products, and telecommunications equipment. Dealing with the detail and specific issues is more to the liking of Japanese negotiators and they would obviously have preferred to continue on the MOSS framework. However, the United States had, by now, become frustrated with this approach as was vividly brought out by the US Undersecretary of Commerce for International Trade, Lionel Olmer, in his testimony to the US Senate in March 1982. In late February 1982, the Chairman of the ruling Japanese Liberal Democratic Party, Esaki, led a diet delegation to the United States to explain Japan's latest measures to expand imports. Testifying before the Senate, Olmer was asked to evaluate the results of the Esaki mission, to which he replied,

in several discussions when we would lay out our case, one or more members of the Esaki mission would reach into a briefcase and pull out large volumes of data to deal with us on a selective issue or other rather than to discuss in a more general basis what I believe and what the administration believes is a pervasive problem of market access generally.[4]

The preference of the Japanese government for dealing with specific issues stems from the fact that the initial identification of the area of concern to the United States facilitates the task of pressuring the domestic industry or ministry to make the necessary concessions. Dealing at the abstract level does not allow pressure to be localized, which is necessary for it to be effective within the Japanese decision-making context. Thus, when the Japanese government complains that the United States fails to show proper understanding, it is not entirely without some justification. As was noted by Timothy Curran,

'foreign pressure is often applied in a wrong way, thus achieving less than maximum liberalization or causing a counter productive backlash in Japan. For example, American demands are often too vague – calling on Japan simply to do something to open its market and ease trade frictions'.[5]

In January 1986, the MOSS talks were successfully concluded, and while the United States expressed satisfaction, Senator Danforth (Republican: Missouri) commented that it was no longer possible to deal with specific issues since there were just too many of them. He added, 'I am absolutely convinced that dealing with these sectoral problems in and of themselves in isolation – that strategy of "ad hocing" the trade problem – is not successful'.[6] But applying pressure in a generalized way has its own problems since it easily leads to an exaggeration of the problem. It can create unnecessary acrimony, and this has indeed been an unfortunate outgrowth of the present crisis in US–Japan relations.

To be sure, this is not simply a bilateral problem since many of the European and non-oil-producing Third World countries have similar trade problems with Japan. While these concerns cannot be ignored, we will focus our attention on the US–Japan nexus because of its relative importance to the overall ability of the liberal trading regime. In chapter 7 we will look at Japanese trade and economic relations with the regional countries of Asia.

Earlier, we noted the importance of a strong and large economy in providing easy access to its market for foreign producers, as protectionism in the large economy tends to spread rapidly and also because of the need to provide a mechanism to balance supply and demand imbalances of other regime members who may otherwise, in times of economic recession, be tempted to raise protectionist barriers. Tensions build up when this vent for surplus is closed, but the problems become compounded when one large economy itself becomes dependent on another to balance its own supply and demand imbalances.

It is often argued that the policies of the Japanese government limited the potential that the Japanese economy had for performing the balancing function by restricting foreign access to the Japanese market. Worse, instead of a positive contribution, the Japanese economy had a net negative effect by relying unfairly on the failing US economy to the detriment of American industry and stability of the trading system. As Hofheinz and Calder noted, even though domestic car sales in

Japan, in 1979, had dropped by 6.3 per cent, production had actually increased by 38 per cent. They went on to suggest that 'Exports have saved the Japanese automobile industry from the slow death presently being suffered by US auto makers'.[7] It is interesting to note that, in 1979, Japan exported about 3 million cars but imported only 64,000 units, and that happened to be a good year for foreign car sales in Japan.

Since the early 1980s, Japan's overall trade surplus as well as the surplus in trade with the United States increased at a rapid pace, as shown in table 5.1.

Table 5.1   Japan's trade balance ($ million)

Year	Total[a]	With USA[b]
1980	2,125(1)	12,200
1981	19,967	18,100
1982	18,079	19,000
1983	31,454	21,700
1984	44,257	36,800
1985	–	49,700

Source: [a] *Japan, 1985*, Keizai Koho Center, Tokyo, p. 48.
[b] The 1985 figure is taken from *Asahi Shinbun* 31 January 1986, p. 1.
Note: This reflects the oil-price hike.

Within the context of the general trade imbalance, Western criticism concerns the low ratio of high-value-added manufactured goods (Standard International Trade Classification [SITC] categories 5–8) in total Japanese imports. Although most experts agree that the Japanese trade surplus with the United States is structural, given the low resource availability and high resource requirement of the economy, it is still alleged that the ratio of manufacturing imports to total imports is too low and that it is not structural but artificial. Table 5.2 shows that, while

Table 5.2   Manufactured imports in total imports

Year	Value ($ billion)	Percentage
1980	32.1	22.9
1981	34.8	24.3
1982	32.8	24.9
1983	34.4	27.2
1984	40.6	29.8

Source: MITI, Tokyo (based on customs statistics).

94

there was some improvement in the 1980s, the ratio was still very low. Only 30 per cent of Japan's total imports were manufactured goods as opposed to 71 per cent for the United States, 52 per cent for the EC, and 83 per cent for Canada.

From table 5.2, it is also clear that in the first four years of the 1980s there was no significant change in the dollar value of manufactured imports, but the ratio did climb steadily. This alerts us to the volatility of the ratio to price changes of primary products, particularly oil, which constitutes a hefty chunk of total Japanese imports. Japan's oil bill, over the period 1980–4, declined from $57.6 billion to $45.3 billion, reflecting both a decline in oil prices and the success of the conservation movement. Accompanying the decline of oil prices, the price index of non-oil primary commodities also declined from 100 in 1982 to 81 in 1984.[8] Going back to the decade of the 1970s, in 1970 the ratio of manufactured goods to total imports was 30.3 per cent and in 1972 29.6 per cent. The oil crisis of 1973 and the quadrupling of oil prices lowered the ratio to 20.3 per cent in 1975. In 1979 the ratio was 26.7 per cent, but after the second oil crisis it again went down to 22.8 per cent in 1980.[9] It could be argued that since Japan is a resource-dependent country and thus unlike all the other advanced industrialized countries, the data presented above distort the reality to the detriment of Japan, since primary imports will necessarily figure prominently in total Japanese imports. As a more standard measurement, we could look at manufactured imports as a percentage of the gross national product (GNP). This is given in table 5.3 along with statistics for the United States, West Germany and the United Kingdom, for comparative purposes.

Japan's manufactured imports were about one-half to three-quarters below the average for developed countries. Matsuda Manabu of the Japanese Ministry of Finance suggested a couple

Table 5.3 Ratio of manufactured imports to GNP

	1965	1975	1980	1983
Japan	2.2	2.3	2.9	2.7
United States	1.6	3.4	5.2	5.2
United Kingdom	6.4	12.1	14.3	14.8
West Germany	7.5	9.8	12.1	13.4

Source: Matsuda, M. (1986) 'O-Bei Shokoku to no Boeki Mondai no ichi shiten: Seihin Yunyu hiritsu Hijo Yoso no Datosei ni tsuite', *Boeki to Kansai* 34: 35.

of factors behind Japan's low manufactured imports as measured above, besides the import dependence of resources.

1. The fact that there were no industrial countries in the region, besides Japan, to allow for a division of labour, as has taken place on the European continent.
2. The fact that Japan had a large domestic market which enabled it to set up and support domestic manufacturing. Therefore, he argued, it was unfair to criticize Japan for importing only as many manufactured products as did Switzerland with a GNP about a tenth of Japan, because the latter obviously could not support a domestic manufacturing base with its small market.[10]

He then went on to argue that American complaints that the Japanese market was closed ignored the fact that Japan was the second largest importer of American manufactured goods, after Canada, and well ahead of the fifth-ranked West Germany. Also, he pointed out that the Japanese ratio was indeed changing for the better. Although the growth in imports of manufactured goods for Japan was 16.8 per cent over the period of 1975–83 compared to 37 per cent for West Germany, he argued that when this nominal figure was adjusted for exchange-rate movements, the true growth rates were 34.9 and 22.9 per cent, respectively.[11] This certainly presents a rosier picture for Japan, but may be as misleading as the one he wishes to correct. This is because the base values for 1975 are much lower for Japan with the consequence that growth appears faster than for West Germany which had already achieved a higher level of imports of manufactured goods.

In his above-mentioned Senate testimony (1982), Under-secretary Olmer tabled a list of factors that he claimed were behind the trade imbalance between the two countries. Included among these, besides the plain bias of the 'buy Japanese' policy, he listed the residual quotas, government standards and certification procedures, the government tobacco and salt monopoly, application of sales tax on a CIF basis for imports and on an ex-factory basis for domestic goods, and the MITI.[12] In the period since then, there has been considerable improvement in some of the problem areas, but others have continued to persist. In 1982, Japan had quota protection for 27 items, including four leather products, but which have since been removed following the MOSS talks, leaving 23 items under quota protection. Also, although the market share of American-brand cigarettes was still low, it had increased in recent years. And, as we shall see, improvements have been made in the standards and certification procedures.

THE NATURE OF THE US–JAPAN TRADE IMBALANCE

A common perception in the United States is that since Japan is a surplus country, the cause as well as the solution could be found in Japanese trade policy and practice.[13] The Japanese, to a large extent, feel that American criticism is misdirected and that Japan is being made a scapegoat for problems internal to the United States, specifically the American fiscal deficit. On both sides of the Pacific there exists a wide perception gap: the Americans tend to view Japan as more closed than it really is, while the Japanese tend to regard their economy as a model of openness. However, it should be pointed out that raising the level of Japanese manufactured imports requires concomitant efforts on the part of foreign manufacturers. Some have found this missing in Japan's trading partners.

According to Lawrence Snowden, former President of the American Chamber of Commerce in Japan, 'the accusations [against Japan] arise more from companies which have taken a look at the market and decided it was too tough based on old wives' tales they have heard over the years about how bad things are in Japan.' He criticized American businesses for not doing their home work: 'if they believe that a widget which is made for a six-foot-four Texan or West Virginian sells well to a five-foot-two dark-haired Japanese, they just haven't understood the market place very well or the consumer, *and that's the problem*'.[14] The perceptual problem is frequently taken up in Japan to rebut Western criticisms. Higashi Chikara, a former Ministry of Finance official and presently a LDP diet member, wrote that American and European critics were not adverse to using 'outdated statistics and arguments' to make their point, a theme taken up also by a group of MFA officials who wrote that, when US Congressmen and Senators claimed that the Japanese market was closed, one got the impression that the image of Japan of 10–20 years ago was still deeply ingrained in their minds.[15] From a different viewpoint altogether, it could be

97

argued that the old image was more deeply etched in the collective Japanese mentality. Comparing Japan today with Japan of two decades ago will surely give the impression of much progress, but the correct comparison should not be with Japan of the past but with conditions in other countries today. Thus, Olsen argued that even though a lot has been achieved in the intervening period, a lot more still remained to be done.[16]

The perception gap is not a new phenomenon. It can exist between countries sharing the same cultural background, but when socio-cultural barriers have to be crossed the problems can become magnified, arising from the difficulty or lack of obtaining accurate information. Snowden, in the above-mentioned interview, explained that, even today, many American executives looking to set up in Japan were unaware of the liberalization measures of 1979 which allowed them to 'do what [they] want in this country in the way of owning a subsidiary.' A few years ago, the Japanese government set up the Office of the Trade Ombudsman (OTO) and as of 6 November 1985 it had received 221 claims of grievances against Japanese trade practices and the legal structure from foreign business organizations, of which about 90 were documented to be a misunderstanding of the actual situation.[17]

Of course, as mentioned, there is misperception in both countries. The Japanese find it hard to understand Western criticism of their system, convinced that their market is more open than any other. In terms of average tariff rates, Japan compares very favourably, even though tariffs on selective items are very high. But with an overall decline in the weight of tariff protection, other forms of non-tariff barriers (NTBs) have become more prominent. However, Higashi Chikara was convinced that the obstacles to import were only assumed ones, not real. He wrote,

> When, in time, they [the foreign critics] accepted the fact that among all industrialized nations, Japan has some of the lowest tariffs, they focused on the assumed non-tariff barriers many of which are in reality traditions rooted in the nation's unique social and cultural history over which the government has no control.[18]

This forms a part of the Japanese response to foreign criticisms: that the West was trying to re-order and change Japanese social structure to conform with Western patterns. This, however, as we shall see, was indirectly acknowledged by the government as necessary to resolve trade frictions, but apart from this there are other NTBs that cannot be explicitly linked to culture or society. One example of a discriminatory NTB concerned shipping containers, an issue which the Japanese government tried to side-step using what one official of the Japan External Trade Organization (JETRO) described to me as the 'giraffe theory'.[19]

In recent years, most shipping companies have started using oversized containers to save on transportation and handling costs, and to improve efficiency. The Japanese government was reluctant to allow these containers into Japan, arguing that the oversized containers posed a safety risk on Japan's narrow and congested roads. Ironically, however, many of these same containers were manufactured in Japan and transported over the road system from the factory to the docks for export. If there was a double standard here, the Japanese government had a very simple and neat answer for it. It argued that a container for export was itself an export commodity which could not possibly be cut into smaller pieces and still be exported, just as the giraffe's long neck could not be cut off to fit into a smaller container prior to export. However, when importing, the container was no longer the commodity, which was what was inside the container and which could, therefore, also be transferred into smaller containers at the port of entry. It was unconcerned that such transhipment at the port of entry meant additional cost for the importer and a handicap for the foreign manufacturer to overcome.

Non-tariff barriers also included many of the technical standards and certification procedures that are generally considered to be relatively more stringent and cumbersome than in other developed countries, especially those relating to product safety and which have the overall effect of discouraging foreign producers or of negating their relative advantage. Also, a slow-moving Japanese bureaucracy is blamed for lengthy delays in product certification that give the Japanese manufacturers time to prepare themselves for foreign competition. In a recent instance, a Swedish pharmaceuticals company applied to the Ministry of Health and Welfare for approval to market a certain drug in Japan which had already become available in the United States some years ago. The Ministry rejected the application, citing racial differences why it could not accept US test data, requiring, in effect, for the drug to undergo a three-year testing period in Japan. The company complained that even if it obtained approval at that time, it would not benefit much because Japanese firms would have surely come out with a similar product and at a cheaper price.[20] Similar stories of bureaucratic red tape which work to the advantage of domestic manufacturers are not rare. For example, the US government, in 1982, made the accusation that the Japanese Ministry of Health and Welfare had a list of approved ingredients for cosmetics which, however, was not readily available, so that a manufacturer could not know prior to submission for certification what would or would not be approved.[21] At a time when technological innovations occur at a fast pace, delays with certification systems can literally wipe out the potential gains for the innovator of the product.

Many of the standards and certifications, as the Gotoda Commission (an advisory body set up by the Prime Minister in January 1983) reported, were not only based on tradition and social customs but also reflected the accepted 'role of government within that country'. This is indeed a major source of contention and it is often argued that the Japanese government had involved itself excessively in controlling the economic system. Prime Minsiter Nakasone, no doubt influenced by President Reagan, in outlining the Action Programme in 1985, suggested that it was time for this to change. However, we should not expect results overnight, nor to the extent of the United States. Acknowledging a need to redefine the role of the government is a major step in itself, but actual results will necessarily take time.

Even as the Japanese government implemented measures to improve market access, it consistently maintained that the trade imbalance was, mainly, the result of the high value of the American dollar. It suggested that the high dollar had made American exports dearer and therefore less competitive on the world market. Normally, the economic fundamentals – the determinants of exchange rates in a flexible exchange-rate system – would tend to suggest a low value for the dollar, but, it was argued, the value of the American dollar had been kept artificially high as the result of the interplay between budget deficits, high interest rates, shortage of capital for private investment, high demand for the dollar, and capital flows into

100

the United States. Indeed, in the period 1980–4, the value of the US dollar had increased by 40 per cent. If we accept this position, correcting the trade imbalance could only be possible through a sustained devaluation of the dollar, which in turn required a reduction of US federal budget deficits. The American government, until the recent G-5 agreement of September 1985 which readjusted exchange rates, consistently rejected this line of reasoning, claiming instead that capital inflows into the United States were the result of high profitability in the United States and not the result of interest-rate differentials. In an interview published in the *Asahi Shinbun*, former West German Chancellor Helmut Schmidt also played down the role of exchange rates and suggested that the real cause of trade imbalance was Japan's low defence spending, high savings rate and the consequential low consumption pattern.[22] We will look at Japanese savings and consumption patterns in chapter 6, but it must be pointed out here that consumption levels are partly determined by socio-cultural variables and, therefore, are less amenable to quick-fix solutions. However, the Japanese government did take important steps to reduce the built-in incentives to save, as we shall see later. The importance of low defence spending in Japan's economic success has been variously debated, but according to Professor James Morley this had only a marginally positive effect.[23] Furthermore, increasing Japanese defence spending by any significant level is not socially feasible, and if we leave it out of our discussion we can identify three main factors that could probably be held responsible for the trade imbalance:

1. a closed Japanese market and resistance to imports;
2. an overvalued dollar and undervalued yen; and
3. low domestic demand in Japan, resulting in export-push growth.

In the remainder of this chapter we will take up the first two points and leave the third for the next chapter. This will allow us to break down the focus of the two chapters in terms of expanding imports, on the one hand, and reducing exports, on the other. The second point, of course, impacts on both the export and import side of the trade equation and will also be referred to in the next chapter.

JAPANESE MARKET-OPENING MEASURES

Up until now, Japan had undertaken market-opening measures seven times, but the fact that so many separate actions were necessary, Kamijo admits, testified to the ineffectiveness of each.[24] The piecemeal, cautious manner in which the problem was tackled only increased frustration in the United States and the announcement of each new measure was met with anticipation of the next. The process, it was suggested, resembled an infinite progression where the goal was never quite attained.

While tariff restrictions in Japan are, on the average, of only marginal significance, the low penetration of foreign manufactured goods suggests the problem may be more basic and at the societal level. In Japan, Western pressure to open the economy is often likened to attempts to alter the Japanese social structure and reshape it in the mold of Western industrialized democracies. While it sounds drastic and arouses a natural hostility, there is some truth to the fact that market opening cannot be completely divorced from social opening. It is true that Japanese society is relatively closed and it is also true that its internal unity comes from maintaining a clear distinction between the 'self' and the 'other'. This distinction, even discrimination, has been held to account for many of the problems confronted by foreign manufacturers in Japan. Koganei Yoshihiro admitted that, until Japanese society was altered, market opening itself could not be expected to resolve the trade frictions. The 'other', therefore, had to be accepted and accorded the same status as the 'self', and foreign products, similarly, given national treatment. He outlined the ideal result saying that,

> If the Japanese are successful in retaining their strong points and, furthermore, if they are able to forge a new social order based on logic and universalism, that will solve our present day problems and will also have the additional significance of allowing us to make a positive contribution to the global society.[25]

Such drastic reordering might require a major crisis as a precondition, but it can be argued that a crisis already exists. As we shall see, an 'international society' (*Kokusai-ka Shakai*) was the basic thrust of the Action Programme of 1985. Necessarily, however, the final realization of the *Kokusai-ka Shakai* will take time, though the foundation has been set.

Not only does the nature of society reflect on the attitudes toward foreign products but they also impinge on the governmental standards and certification procedures (non-tariff barriers) which have come to the forefront of US–Japan trade disputes. Unfortunately standards and certification procedures are not governed by any internationally agreed codes. The Tokyo Round Agreement on Technical Barriers to Trade stated in very broad and general terms (Article 7.1) that

> Parties shall ensure that certification systems are not formulated or applied with a view to creating obstacles to international trade. They shall likewise ensure that neither such certification system themselves nor their application have the effect of creating unnecessary obstacles to international trade.[26]

In looking at market-opening measures, we will concentrate on the Nakasone administration because it appears that, apart from foreign pressure, strong political leadership is equally important in making effective progress. Suzuki did implement a number of market-opening measures, but these were quickly labelled by Senator Heinz as 'thin gruel masquerading as beef stew'.[27] When Nakasone became Prime Minister in late 1982, expectations were high that significant steps would be taken. On 13 Janaury 1983, several days prior to Nakasone's visit to Washington, the Ministerial Conference for Economic Measures released the duly awaited package of measures to liberalize imports. The package contained a liberalization programme for a number of tariff and non-tariff barriers.

On tariffs, it was announced that there would be either a reduction or an elimination of tariffs on 47 agricultural and 28 manufactured products, bringing to 323 the number of items on which tariff reduction/elimination was to be implemented, from FY1983 (the 323 items included 215 items covered in the measures adopted the year before). While the package was not as radical as expected, it did include such items of interest to the United States as tobacco, biscuits, and chocolate.

With regard to NTBs it was agreed, for instance, that the government would accept foreign test data on electrical applicances, animal pharmaceuticals, and food additives, obviating the need, as before, for re-testing and inspection. Such test data, however, had to be generated by foreign laboratories that had been inspected and approved by the appropriate Japanese authorities. Despite the cumbersome procedure of approving foreign testing agencies, it was still an improvement over the system that refused to accept any foreign data as valid. Another area where improvement was made was in the import procedures for autos. Under the system in place, auto imports of 100 units per model type qualified for simplified handling procedures, and this maximum limit was now raised to 300 per model type. If this appears to be insignificant, it was not so by Japanese standards. In 1982, Japan imported 463 passenger cars from France, 1,275 from Italy, 1 from Belgium, and 876 from Sweden. The largest exporting country was the United States with 3,051 units, and Canada exported only 103 units. It was reported that as a result of the changes announced in this area there would be a 30 per cent reduction in the number of documents to be submitted to the authorities.[28] Much of this documentation referred to inspection certificates attesting to compliance with the many safety and anti-pollution regulations. Compared to the low volume of imports, a 30 per cent improvement does seem to be a significant concession.

It was also announced that standards would be modified following a review of forty related laws and that import procedures would be revised in respect to sixteen items.[29] Accordingly, a committee was set up under the Chief Cabinet Secretary, Gotoda Masaru, and charged with the preparation of a final report by the end of March. When the Gotoda Commission formally submitted its report, it was somewhat more modest than what it had originally set out to do. It proposed revision of only seventeen existing laws, and the government explained that, 'the principle of equal treatment can be maintained without changing many of them'.[30] The revision of the laws was to 'ensure legal non-discrimination between nationals and non-nationals in certification systems; to ensure transparency of standards; to promote internationalization of standards; to promote the acceptance of foreign test data; and to simply and speed up certification procedures'.[31] Transparency referred to clarity and openness of standards, considered to be a problem with the existing system, as Undersecretary Olmer had pointed out with reference to standards established by the Ministry of Health and Welfare.

On 18 May 1983 the diet approved and amended the necessary laws and these became effective as of August of that same year. A few concrete examples of the improvements made are listed below.

1. A foreign manufacturer exporting to Japan could not apply directly for certification, where such certification was required by law.
2. Where a foreign manufacturer had already obtained proper certification, an importer of the products was to be waived from certification requirements.[32]
3. The obligations specified under the law would apply equally to both domestic and foreign manufacturers.

Prior to the revision of the certification system based on the Gotoda Commission report, the existing law specified that certification of foreign products could only be obtained by a Japanese company, that is, the importing agent. This had the effect of practically holding the foreign manufacturer hostage to the local importer, and if for some reason the importer broke off an existing agreement, the manufacturer was automatically forced to cease exports until such time as it had found a new importer and that new importer had applied for and obtained certification. The effect was particularly disadvantageous for those foreign manufacturers that had entered into a sole-agency agreement. The revision of the law freed the manufacturer to switch importers if it was dissatisfied with its existing Japanese agent, since it and not its agent held the certification.

Another improvement was in the law pertaining to type approval for certain products. For example, the Consumer Product Safety Law[33] enacted in 1973, and among the seventeen laws that were amended, specified that certain products like pressure cookers, cribs, roller skates, and mountain-climbing ropes, deemed to bear on the safety of the consumer, had to be inspected and carry a special seal of approval issued by the relevant testing authority in Japan. In Article 4, the law stated that either the foreign manufacturer or the Japanese importer could submit the product for inspection, but it barred the foreign manufacturer from applying for type approval for the product. This made it necessary for each import shipment to be inspected separately. In practice, the Japanese importer would submit the product for inspection, but there was always the risk that the product in question might not pass the rigorous inspection, in which case the importer would be left with a shipment of goods that could not be sold. In the revised law, Articles 32.2 to 32.5 specifically provided for type approval for foreign manufacturers with the same application procedures as for domestic manufacturers. A foreign manufacturer that had obtained type approval could affix the approval seals at the factory and prior to actual shipment. Under this law, in 1985, the Lobo Industries of France received registration as manufacturer and type approval for the export of protective helmets. Under the Electrical Appliances and Material Control Law, Rexair Inc. and Ekco Housewares Inc. of the United States received registration as manufacturers of AC motors and electric heating devices, respectively. Also in 1985, Creative Appliances Corp. Ltd of Canada was granted registration and type aproval for electric kettles.[34] The above is just a sample of those manufacturers that had received registration or type approvals, but the total number is still very small – fifteen registrations and seven type approvals under the Electrical Appliances and Material Control Law. A revision of the Motor Vehicles Act also made it possible for foreign car manufacturers to obtain type approval, thus removing the need to submit each car for individual test and inspection.

While a system for type approval was introduced and some foreign manufacturers were able to obtain such approval, the total number remained small. This was the result of the requirement that prior to granting type approvals, a thorough inspection had to be done either by an approved foreign testing agency (like, for example, the Underwriters Laboratory) or by an inspector sent from Japan. Granting of inspection authority to a foreign testing agency also depended on inspection by an inspector sent from Japan, and all the costs had to be borne by the foreign party seeking inspection.

To ensure transparency of standards and national treatment of foreign products, the Gotoda report stated that, 'Opportunities to hear the opinions of interested parties both domestic and foreign will be provided from the initial stages of the standard-drafting process so as to fully reflect their opinions in the process'. It was not that this equality was denied before, for the Cabinet decision of 22 May 1975 made clear that advance notice would be given to all interested parties, including foreign ones, prior to initiating revisions of safety standards.[35] Somehow, however, it did not work as effectively as it should have and it remains to be seen whether the renewed commitment will make for any improvement.

The process of market-opening measures did not end with the Gotoda report. On 21 October 1983, a set of Comprehensive Economic Measures was announced and two External Economic Measures were adopted on 27 April 1984 and on 14 December 1984. These measures constituted further steps to promote imports through, for example, expanding the scope of the import-financing role of the Export–Import Bank of Japan, and by strengthening the import-promotion function of the Japan External Trade Organization (JETRO) that had, in the past, busied itself exclusively with the expansion of Japanese exports.

However, the overall trade picture continued to deteriorate. The Japanese surplus continued to increase and so did the level of American hostility toward Japan. Anti-Japanese sentiment was particularly strong and vocal in the Congress. On 28 March 1985, the House of Representatives passed a unanimous resolution condemning Japan, and this unprecedented action was followed up with a similar resolution on 2 April in the Budget Committee of the Senate.

On 9 April 1985, the Advisory Committee for External Economic Measures, led by Dr Okita, and including such eminent personalities as Morita Akio of Sony and Maekawa Haruo, former Governor of the Bank of Japan, submitted a report to the government. In light of the gravity of the trade situation, the report emphasized the imperative for quick and more effective measures.

> To avoid a crisis in the world of free trading system and to ensure global economic progress and stability, Japan must take concrete measures . . . in such areas as improving market access, fostering sustained economic growth driven by domestic demand . . . and encouraging manufactured imports. The basic approach must be a bold one of 'freedom in principle, restrictions as exception', one designed to open Japan to the world.[36]

On 30 July 1985, the Government–LDP Headquarters for the Promotion of External Economic Measures finalized the 'Outline of the Action Programme for Improved Market Access' and, on that same day, also set up a special committee to

107

oversee and facilitate the implementation of the Action Pro-gramme headed by the Chief Cabinet Secretary.

Various MITI and MFA officials were quick to classify the Action Programme (AP) as a package totally different from those that had preceded it and not entirely without justification. It was different not only in the sense of being a more comprehensive measure, but also because it pointed to an eventual readjustment in the state–society relationship. The latter will probably take much longer than the three-year time-span for the implementation of the AP. Among the different measures, the package introduced concessions and improvements in such areas as tariffs and quotas, standards and certification, government procurements, financial and capital markets, services, and import-promotion measures.

For tariff reduction or elimination, the government list contained 1,850 industrial and agricultural items, 36 for tariff elimination. Most of the items slated for tariff elimination, however, were products in which Japan had a strong competi-tive advantage, like cameras, auto parts, Telephone and Telecommunications equipment, etc. A 20 per cent tariff reduction was also proposed for 1,670 industrial and mining products, and 110 agricultural products, to be phased in over the period of the AP. These reductions were made subject to the safeguard clause (GATT, Article 19); in other words, the tariff reductions could be withheld or withdrawn if it resulted in significant damage to the local industry.[37]

To simplify the standards and certification procedures further, a total of eighty-eight amendments to twenty-three laws were proposed. The main objective was to expand the scope for self-certification, 'to allow manufacturers to check compliance with standards, instead of inspection and other check-ups by the government or other entities' on specific products.[38] The ceiling on motor cars qualifying for simplified import procedures was raised to 1,000 units which, because of the low Japanese auto imports, promised to 'bring virtually all imported vehicles within the scope of the simplified certification system'.[39] This will probably not have more than a minor effect on the import of foreign cars in absolute terms, because of the low existing levels of imports. In percentage terms, however, auto imports for the first nine months of 1986 did increase by approximately 25 per cent over the corresponding period in 1985.[40]

To facilitate the import of pharmaceuticals it was decided

that, 'foreign clinical test data shall be accepted for all examination/testing items except for the following three items not immune to differences between Japanese and foreigners: comparative clinical trials; dose finding tests; absorption, distribution, metabolism, and excretion tests.' This was no doubt an improvement, but it is still hard to understand the rationale behind the exceptions, based on biological differences between the races. At the time the AP was being formulated, there was some contention on this point between the Economic Planning Agency (EPA), responsible for the overall content of the AP, and the MHW. When pressed by the EPA, the MHW produced test data to show, for example, that because of dietary habits the average Japanese had longer intestines, by as much as 20 per cent, and that this had to be taken into consideration since it bore directly on the absorption rate of drugs. The EPA eventually had to defer to the MHW, recognizing their competence in this area.

There were two particular features in the AP that separated it from the market-opening measures of the past and that could prove to be the most promising aspects of it, from the point of view of foreign manufacturers. These were:

1. redefinition of the role of government; and
2. national treatment of foreign products.

The first point referred to existing state–society relationships and to certain specific aspects for the micro-level regulatory intervention in the economy.[41] Traditionally, the role of the government within Japanese society had been wide and unquestioned. The government enjoyed far greater latitude than in any of the Western democracies, a fact that can be gleaned from the highly regulated and ordered Japanese society. In the economic sphere, the government had established a wide range of product safety standards to protect the interests of the consumers, and the consumers in return have come to look upon the government to provide this function, which it did, through its testing agencies.

Although international comparisons of governmental regulations are difficult, about 15 per cent of all Japanese laws, as of November 1984, were judged to be regulatory laws. The weight of the regulated sector of the economy was approximately 53 per cent of the GNP in 1980. The weight of those areas of the economy where governmental regulations were particularly severe was 26.2 per cent in 1975, but had declined to 25 per cent in 1980. In the United States, the weight of the regulated sector of the economy was 23.7 per cent in 1975 and presumably much lower in the 1980s under the Reagan administration.[42] However, as the EPA's report, from which these statistics are taken, cautioned, strict comparability should not be assumed since regulatory mechanisms in the two countries differed.

To illustrate the difference in the Japanese and Western conceptualization of the role of the government, we can look at the regulations governing certification of foreign autos. For much of the post-war period and until very recently, the Ministry of Transportation refused to allow self-certification by foreign auto producers feeling that, 'the Ministry, rather than the foreign firm, would be at fault if an error was made and an accident resulted'.[43] Whatever the merits or demerits of this sytem, it did work to the disadvantage of foreign firms producing in a less regulated environment.

The AP report contained the important point that, 'On the basic standpoint of "freedom in principle, restrictions only as exceptions", government intervention shall be reduced to a minimum so as to leave the choice and responsibility to consumers'.[44] Of course, this did not cover all products, nor was it to mean that the government would lower or eliminate the standards that were already in place, but that it would leave it as the responsibility of the manufacturers to ensure compliance with the standards. Whereas in the past the government would, based on its own tests, ensure compliance, the AP announced that the government would be willing to accept test results generated by the manufacturers themselves to determine whether the products complied with the established standards. The government would reduce its role of testing and granting of permission to affix quality seals certifying minimum-quality standards. The consumers would be left to make their own choices and market forces would be given greater play in determining product success or failures. For example, it was decided that the Industrial Standards Law would be reviewed with the aim of reducing the number of products that currently reuqired the 'JIS' quality seals. This law applied to products under the jurisdiction of MITI, but the scope of self-certification was to be expanded to other areas as well, like fire-fighting equipment (Ministry of Home Affairs), microwave cookers

(Ministry of Post and Telecommunications), etc. On 13 December 1985, the diet accordingly revised three laws covering consumer goods, gas supplies, and fire-prevention equipment.[45]

With respect to the second feature of 'national treatment', it is true that Japanese buying habits have been strongly influenced by the 'buy Japanese' policies (*kokusan hin aiyo*) and by the socio-cultural importance of distinguishing between 'them' and 'us'. Thus, it was typical for foreign products to be displayed separate from competing local products in the 'import section' of stores. The practical effect was that a consumer was, thus, denied the opportunity for comparative shopping, restricting sales of foreign products. Unless the consumer had determined in advance to buy an imported product, it was likely that the final choice would be made from a group of competing Japanese products. Attempts to change this had not gone much beyond verbal exhortations and, understandably, with little effect. Prime Minister Suzuki, in May 1982, urged his countrymen to change their outlook on imports, saying, 'we have not shed out misperceptions that export is good, import is bad. Instead of discriminating against foreign products, we should adopt a more welcoming attitude'.[46] Nakasone went a small step further. In his television address announcing the government's intention to formulate the AP, he not only urged viewers to buy more imports, but also suggested a shopping list to help them spend an additional $100 on imported goods.

To increase corporate purchase of imports, the MITI Minister Murata called in representatives of Japan's leading firms in April and again in August 1985 to urge them to increase their planned imports for the year, including their own corporate procurement of parts. In an interview afterwards, the Minister said that the time had come for Japan to move away from the 'buy Japanese' to a 'buy foreign' policy.[47] The 134 companies to which MITI made the special appeal reported that they intended to increase imports by an estimated $7.4 billion in FY1985 as compared to the year before.[48] Their FY1984 imports had been about $97.3 billion. In a follow-up of their import performance in late March 1986, it was learned, however, that their imports would increase by only $3.1 billion, less than half of what had been initially anticipated,[49] due to the rapid decline in the price of oil and of other primary commodities. Also, in so far as procurement of foreign parts was concerned, the difficulty here was the practice of intragroup buying in Japan and the policy of maintaining low inventory levels to ensure maximum cost efficiency. This would not be possible if manufacturers in Japan were to rely more on foreign parts since they would have to maintain higher levels of fixed inventory to account for possible shipment delays, etc. According to US Commerce Secretary Malcolm Baldridge, the practice of intragroup buying was a major hurdle for foreign companies to overcome and one that the AP had not touched upon.[50] However, since this practice also affected Japanese firms standing outside the group, one cannot readily denounce it as discriminatory to foreign manufacturers alone.

Government procurement policies, too, had been resistant to change. Here, the main dispute between the United States and Japan was on the procurement of the Nippon Telephone and Telegraph (NTT) which until 1984 was a public monopoly. NTT's procurements had almost wholly been restricted to domestic suppliers, and at one time the NTT Chairman Akigusa had arrogantly brushed aside American pressure to buy American telecommunications equipment saying that the only things that the United States could offer to the NTT were 'mops and buckets'.[51] The American interest in selling to the NTT was part of a general strategy to boost its high-technology exports to Japan. The Americans argued that Japanese procurements should be as open as they were in the United States or Canada, to which the Japanese counter-argument was that procurement policies in the United States and Canada were the exceptions rather than the rule. Such an argument, understandably, made little sense in bilateral negotiations and, confronted with increasing pressure, the Japanese government had to concede to the American demands. NTT's foreign procurements (table 5.4) have shown rapid growth in recent years, although still low in absolute terms. Over the four-year period 1981–4, NTT's

Table 5.4 NTT foreign procurements (Y billion)

Year	Total	From USA
FY1981	4.4	3.8
FY1982	11.0	8.6
FY1983	34.8	31.2
FY1984	36.0	32.0

Source: MFA, Tokyo, Japan.

procurement from the United States registered an eight-fold increase, although procurement in the final two years appeared to have levelled off. Also, as the statistics show, the United States accounted for nearly 90 per cent of all foreign procurement by the NTT.

Considering that, in 1982, total NTT procurement was about Y700 billion, the absolute amount of NTT foreign procurement is still quite small. Also, until recently, the NTT had not purchased any core equipment. The first major purchase was in December 1985, when it announced its decision to purchase digital switches from Northern Telecom.

To assess the impact of the AP, it should be emphasized that the most hopeful feature was perhaps the fact that it tried to establish new directional objectives. At the same time, there should be no illusion that it will be easily achieved. To given an example, with respect to the elimination of the 'JIS' marking system, only about 10 per cent of the total number of products under MITI jurisdiction will be affected in the three-year phase of the AP.[52] Also, bureaucratic foot-dragging in the implementation phase cannot be ruled out either. The bureaucracy's attitude to the entire process will be largely determined by its interpretation of the political will. Bureaucratic foot-dragging could result from a number of other factors as well, including the preservation of traditional prerogatives. For example, the AP stated that all standards and certification requirements not based on specific laws, that is, those based on public notification (*kokuji*) or directives (*tsutatsu*) issued by the various ministries, would be abolished and that the Committee to Promote the Implementation of the Action Programme (Chairman: Gotoda) would complete all the necessary procedures by November 1985. This generated considerable bureaucratic hostility since it would reduce the number of special institutions that currently oversee the observance of these directives and jeopardise also the *Amakudari*[53] chances of senior bureaucrats. The opposition was rationalized on the belief that this was an area of little relevance to import promotion and because there had been little or no foreign criticism of these practices. As a result of this dispute, agreement on the implementation phase of this part of the AP was only reached in March 1986 and it was decided that such standards would now be abolished in July 1988.

Problems in the implementation phase could also arise because, while the AP was formulated by the Economic

Planning Agency (EPA), which is attached to the Prime Minister's Office, implementation would depend on and require the co-operation of the regular bureaucracy and here special interests could delay the process. It is possible that undue delays may lead to a negative interpretation in the West of the government's sincerity, and mindful of this, the Keidanren, in a recent report, urged particular attention to the task of carrying out the implementation according to the original schedule, 'so as not to betray the expectations, domestic and overseas, and realize the originally intended effect'.[54]

In the final section we will return to the question of effectiveness, but in the next section we will look at the distribution network in Japan and the role it plays in determining market access for foreign manufacturers.

THE JAPANESE DISTRIBUTION SYSTEM AS AN IMPORT BARRIER

No study of the problem of expanding Japanese imports would be complete without touching on the complicated distribution system in Japan. Foreign businesses often complain that this distribution system is closed and largely responsible for the low penetration of foreign goods in the Japanese economy. The Japanese distribution system, like the economy in general, can be classified into two categories: the efficient modern sector; and the more numerous and inefficient traditional sector. The former, because it is usually controlled by the large manufacturers, is difficult for an outsider to penetrate, while the latter is much too inefficient to handle large sales volume. This dualistic feature of the distribution system has been the crux of the problem for foreign manufacturers wishing to enter the Japanese market. Although the Committee on Distribution within MITI prepared a guideline in the late 1960s to rationalize/modernize the cumbersome distribution system, the programme appeared to have had little major success. Anticipating the difficulties in achieving this rationalization, Yoshino noted the following as one major problem area: 'Given the strong traditional orientation toward large-scale manufacturing firms, it is by no means certain that those charged with the distribution programmes will enjoy the most influential position, even within MITI'.[55]

Interestingly, the distribution system in Japan has also been a handicap for many Japanese firms. The most prominent examples would be Sony and Honda, which were forced to rely on export sales because of the difficulty of breaking into the domestic group-oriented distribution network. Presumably, therefore, an open distribution system would work both to expand imports and reduce export dependence for many local firms. To illustrate the difficulties faced by foreign and domestic non-group manufacturers, let us take an example in the electronics industry. In 1982, there were about 60–70,000 electronics retail outlets of which about 40,000 carried Matsushita (National) products, exclusively or otherwise, and only 3,000 carried Sony products.[56] The barrier for new entrants into an established industry, like Sony, was the domination of the distribution system by the *Keiretsu* (intrafirm) groupings which block out the products of companies outside the *Keiretsu* group. According to Woronoff

> The distribution *Keiretsu* tied up the market even tighter as regards most consumer goods. Where manufacturers controlled the wholesalers or retail outlets, they would determine which articles were sold and easily veto the sale of imported products that competed with their own. Indeed, in many of the distribution networks the rule was exclusive dealers and even in some supposedly independent outlets, the owner would be wary of upsetting his customary supplier. Where wholesalers dominated the retailers, and either belonged to or themselves owned manufacturers, they would refuse to serve as channels for competing imports or, at most give them second-best treatment.[57]

The *Keiretsu* is a pre-war legacy of the Japanese economy and one area that the allied occupation forces failed to reform, although this was on their original agenda.

Because of distribution problems, the sales volume of foreign products remained typically small and this fostered the practice of overpricing. In turn, it required that foreign products be adorned with an exclusive 'brand' image to make the product saleable. Exclusivity and separateness, again partly determined by social structures, became the selling points of foreign goods. Only if it was expensive was it any good. An interesting example of this was Johnnie Walker Red Label scotch whisky which, when it was priced high and therefore 'exclusive', was the best-selling scotch whisky in Japan, but as its price dropped it also lost its market standing.

Surrounded by an air of exclusivity foreign products, being overpriced, were unable to compete with equivalent Japanese substitutes. It is often argued that lowering prices of imports would have only a marginal effect on sales volume because Japanese substitutes were readily available. There are exceptions, of course, like Kodak and Procter and Gamble, which have been very successful in Japan, but even here it is not uncommon to hear murmurs of discontent.

One measure of the efficiency of a country's distribution network is the *W/R* ratio, which is the ratio of total value of wholesale sales to the total value of retail sales. A high *W/R* ratio would thus indicate a lengthy distribution process or a lengthy intermediary stage before a commodity reached the retail level. This would naturally be reflected in a higher retail price. Table 5.5 compares the *W/R* ratio of Japan and a number of other advanced industrialized countries.

Table 5.5 W/R ratio

	Japan	USA	UK	France	West Germany
	1982	1982	1983	1982	1979
W/R ratio	4.21	1.87	2.03	1.57	1.67

Source: 'Yunyu hin no Ryutsu Oyobi sho Kanko ni tsuite', *Bukka Antei Seisaku Kaigi Seisaku Bukai'*, 28 March 1986, p. 16.

Even allowing for discrepancies in cross-country statistics, the high *W/R* ratio in Japan indicates a more complicated and lengthy distribution stage. Of the five countries, France had the most efficient distribution network as measured in terms of the number of stages before a product reached the retail level. We should, however, be careful in our use of such comparative statistics. The Republic of Korea, for example, has a *W/R* ratio of only 0.7, but this was mainly due to the fact that the distribution system was not well estbalished at all and many retailers bought directly from the manufacturers, thus bypassing the wholesale stage.[58]

The *W/R* ratio, as given above, does not discriminate between domestic and imported products and, indeed, if equal treatment is given to all, regardless of country of manufacture, the system, even if inefficient, cannot be called unfair. In late

1985, the EPA, in co-ordination with MITI and MOF, conducted a survey to assess whether imported products received the same treatment as domestic, or whether they were discriminated against, as foreign manufacturers allege. The survey was conducted over the period of July to September and the final report and conclusions were released in November 1985. The report acknowledged that the small number of product categories included in the survey could not be the basis for a definitive conclusion, but it nevertheless felt confident enough to conclude that, while the distribution system tended to overprice imports more than domestic products, the margin retained by wholesalers and retailers was about the same.[59] The disadvantage of imports over domestic products, however, can clearly be seen from table 5.6, compiled from the survey results. The table compares the mark-up resulting from the distribution system; in other words, the percentages represent the weight of the distributors' margin to the retail price of the products.

Table 5.6 Distributors' margin as weight of retail price

Product category	Imports[a]	Domestic[b]
	%	%
Glass products	61– 3	30
Cutlery	60– 5	60
Pots and pans	66–74	45
Bedding	42–57	50
Furniture	51–66	35
Attaché cases	68– 9	35
Toys	64– 7	45
Men's coats	56–71	35–8
Shoes	61–71	35
Sports shoes	60– 5	50
Shirts	67–71	40
Tyres	40– 6	50
Musical goods (speakers)	55–60	23
Spaghetti	29–64	28
Bottled and canned goods	36–45	45

Source: Compiled from EPA (1985) 'Yunyu hin Ryutsu Jittai Chosa Kekka no Matome', November, pp. 257–85.
Notes: [a] Survey of 2–3 products. [b] Survey of one product.

There is a wide margin in the mark-up on particular product categories, but if we look at the average, domestic products received a mark-up of 40 per cent while the mark-up for imports ranged from 54 to 64 per cent. Another criticism of the Japanese distribution system was that it was too inflexible to pass on benefits to the consumers. Even after the rapid devaluation of the dollar against the yen, the reduced price for imports had not been passed on to the consumer but had rather been retained by importers and distributors. A MITI survey which examined price changes in the period between August 1985 and March 1986 found that, in spite of the decline in import prices of such products as jeans, athletic shoes, electric razors, and watches, the prices of these good at the retail level remained unchanged. This essentially made it difficult for exporters of products to Japan to increase their sales volume and market share. It should be mentioned, however, that not all foreign manufacturers were equally concerned about increasing their market share. For the giant chemical company, DuPont, the devaluation of the dollar was used as the long-awaited opportunity to recoup profitability after years of operating with small profit margins when the dollar was inflated.[60]

The government, understandably, has little control to alter the distribution system because it reflects the paticular socio-economic condition of Japan. However, a recent report released by MITI expressed the hope that the distribution network would more clearly balance the interests of the producers and the consumers. One feature of the distribution system, as noted above, was its domination by the major *Keiretsu*. Obviously, therefore, the distributors were more sensitive to the interests of the producers, resulting in a restriction of products handled and consequently constraining the choice available to consumers. In its 'vision' for the distribution system, MITI observed that, with the increasing internationalization of the Japanese economy, the distribution system should more accurately reflect the diversity of 'needs' of the consumers and respond in a like manner, hopefully resulting in expanded imports of manufactured goods.[61]

Earlier MITI policies of rationalization/modernization of the distribution system had been directed at the traditional sector which, by its very nature, was less amenable to 'direction and control' given its numerical and regional diversity. The present outline of the 'vision' was aimed at the modern sector dominated by large manufacturing concerns, and because MITI's clout with big business is greater, its chances of success should be much improved.

OFFICE OF THE TRADE OMBUDSMAN

As part of the January 1982 market-opening measures, the Japanese government established an Office of Trade Ombudsman (OTO) to handle and process complaints from foreign companies and other interested parties on Japanese import procedures, inspection systems, or any other specific issue. The OTO was an interministerial mechanism with the secretariat located within the Economic Planning Agency (Prime Minister's Office, PMO). Its main purpose was to ensure that the market-opening measures were faithfully implemented and for this it depended on foreign exporters and importers in Japan to bring to the government's attention any discrepancy in principle and practice. The principal functions of the OTO are listed below:

1. Strive to reduce government intervention in the economy.
2. Internationalization of standards and certifications.
3. Simplification of import procedures.[62]

From the very inception of the OTO, there were complaints from foreign sources about its structure. They argued that it was impossible to expect the bureaucracy to respond to and handle complaints on the practices of the bureaucracy in a fair manner. Even though the secretariat of the OTO was in the PMO, it was only responsible for co-ordination and did not have any authority or jurisdiction over the respective bureaucracies. the actual and/or preceived problems as to the fairness of the OTO prompted the government to set up, in January 1983, an Advisory Council to the OTO, to oversee its activities and ensure fair handling of complaints. It is difficult to imagine, however, how the Advisory Council can do more than oversee the procedural aspects of problem resolution. The Advisory Council is composed of private individuals; although its chairmen, to date, have had past association with the official bureaucracy. Although the OTO Advisory Council does not have any administrative authority, Okita Saburo, the current Chairman, wrote that, 'the stature of its members gives it considerable influence within the Government of Japan'.[63]

As of February 1986, the OTO had received 234 complaints (88 in 1982, 50 in 1983, 25 in 1984, 68 in 1985, and 3 in the first two months of 1986), of which 119 had been filed domestically. In terms of the general nature of the grievances, table 5.7 provides a summary.

Table 5.7 Nature of OTO Complaints

Ministry concerned	No. of complaints
MHW (pharmaceuticals, shokuhin eisei, etc.)	98
MITI (high-pressure gas, etc.)	48
MOF (import procedures)	41
MOAFF (live-animal inspection)	24
MOT (shipping containers)	9
Others	36
Total	256

Source: 'OTO no . . . ni tsuite', p. 7.
Note: The total exceeds the number of cases (213), because some complaints concerned more than one ministry.

It is not surprising that the Ministry of Health and Welfare had the most number of complaints because of its close association with the powerful and conservative Japan Medical Association (JMA). The JMA has not been very receptive to the government's attempt to open up the pharmaceuticals industry to foreign competition and according to one report, the JMA even refused to accept foreign test data on pharmaceuticals even though these were included in the AP. One EPA official, however, conveyed the determination of the government to proceed with the measures contained in the AP although they acknowledged that the opposition of the JMA could hold back the sale of imported prescription drugs.[64]

In terms of the resolution of the complaints lodged with the OTO, according to figures available, 224 of these had been resolved, mostly to the satisfaction of the aggrieved party. The breakdown of the outcome of complaints is given in table 5.8.

It is worth noting that misunderstanding was the single most common source of complaint to the OTO. This suggests that there was considerable confusion concerning the legal structures and import regulations. In providing a venue for the

Table 5.8 Outcome of complaints to the OTO

Cause of complaint removed	79
Complaint result of misunderstanding	93
Removal of misunderstanding had import facilitating effect	(65)
Other	(28)
Existing practice continued	56

Source: 'OTO no Saikin no . . .', p. 8.

removal of misunderstanding, the OTO does seem to have a role to play in the Japanese economic system, and as Okita Saburo observed, 'There is nothing quite like it anywhere else in the world and it is hoped that foreign manufacturers and governments will take advantage of the OTO's availability'.[65] This quotation sums up the strength of the OTO, but it also points to its existing weakness.

The complaints to the OTO have come mostly from foreign manufacturers, even though many were lodged domestically by foreign subsidiaries and the like. However, for the OTO mechanism to be fully effective, it will be necessary for local importers to get more closely involved since they are in a better position to understand the problems confronting imports. Of the 234 complaints that had been lodged with the OTO, 119 had been from within Japan, but a senior MITI official confirmed that hardly any of the 119 complaints had come from Japanese companies. Indeed, in the initial stages, the OTO specifically denied access to Japanese firms, but in early 1983 this restriction was removed to allow both foreign and local business equal opportunity to voice their complaints, either directly or through the Chamber of Commerce. The latter option was provided so as to ensure anonymity, but this did not allay the fears of domestic companies. Japanese firms have been reluctant to utilize the OTO for fear that they could be subject to persecution or harassment from the bureaucracy, making things even more difficult for them. The other reason why Japanese firms have been relatively absent from the list of complainants can be attributed to cultural values. The OTO is a formal apparatus for handling disputes, but social values in Japan have a distinct bias in favour of informal means.

The cultural barrier may be difficult to break, but officials tend to deny emphatically that by resorting to the OTO Japanese firms leave themselves open to harassment. However, the perception may be too deeply ingrained and this may prove to be a long-term disadvantage for the OTO even though, as it is, it still serves a useful purpose, albeit mostly for foreign companies.

EXCHANGE RATES AND TRADE IMBALANCE

It should be emphasized that there are some differences of

opinion between Japan and the United States as to the real significance of market-opening measures. For Japan, they are just that, namely, measures to facilitate the entry of foreign products into Japan. For the United States, however, no market-opening measure is complete unless it also translated into expanded imports. From the Japanese point of view, the latter is outside the scope of the government, and Western expectations, therefore, are unreasonably high. Both the EC and the United States have been urging Japan to establish import targets and ensure its fulfillment.[66] One MFA official reacted to these demands in the following words: 'They, perhaps, are under the impression that we are a communist country'.[67]

The Japanese government also insists that it was not entirely up to Japan to bring about a balance in trade. Prime Minister Nakasone repeatedly asserted that a portion of the blame must be apportioned to American businesses that had not made 'sufficient' efforts to penetrate the Japanese market. Thus, even in the case of the AP, which was unveiled with such fanfare, the most optimistic assessment was that it would lead to some increase in imports over time if the implementation phase proceeded smoothly and provided foreign manufacturers took the Japanese market more seriously than they had in the past.

As mentioned earlier, the trade imbalance cannot be attributed to any one single factor and it will be necessary to tackle the problem on all fronts. One area that the Japanese government had emphasized was the macro-economic policy differences between the two countries, tight fiscal and easy

Table 5.9 Budget deficits in the United States and Japan ($ billion)

	United States		Japan			
Year	Budget deficit	Outstanding debt	Budget deficit		Outstanding debt	
1980	59.6	914.5	78.7	(14,170)	391.7	(70,510)
1981	57.9	1,003.9	71.7	(12,900)	457.1	(82,273)
1982	110.6	1,147.0	78.0	(14,045)	480.5	(86,482)
1983	195.4	1,381.9	74.9	(13,486)	609.4	(109,695)
1984	175.4	1,576.7	71.5	(12,865)	676.1	(121,694)
1985	203.0	1,841.9	64.9	(11,680)	738.3	(132,900)

Source: Japan, 1985, pp. 82–3.
Notes: Figures in parentheses are Japanese yen (Y180=$1). 1985 figures are estimates.

monetary policies in Japan, and easy fiscal and tight monetary policies in the United States. First, let us take a look at budgetary trends in the two countries.

Table 5.9 does somewhat exaggerate the annual Japanese budget deficits for the early 1980s because of exchange-rate movements. If we use the average exchange rate for the year 1980, which was Y226.7=$1, Japan's budget for the year is somewhat lower at $62.5 billion, but still more than the US deficit for that year. The trend, however, has been unmistakable. With the massive increase in US federal spending, together with the tax cuts in 1981, the first year of the Reagan administration, the US deficits have literally soared. During this same period, the Japanese government succeeded in bringing down the yearly deficits with strict fiscal austerity. This period also corresponds to the rapid deterioration of the trade imbalance between the two countries. One result of the continuing US deficit has been the phenomenon of 'crowding out' in the financial markets, and the effect was particularly noteworthy since private sector investment needs had increased with the economic recovery and growth beginning in 1983. Domestic personal savings in the United States have always been low and declined even further in 1983,[68] and even though the corporate savings rate has traditionally been high, the imbalance between gross domestic savings and investments continued to worsen, pushing up interest rates in the process. The IS (investment and saving) imbalance can be seen in table 5.10.

In Japan, on the other hand, helped by a high rate of personal savings and low domestic investment demand, both public and

Table 5.10   US savings and investment ($ billion)

Year	Total net savings[a]	Gross domestic private investment
1980	405.9	401.9
1981	484.3	484.2
1982	408.8	414.9
1983	437.2	471.6
1984	551.0	637.3

Source: Economic Report of the President, February 1985, table B-25, p. 262.
Note: [a]Net of personal & business savings; and federal & state/local deficits/surplus.

private, the economy has enjoyed a net capital surplus. The capital shortage in the United States and the surplus in Japan is reflected in interest-rate differentials (see table 5.11).

Table 5.11 Interest-rate differentials in Japan and the United States

	Official discount rate	T-B rate 3 months	Official discount rate	Call rate no. cond.
1980	13.0	11.43	7.25	10.93
1981	12.0	14.03	5.50	7.44
1982	8.5	10.61	5.50	6.94
1983	8.5	8.61	5.00	6.39
1984	8.0	9.52	5.0	6.10
1985	7.5	–	4.5	–

Source: *Ekonomist* (Tokyo), 17 September 1985, p. 101.
Note: The official discount rate is for the year end; the short-term rate is the year's average.

Although interest-rate differentials are not the sole determinants of international capital flows, they do influence such movements and it is no surprise that Japan's basic balance has consistently been in deficit with the United States. The demand for the US dollar also inflated its value beyond the levels that would be reasonable given the economic fundamentals, trade deficits, etc. Needless to say, a high dollar value made imports cheaper and exports costlier and this deterioration of the competitive position made a correction of the trade imbalance even more difficult. The IS imbalance and the high demand for the dollar could be traced back to the fiscal splurge which, in essence, meant that no solution would be complete unless it was also accompanied by fiscal order in the United States. Indeed, this was one of the articles of agreement at the recent G-5 meeting.

According to a recent US Data Research Institute (DRI) report, a 1 per cent interest-rate differential between the United States and other countries results in an overvaluation of the dollar by about 4–5 per cent.[69] The DRI had been commissioned by the US Congress to assess the impact of the 40 per cent increase in the value of the dollar since 1980. The report, released in March 1985, concluded that there had been an adverse impact on the American balance of trade to the tune of $60–70 billion. It also argued that Japan's cost advantage, as a result, had improved from 88 in 1980 to 71 in 1984 (United States=100), reversing the trend of the previous decade (see table 5.12).

Table 5.12 Japan's manufacturing costs (United States=100)

	1965	1971	1975	1980	1984
Labour costs	60	54	92	79	60
Capital costs	95	64	51	90	96
Energy costs	184	168	192	243	188
Overall	72	60	86	88	71

Source: (1985) 'Bei-koku no Kokusai Kyoso Ryoku' *Chosa Geppo* (Ministry of Finance), vol. 74, no. 8, p. 47.

To counter the argument that interest-rate differentials were responsible for the growing trade imbalance, the US administration argued that the trade imbalance had grown despite a narrowing of the differential in recent years. To curb capital flows to the United States, it argued that the Japanese government should be more flexible in its fiscal policies and reflate the domestic economy. According to this position, the restraint on fiscal spending in Japan had forced the Japanese economy into an export-led growth pattern when, in fact, it should act as the engine of growth to lift the world economy out of the recession. There is, indeed, ample evidence to suggest that Japan's own economic recovery was based on the American economic recovery. During the latest recovery period (1983) the contribution ratio of export to GNP growth was much higher than in the earlier recovery periods of March 1975 and October 1977. The export growth had gone mainly to the United States, pulled in by the boost in consumer spendings there. Exports to the United States increased by an enormous 45 per cent in FY1984.[70]

In all previous recoveries from recessionary periods, Japan's economic growth was led by exports. This dependence on export-led growth has been explained in terms of the commitment to permanent and secure lifelong employment in the modern sector of the economy. Due to the fact that employers, at least in the modern sector, were constrained from laying off workers during a recession, labour costs for a typical large Japanese firm tend to be treated as a fixed cost rather than as variable costs. This meant that during a recession, when there was surplus productive capacity, the marginal cost of production was very low and firms would try to take advantage of this by a concerted export push.[71]

In the United States autumn is an especially difficult time for defenders of free trade. The administration releases its trade figures for the fiscal year ending in September and, in recent years, with little to be cheerful about, there was always the danger of tipping the balance in favour of the protectionists. The year 1985 was a particularly ominous year, partly because of the anticipated worsening in the trading position, but also because the Congress, in censuring Japan so strongly earlier in the year, held out the spectre of more concrete steps to safeguard the US economy from the flood of imports. This worried both the Japanese and US administrations, which were equally committed to avoiding legislated protectionism. As we saw, the measures taken by the Japanese government to liberalize its economy provided no firm guarantees of improving the trade situation in the short term and any beneficial effect was only likely to become apparent in the longer run. This made it essential to rely on other mechanisms to overcome the protectionist forces during this transitory phase. No matter how significant the Japanese market-opening measures, unless the transitory period was carefully managed, the potential long-term benefits could not be realized. It was in this background that we can analyse the decision taken at the G-5 meeting in New York to adjust international currency rates. The dollar, through the 1980s, had become clearly overvalued and the G-5 agreement was only a necessary adjustment. The reason why the United States agreed to currency readjustments, despite earlier opposition, can partly be attributed to Japan's consistent emphasis on this point and partly to the nomination of James Baker as the new US Secretary of the Treasury.

Under a system of floating exchange rates, we would expect trade imbalances to be automatically adjusted by appreciation in the value of the surplus currency and depreciation in the value of the deficit country. But even though the fixed exchange-rate system collapsed in the early 1970s, adjustments did not take place smoothly, presumably because of the magnitude of capital flows between countries. Capital flows today are less determined by the flow of goods as they are by differential interest rates, varying levels of profitability, and economic performance. The increase in speculative capital

126

flows across national boundaries made it less likely that exchange rates, as determined by the market, would accurately reflect the trade picture. Ever since the global trade imbalance became a threat to the system, the surplus countries of Europe and Japan argued on the need to take joint action to bring about exchange-rate changes. However, the United States, in particular the Federal Reserve Board, was less than sympathetic to this argument, fearing that a lower dollar value would lead to a resurgence of inflation at home. This had, indeed, been the American experience in the decade of the 1970s. Beginning in 1979, the Federal Reserve Board (FRB), under Chairman Paul Volcker, instituted tight monetary policies and succeeded in bringing down inflation levels. In 1983–4, the rate of inflation in the United States was below 4 per cent compared to 9 per cent in 1981. Quite understandably, the FRB was extremely reluctant to deviate from what it considered to be good policy.

The fear that a lower value of the dollar would revive inflation was based on two assumptions: first, that it would translate into higher import prices; and second that an increase in export demand for American products coupled with consumer substitution of domestic products for imported products would create an excess of demand over supply, at least in the short run because supply could only be expected to increase with a time-lag. This was the standing argument of the FRB against using exchange rates as an instrument of policy, although it was reported that Paul Volcker had been reduced to a minority position with recent Reagan appointments to the Board by President Reagan. The US administration, under pressure to demonstrate to Congress that active measures were being taken to reduce the trade deficit, eventually came around to the position that such readjustment was inevitable. While the effects of exchange rates are also lagged, there is greater certainty that eventually the desired outcome would be realized.

At the G-5 meeting, the five member countries agreed to intervene in the financial markets to lower the value of the dollar relative to other currencies. The agreement had an immediate effect and the dollar went on a tumble in international currency markets, declining 30 per cent by March 1986 and 40 per cent by August 1986. Table 5.13 shows the movement of the dollar against the yen.

At the G-5 meeting, it was also agreed that Japan and West Germany would implement policies to raise domestic demand

127

Table 5.13 Exchange-rate changes
between yen and dollar

4 January 1985	Y252=$1.00
2 February 1984	Y263=$1.00
18 July 1985	Y236=$1.00
20 September 1985	Y242=$1.00
4 October 1985	Y211=$1.00
25 November 1985	Y200=$1.00
28 January 1986	Y195=$1.00
10 March 1986	Y179=$1.00

levels. It was this aspect of the agreement that the FRB was particularly careful to emphasize. Testifying before the Sub-committee on Domestic Monetary Policy of the House Committee of Banking, Finance, and Urban Affairs in November 1985, Staff Director for Monetary and Financial Policy, Board of Governors of the FRB, S. H. Axilrod, stated that members of G-5 had agreed on the 'need for more fundamental macroeconomic policy adjustment here and abroad . . . Intervention and exchange rate changes are no substitute for sound underlying policies'.[72]

Despite the wary, cautious approach of the FRB, USTR Clayton Yeutter, for the administration and testifying before Congress, hinted to the lingering disagreement. Yeutter explained the expressed hope for a further decline in the value of the dollar. FRB Chairman Volcker, however, contradicted him by saying that the decline had already gone far enough. It was also Paul Volcker who, at the London G-5 meeting in January 1986, ruled out a concerted cut in interest rates, sought by Japan, fearing that such a move would revive inflation by lowering the value of the dollar and boosting domestic consumer spending. The dollar, however, continued to decline still further and Japan felt confident enough to reduce its own discount rate unilaterally.

As a result of the appreciation of the yen Japan had been under considerable pressure from domestic sources to lower interest rates to avoid a recession. The government, however, did not wish to widen interest-rate differentials that might lead to an increased demand for the dollar. The 0.5 per cent rate cut had no visible impact on the exchange rates and the dollar continued to fall. By late January, the yen had appreciated to under Y200 to the dollar, exceeding the anticipated increase in its value. Industry sources bitterly complained that they would not be able to compete if the yen continued to rise and applied constant pressure on the government to cut the discount rate even more. On the earlier occasion, the Japanese government was concerned not to strengthen the dollar, but the second time the discount rate was reduced, there was at least the implicit hope that it would lead to a stabilization of exchange rates.

The rationale behind using the exchange rate as the mechanism to bring about trade adjustments was that it provided a degree of certainty, although, by usual estimates, the effect takes from four to six quarters to work through the system. Accordingly, an improvement in the US–Japan trade situation could, at the earliest, only be expected in the latter part of 1986 or in early 1987. It actually took a little longer to realize the trade-corrective effects due to a number of factors. The most important was that the currency adjustment took the form of creeping adjustment and was stretched out over a long period of time, whereas the six-quarter lag is assumed true for a one-shot exchange-rate change. Also, during the period of the weak yen Japanese manufacturers had built up a high profit margin and it was easier for them to lower profit margins and to postpone price increases. Also, US exports hardly showed any increase because the Latin American (Brazil, Mexico) countries, which had always figured prominently in the past export surges, had been forced to tighten their belts due to their debt crises. As to the extent of the corrective effect of the rise in the value of the yen, C. F. Bergsten, former Assistant Secretary of the Treasury, and currently Director of the Institute for International Economies, suggested that it would eventually produce a reduction of about $20 billion in the US trade deficit with Japan. Speaking before the Japan Society of New York on 12 March 1986, he said a further rise in the yen was desirable, to about Y160 to the dollar, citing the sharp drop in oil prices as one factor why the currency should be further revalued.[73] Apart from the normal balance of payments effect, the American business magazine *Fortune* noted another favourable effect of the currency revaluation. A stronger yen, it argued,

> would make it cheaper for Japanese companies to buy land and cement and pay wages in the United States, speeding up the Japanese expansion of manufacturing in the United States. The Japanese industrialization of America may do more than anything else to bring trade into balance.[74]

CONCLUSION

At this stage, it is necessary to assess the extent to which the material presented above on market-opening measures constitutes evidence of system support. In the case of the auto dispute, we argued that an analysis of MITI's intentions and support for VER could be taken as clear indications of the recognition of Japan's responsibility in maintaining and strengthening the liberal economic order. Aside from the intentions behind the VER, the policy was also effective in terms of its objective, but only because the American car manufacturers did undertake the investment necessary to retain international competitiveness. But, regardless of whether the VER actually achieved its objective, a simple analysis of the intentions would still be sufficient to show that, at least, the Japanese government was concerned about system stability. It provided the opportunity, the breathing space, but it could not, obviously, be held responsible for the actual revitalization of the American auto industry. Similarly, in assessing the significance of the market-opening measures, we could use either one of the following two criteria:

1. actual reductions in US trade deficits with Japan;
2. market-opening measures as an independent criterion.

This, perhaps, frames the question in terms similar to whether Japan is a democracy. If, by democracy, we mean an alternation of political power, then Japan is not a democracy since the conservatives have continued to dominate the government in the post-occupation period. At the same time, it cannot be denied that elections have been held regularly and elections have been as fair and free as can be expected, given the advantage of incumbency. Most analysts, on the basis of the latter, accept that Japan is a democratic society. If by an effectively open economy we mean relatively balanced trade, then the Japanese economy is not open; but if we were to use openness as an independent criterion, the answer would still have to be cautiously worded. We do not hold Japan to be a paragon of openness but, instead, what we tried to demonstrate was that serious attempts, unlike in the past, were being made to address the basic conditions behind the limited access to foreign manufacturers. The Action Programme was the first to deal comprehensively with the socially determined barriers to imports. We also identified, however, areas of remaining problems, such as distribution, which need to be streamlined and improved.

Unquestionably the protectionist sentiment in the United States is being fuelled by the growing trade imbalance with Japan and a solution to the present crisis would, logically, have to come through an easing of this trade imbalance. However, the difficulty with this is that the US trading imbalance is a global phenomenon and not just restricted to trade with Japan. The deterioration in the US trade balance over the period 1982–6 extends beyond Japan to Western Europe, Latin America, and the Asian newly industrializing countries. While the trade deficit with Japan widened from $19 billion in 1982 to over $55 billion in 1986, in trade with Western Europe there was a reversal from a surplus of $5 billion to a deficit of over $30 billion over the same period. On the basis of the general nature of the problem, it would be unfair to single out Japan as the source of the problem. The global nature of the US trade deficit suggests that there must be factors internal to the United States that are also responsible for the worsening of its trade position. In the G-5 agreement the respective finance ministers and central bank governors, recognizing the destabilizing nature of the trading imbalance, agreed on a couple of points designed to restore balance. One was currency readjustment and the second was fiscal responsibility in the United States. Since the G.5 agreement the dollar had depreciated by about 50 per cent against the yen, but there was no indication to suggest that the US government had found the political will to tackle the massive federal fiscal deficit, at least until the stock market crash of 1987. The budget deficit in the United States was an important factor behind the US capital account surpluses and trading deficits. Since international capital flows are closely interlinked with flow of goods, both have to be dealt with if the deficits in merchandise trade are to be reversed. The blame cannot be placed entirely upon Japan and Japanese government actions alone would, therefore, be insufficient to balance trade.

With respect to the second evaluative criterion, we should mention at the outset that blame on Japan resulting from the trade imbalance is intermediated by the perception of a closed Japanese economy. However, with respect to tariff and quota barriers, at least, Japan has an open, if not more open,

131

economy than the other advanced industrialized countries. As such, the perception of a closed Japanese economy can be related to other invisible trade barriers like, for instance, the system of standards and certification. Standards and certifications, in any country, are based on an acceptable and traditionally defined state–society relationship. In Japan the state had generally assumed an intrusive role, more so than in the West, and the absence of well-developed societal consumer-interest groups had forced the state into a role where it was seen as protecting the minimum interests of the consumers. This function has been performed through an elaborate (safety) certification system and the standards are often so strict as to become an effective barrier to imports from other countries, which rely more on market forces to determine product survival.

In the discussion on the Action Programme, we suggest that the two features of the AP that could be important for foreign manufacturers were (1) a clearly defined commitment to reduce state intervention through a revision of the standards and certification procedures, and (2) national treatment of foreign products. The AP, drafted and formulated by the Economic Planning Agency, which is part of the Prime Minister's Office, reflected a willingness on the part of Japan's political leadership to play a more supportive role in the international system. However, since the AP was drafted outside the normal bureaucratic structure, problems could arise in the implementation phase. As we indicated, it is not yet clear that all the concerned ministries are equally committed to implement it in conformity with the principles contained therein. It is also clear that political leaders in Japan have much less control over the bureaucracy than do their counterparts in other countries. The relative autonomy of the bureaucracy in Japan and the lack of well-defined consensus could detract from effectiveness, at least in the short term and until a consensus had been formed. But, in so far as initiative had been taken, it indicated a new-found sense of responsibility, although the government now faced the difficult task of consensus building.

Nevertheless, unless there was some improvement in the trade situation, it was unlikely that the foreign perception that the Japanese economy was closed to imports would change. Since it was the perception that was indirectly contributing to protectionism, it was unlikely that the trade regime could be stabilized without changes in Western perception about Japan. Such changes in perception will, furthermore, depend on at least reversing the trend of growing Japanese surplus. There has, indeed, been some improvement in the trade position. In August 1987 the Japanese surplus against the United States declined for the fourth month in a row. Japanese exports to the United States in that month declined by 1.6 per cent over a year earlier, while imports from the United States registered a 27.5 per cent gain.[75] On a volume basis, starting in 1986 the rate of growth of Japanese imports has been well above that of exports and OECD forecasts suggests that the trend was likely to continue in 1987 and 1988.[76] No one expects trade to balance completely, for the US–Japan trading imbalance is part of the structurally determined Japanese surplus against the West to compensate for Japanese deficits with the primary and raw-material-exporting countries. Additionally, as we shall discuss in the next chapter, we can also expect improvements to flow from the government's policy to reduce domestic savings and raise real consumption levels, which should reduce the pressure to export and contribute to expanded imports.

To facilitate the process of balancing trade, the Reagan administration, too, must acknowledge the trade effects of its budget deficits. So part of the blame must go to the tardiness of American business. In the first half of 1987, South Korea, for example, lifted import restrictions on twenty-four items under American pressure, but of the resulting 'new' business Japan captured 57 per cent as opposed to only 18 per cent for the United States. The South Korean Ministry of Trade and Industry blamed the slowness of US industry, and a US embassy official concurred, 'A lot of the Japanese companies are next door and very ready to take advantage, while some American companies are less aggressive and export-oriented than we would hope'.[77]

There is no denying that improvements in market access had been made and that further change for the better could be expected. The problem is that during periods of change, the expectation of change often runs far ahead of the change itself. Radical change will do much to solve the problem, but it has to be admitted that practice and custom established over the years cannot be done away with in one fell swoop. As well as understanding the functional aspect of foreign pressure, there is also a need to exercise patience and understanding. Western critics understand well the usefulness of pressure, even though, at times, it seems to run out of control; but for the importance of patience, they might want to learn from their own history.

At the end of the First World War, the United States, instead of accepting responsibility concomitant with its economic strength in the world economy, withdrew inside its own shell and only started to take a more positive role after the Second World War. That was how long it took to forge a domestic consensus on liberal trade under American leadership. The British experience was quite similar. At the close of the Napoleonic Wars and the beginning of the 100 years of 'peace', Britain was the strongest economic and industrial power, but in the beginning the earlier mercantilist spirit continued to dominate trade issues. Even as the British government realized the wisdom of trade liberalization, Parliament continued to hold steadfast to the protection of domestic industry. Imlah provided an example. He wrote,

> The President of the Board of Trade, Frederick J. Robinson, frankly admitted in Parliament in 1817 the harm which import restrictions worked on British export trade but lamented that whenever he proposed to lower barriers half the manufacturers in the country presented petition and sent delegations against any liberalization of the laws.[78]

Things began to change for the better in the mid-twenties following the business upswing, but it was not until a couple of decades later that the principle of free trade was realized.

The evidence indicates that Japan is making a concerted effort, but it needs time before these efforts will start to bring any effective result. There are no easy short-term solutions, but the big unknown is whether the West will wait patiently for long-term solutions to become effective.

6

Industrial Restructuring and Demand Expansion

FOREIGN DEMAND AND JAPANESE ECONOMIC GROWTH

For a supporter, we emphasized the importance of supplementing the hegemon's ability to provide a large open market to balance global supply and demand imbalances. In the past, Japan, instead of doing this, itself relied on the hegemon's market to balance its supply and demand imbalances as part of its export-led growth strategy. According to Inoguchi Kuniko, if Japan was to become a supporter it had to provide: first, an open market by liberalizing its standards and certification procedures and rationalizing its distribution system; and second, a large market by boosting existing levels of domestic consumption.[1] We looked at the former in chapter 5 and this chapter will concentrate on the latter aspect of increasing domestic demand. We will also consider the importance of economic restructuring in Japan. Economic restructuring can be expected to contribute to a reduction in the dependence on exports and promote reliance, instead, on internal stimulus for economic growth. The presence of a large open economy, we argued, was essential to the stability of a liberal trading regime because it provided a vent for occasional global supply and demand imbalances. The importance of a hegemon with a large and open market was explained in these terms. The present crisis of the LIEO stemmed from the American perceptions, based on its worsening trade position, that the openness of the US economy was being unfairly exploited, not only by the NICs whose development strategies were based on perpetuating an internal supply and demand imbalance, but also by countries like Japan which used market penetration in the United States to ensure prosperity at home. Thus, Gerald Curtis suggested that Americans tended to perceive the success of Japanese economic growth as being the result of an 'export-to-the-United States-led growth'.[2] The resulting protectionism was a signal that the United States was no longer willing to continue in that role as a vent for sustained global supply and demand imbalances. This necessitated not only economic restructuring in Japan, but also, as its positive contribution to the stability of the LIEO, the provision of an open economy to relieve the burden on the United States. Japan's ability to play this regime-supportive role was based on the fact that Japan had the third largest GNP in the world.

It should be emphasized that a large economy was not a sufficient condition in itself. A supporter had to be a large and an open economy. In chapter 5 we looked at the policies recently adopted by the Japanese government to open its economy to imports and in this chapter we shall consider what Inoguchi suggested was necessary for the creation of a large market – a high consumption pattern as opposed to the existing high savings pattern. Of course, Japan already had a large economy, but expansion of domestic demand was essential not only to promote and create new demand for imports but also to reduce the reliance on exports. We will, in this chapter, consider measures introduced by the government to expand demand and to restructure the economy to reduce dependence on exports and increase reliance on internal growth stimuli. The export dependence of the Japanese economy, in terms of its contribution to GNP growth, had deepened during the late 1970s and early 1980s as a result of a poor business climate at home and lack of demand expansionary measures by the Japanese government. As well, we could cite the strong dollar as contributing to Japan's export dependence. The decline in the value of the dollar since late 1985 was likely to reduce this dependence, but demand expansion remained important because of its potential benefit to the international system through global economic revitalization and promotion of imports. A similar course of concerted action was attempted once before in 1978 when, under the so-called 'locomotive thesis', the United States called on Japan and West Germany to reflate their economies and thereby act as engines of growth, in conjunction with the United States, to pull the world out of the recessionary slump. The United States was unable to do so on its own because of the fear that it might worsen its trade imbalance.[3] West Germany carried through its commitments, but Japan reneged on its promise to achieve a 7 per cent economic growth in FY1978, fearing that such a high growth rate would stimulate inflation. In the mid-1980s, Japan was again asked to act as a locomotive and to expand domestic demand and reduce its economic dependence on foreign demand, particularly American demand. The Unites States pressed for this because a reduction in Japanese exports and a boost in their own exports to Japan would help revitalize their own economy.

Some economic restructuring could be expected as a result of market mechanisms and revaluation of the yen, which provided incentives for domestic manufacturers to locate production facilities in foreign markets. Demand expansion was important, however, to forestall economic deflation which could consequently dampen import demand. At the same time, demand expansion and reflation of the economy could also generate 'new' import demand, and there were repeated calls from Western sources for Japan to stimulate its economic growth.

Domestically also, there was considerable pressure on the government to increase demand and thereby compensate for the expected decline in foreign demand for Japanese goods. This pressure came both from industry sources and from within the ruling Liberal Democratic Party (LDP). It would be normal to assume, therefore, that since demand expansion was being proposed by both internal and external sources, the task of the government would have been that much easier. In reality, however, the government found it very difficult to act on these pressures. First, there were the critics of demand expansion, like Shinohara Myohei of the Institute of Developing Economies, who warned about the dangers of reviving inflation and who argued that Japan should stop pandering to the demands of its trading partners, especially since it was not entirely to blame for its trade surplus. Second, the Ministry of Finance was hesitant and apprehensive because fiscal expansion could jeopardize the objective of restoring fiscal balance by FY1990. The MOF was not necessarily opposed to demand expansion as such, but wanted instead to rely on non-fiscal means, even though fiscal measures were generally regarded as more effective in stimulating demand.

The first demand expansion package to include fiscal outlays was announced in September 1986. The question arises as to why the government chose to wait for so long after the currency adjustments had been initiated. However, while fiscal measures were long delayed, the government did attempt to compensate for the revaluation of the yen through monetary mechanisms. It should be pointed out that, however logical, Western pressure on demand expansion was never clearly interlinked with fiscal expansion. This might have given the government an excuse to continue with fiscal austerity, but, of course, a supporter should not be looking for excuses. Indeed, it was not; but it was hamstrung by constraints on its freedom of action. Although we elaborated on these constraints in chapter 3, it might be worthwhile to review them briefly at this point.

First, it should be noted that there was no clear-cut consensus in Japan on its role within the international system. Given the decision-making style in Japan which emphasized consensus amongst all participants, disagreement from even a solitary source was enough to block effective action. The lack of consensus was obvious both within and outside the government although, as we would expect, the former was more crucial. Within the government, the MOF insisted on the priority of eliminating government debt, which ruled out effective fiscal expansion at an earlier stage.

All democratic systems are constricted, to some extent, in their foreign-policy making by domestic constraints, but the Japanese consensual style of decision making made the internal constraints more difficult to manage and overcome. Consensus building is an on-going process and its thrust could be clearly discerned both in the Maekawa Commission report that we will discuss below and in the Action Programme discussed earlier. Before fiscal measures could be taken, the position of the MOF had to be reconciled with the objective of demand expansion. In this regard, we believe it was significant that in the Cabinet reshuffle, after Nakasone was granted a one-year extension to his term in office, he appointed Miyazawa Kiichi as his new Finance Minister. The appointment of Miyazawa, Nakasone's rival for the leadership of the LDP, was interpreted by some as a move to silence his opponent by putting him in charge of a Ministry committed to an 'unpopular' position. This interpretation would be credible only if we could expect a second extension of Nakasone's term in office, but this was unlikely given the nature of factional politics within the LDP. A more likely explanation would be that Miyazawa's appointment was an attempt to force a change in the MOF position, as Miyazawa had already indicated his position in favour of fiscal expansion when he met the Prime Minister in March 1986 and presented to him a list of proposals for demand expansion. Prime Minister Fukuda had done much the same in late 1977, when he appointed Miyazawa as the Director General of the Economic Planning Agency (EPA), hoping thereby to strengthen the hands of the fiscal expansionists in the government.[4]

Second, and as we emphasized earlier, especially when there was a problem of domestic consensus formation, foreign pressure not only became functional but was also welcomed as a way of breaking the deadlock. Thus, the absence of official American pressure in the initial stages of the auto dispute prevented an early resolution of the dispute. In so far as fiscal expansion was concerned, while there was pressure on Japan to increase demand, there was no specific pressure to raise fiscal spending (see p. 149, on the Baker–Miyazawa meeting). This enabled the MOF to insist on delinking fiscal and demand expansion.

To appreciate fully the issues of demand expansion and economic restructuring, it will be necessary to look at the nature of the constraints, particularly the determinants of the high savings rate in Japan and the fiscal crisis. But, first, let us look briefly at the nature of the export dependence of the Japanese economy. Figure 6.1 shows the contributing share of foreign and domestic demand to GNP growth in Japan from which it is easy to assess the importance of the foreign sector. In FY1976, for example, when Japanese economic growth had recovered to about 6 per cent after two years of slow growth, it was mainly led by foreign demand as domestic consumption remained sluggish. In contrast to the Japanese experience, the US recovery during that period was primarily led by domestic demand.[5] Again, in the 1980s, according to *The Wall Street Journal*, without Japanese exports to the United States there would have been no economic growth in Japan in the period since 1983.[6]

It is often suggested that post-war Japanese economic policies had been dominated by mercantilist ideals that glorified exports and relegated imports to a necessary evil which should be kept to a minimum. In fact, in the early 1970s, Japan's export dependence was low compared to the other advanced industri-

Figure 6.1 Foreign/domestic demand component in GNP growth

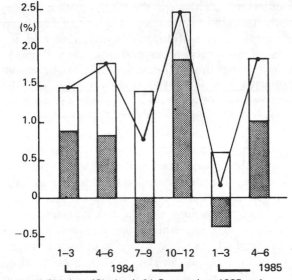

Source: *Asahi Shinbun* (Chokan), 21 September 1985, p.1.
Notes: Shaded area is the foreign demand component; unshaded area is the domestic demand component. Trend line is real GNP growth over previous period, seasonally adjusted.

alized countries but grew rapidly as export growth continued to outstrip GNP growth. Average export growth during the period 1976–80 was 18.6 per cent a year, while GNP growth in the period 1977–80 was only about 5 per cent a year.[7]

In real terms, exports made up to 10.1 per cent of the gross national expenditure (GNE) (1975 prices) in 1970, but went up to 13.8 per cent in 1975 and to 17.8 per cent in 1980, reflecting the increased dependence on exports for economic growth. Exports were replacing private domestic investment as the stimulant to economic growth. Private investment, which had played the leading role in economic growth in the 1960s, declined from 19.6 per cent in 1970 to 16.4 per cent in 1975, recovering slightly to 16.9 per cent of GNE in 1980.[8]

As was mentioned earlier, Japan's trade problems with other countries were the result of a dual imbalance in the Japanese trade structure. Not only was there an imbalance in the overall levels of trade, as reflected in the balance of trade position (see table 6.1), there was also an imbalance in the composition and direction of trade.

Table 6.1 Japan's trade with the West

Year	Exports		Imports		Total balance
1981	62.97	(41.4)	36.59	(25.6)	9.20
1982	57.42	(42.0)	33.00	(25.9)	9.33
1983	70.06	(45.8)	37.60	(29.0)	23.33
1984	84.41	(49.7)	39.77	(29.0)	35.09
1985 provisional	90.46	(51.5)	38.10	(29.4)	46.15

Source: Compiled from *Zaikai Kansoku*, NRI, March 1986, page statistics 3.
Notes: Units: $ billion. Figures within parentheses are the percentage share of total exports and imports.

Japanese imports were concentrated mainly in primary products and raw materials with relatively low levels of manufactured imports, lower still if we consider only finished products, excluding semi-processed items. In contrast to this, even though West Germany was also a trade surplus country, its trade structure was more evenly balanced and, therefore, less problematic. This is not to suggest that trade, at the micro level, must always be symmetrical. Indeed, Britain's foreign trade in the nineteenth century was not balanced. The difference between Britain then and Japan today, however, is that the former, to compensate for low manufactured imports, liberalized the agricultural sector of the economy, whereas the latter, for political reasons, maintained high tariff and non-tariff barriers against agricultural imports.

Looking closely at the imbalance in the Japanese export structure, we find that only a handful of industries accounted for the bulk of total exports. In the decade of the 1960s, export concentration was mainly in heavy industry and petrochemicals. In the 1970s, and particularly since the oil crises, there was a shift in favour of precision goods and high-technology industries. In any event, the industries at the leading edge of the economy predominated export trade. For example, the top ten leading industries accounted for over 50 per cent of total Japanese exports.[9]

The direction of exports showed a similar concentration in terms of destination. This concentration, instead of weakening over time, had become more pronounced. In 1981, 26 per cent of Japanese exports went to the United States, but this increased to 36 per cent in 1984 and, by provisional estimates, to 37 per cent in 1985. Several factors could be cited for this concentration, including the facts that the US economy was more open than the European markets and the overvaluation of

141

the dollar. After the auto dispute and following the VER with the United States in 1981, an effort was made to develop new markets in the Middle East and South East Asia, but this had only a limited success. In 1979, Japanese automotive exports (cars and commercial vehicles) to the United States held a 45 per cent share in 1983, the share crept back up to 45 per cent share of local automotive exports, and while it declined to 37 per cent in 1983, the share crept back up to 42 per cent in 1984. The export destination of other export commodities was similarly concentrated in the United States, and this high penetration of the American market was the reason that trade disputes usually started there and would later spin off to other areas.

This created no major problems for the Americans initially, but as economic performance faltered there was a general backlash against what was perceived to be excessive Japanese penetration of the American market, to the detriment of American industry and levels of employment. Critics were incensed that Japan not only failed to improve access for others to its own robust economy and, thereby, to overcome the recessionary spell in the global economy, but also that it was, in a negative sense, exploiting the weakness of the leader.

DOMESTIC DEMAND AND EXPORTS

In this section we will look at the factors that led to the deepening of export dependence in Japan. We hope, thereby, to facilitate an understanding of how a more balanced economic structure could be achieved. In the main, we will centre our discussion on an analysis of the low consumption levels in Japan (i.e. the causes behind the high savings rate) and on the issue of the debt burden of the Japanese government.

The high savings rate has often been blamed as the leading cause behind Japan's export-push growth. The personal savings rate in Japan in 1982 was about 17 per cent compared to only 5 per cent in the United States. In the early post-war period, the high savings rate was the forte of the Japanese economy because it made available capital for plant and manufacturing investment when the economy was in the high-growth phase. Since then, as the economy entered a slow-growth phase, investment demand for capital declined, but savings remained at the earlier high level. The continued high savings rate kept domestic demand low, forcing industry to become more reliant on foreign demand. Also, the surplus capital which flowed overseas contributed to a surge in exports by keeping the value of the Japanese yen down. It was natural that, in time, this pattern of economic growth in Japan would come in for criticism from its trading partners. Accordingly, it became necessary for the government to attempt to lower the high savings rate such that economic growth could be based more on domestic consumption.

The possible explanations for the high savings rate include, among others, the relatively underdeveloped old-age security and welfare system, high real-estate prices, and the pay structure. In Japan, a large portion of annual income is received in the form of semi-annual bonuses that often exceed six months' salary and in specific business sectors, insurance for example, may approach a year's salary depending on business conditions. This, however, was variable income, and since expenditure and consumption was usually budgeted in terms of fixed income, a large part of the bonus received often ended up as savings, which because of the size of the bonus could be a considerable amount.[10] Also, the price of land in the urban centres of Japan was several times that in the United States or Canada, and now that the 'my home' age had superseded the 'my car' age, there was a strong built-in incentive to save. There were culturally based factors, as well, that may help to explain the high savings rate in Japan. In the competitive and individualistic Western society, the emphasis on 'keeping up with the Joneses' provided a ripple effect boosting consumption patterns, whereas the emphasis on group conformity in Japanese society provided no such stimulus. Also, since simplicity was an important measure of aesthetical standard in Japan, an increase in income levels often only added to personal disposable income (PDI) available for savings. While there was no major discrepancy between Japanese and Western ownership of consumer durables (colour TV 99.1%; washing machines 98%; VCRs 28%; refrigerators 98.4%, etc., in 1985), because of space limitation, cultural, and other factors, Japanese homes tend to be rather simple and bereft of furniture. Many of these socio-cultural determinants to high savings in Japan are beyond the immediate control of the government and there was little it could do in this regard. Western critics, however, were more likely to attribute the high savings to the specific policies of

143

the government, and this will be considered in some detail below.

The tax incentives to save provided by the Japanese government have attracted much critical attention. In Japan, interest earnings on savings of up to Y3 million ($20,000 at Y150 = $1 approximately) per type of financial institution were non-taxable. This meant that an individual could deposit about Y6 million in postal savings and commercial banks and receive tax-free income. On top of that, if bond holdings were included, an individual, with prudent money management, could save up to Y10 million and not pay tax on the interest. This was the direct opposite of the tax system in the United States, which encouraged personal consumption beyond the parameters of PDI by making interest on borrowings tax deductable.

Since raising private consumption was related to lowering the savings rate, the logical place to begin would be with the tax incentives to save. The dilemma for the Japanese government was that such a move was fraught with potential dangers. Tax-free savings had become a necessary concession to wage earners to compensate for a tax structure that was regarded as 'unfair' to fixed-wage earners. Removal of the tax benefit was, therefore, difficult and could only be attempted as part of a major overhaul of the entire tax structure. Indeed, reform of the tax structure did become a major issue in Japanese politics and, in September 1985, the government established a Tax Commission to advise on ways to reform the existing system.

Under the existing tax structure, set up during the period of occupation, the weight of direct tax to total revenue had increased and constituted 73.4 per cent of total revenue in 1985.[11] Those on fixed income considered this high reliance on direct taxation unfair, even though the average tax burden of the Japanese was only about 36 per cent (including the social security component) in 1985 – certainly not unbearably high by Western standards. The feeling of 'unfairness' resulted from the fact that the self-employed (those not on fixed income) were better able to utilize tax loopholes to lower their total tax burden, for example, by shifting income earned to members of the family. Because the tax structure itself was relatively more progressive in Japan, it was possible to benefit from a more than proportional tax break by moving into a lower tax bracket, an avenue not open to those receiving fixed incomes, such as the salaried worker whose taxes were withheld at source. As a measure of the inequitable distribution of the tax burden, the National Tax Agency reported the result of a survey in September 1986 which showed that, while 89 per cent of salaried workers paid taxes in FY1985, only 42 per cent of the self-employed and only 22 per cent of farmers paid any taxes at all.[12] As this perception of unfairness became more widely entrenched, the tax break on 'small' savings acquired more than a symbolic value, not to be easily tampered with. One possible solution would be to balance the tax burden of each group by increasing the scope of indirect taxation as in European countries (sales tax, value-added tax, wholesale tax, etc.), but this could only bring about 'fairness' if it was accompanied by a lowering of the tax burden of 'salaried workers'. As presently constituted, indirect taxes contributed only 26 per cent to government revenue (FY1986 budget), well below the levels in other advanced countries. However, there was strong opposition to any measure that simply imposed indirect taxes on top of the existing tax burden. Prime Minister Ohira had found this out the hard way when he proposed levying a general consumption tax, modelled on the European value-added tax, in late 1979, and took the country to the polls.

Thus, it was not surprising that when the earlier Tax System Study Group (*Zeisei Chosa Kai*, Chairman: Ogura) submitted its final report to the Prime Minister in late 1983, it recommended that the government should consider the possibility of expanding the base of indirect taxation, given the low average tax burden in Japan, but added the cautionary statement that such taxes should only be introduced with the understanding of the people and with maximum regard for fairness of the system.[13]

The Tax Commission set up in 1985 was composed of about fifty members. One member, Sakaiya Taiichi, openly expressed his position that the incentives on savings had outlived their purpose and that at least a part of the interest income should be subject to a uniform tax. In return, he advocated lowering the income-tax and corporate-tax burden by about Y5 trillion, the lost revenue being made up by expanding the tax base.[14] (The terms 'billion' and 'trillion' are used in the American sense. A trillion, therefore, is equal to a British billion).

The report of the committee was submitted in late 1986 and shortly thereafter the LDP, in early December 1986, announced tax-reform proposals that contained two important features.

145

Besides simplifying the tax structure and reducing the number of tax brackets, it proposed the introduction of a value-added tax (VAT) and a total abolition of the tax incentives on savings. The proposals were tabled before the diet in Spring 1987 for implementation from FY1988. To make sure that this did not simply end up as a tax-increase package, and thereby adversely affect consumption levels, the government also declared its intent to lower personal income-tax rates from the maximum of 70 per cent to 50 per cent and corporate taxes from 53 per cent to 49.99 per cent.[15]

The government's tax-reform proposal was formalized in two separate parts, one dealing with tax reduction and the elimination of interest-free savings and the other dealing with a revamp of the tax structure, including the introduction of an indirect value-added tax. During the elections for both the Upper and Lower Houses of the Japanese Diet in the summer of 1986, Nakasone had pledged tax reduction and given his commitment not to introduce large-scale indirect taxation. However, buoyed by the massive election victory of the ruling LDP, Nakasone felt confident that he could force through legislation restructuring the tax system and introduce VAT. The introduction of VAT was considered necessary to stay within the governmental guideline to eliminate fiscal deficit by the year 1990. To justify the about-turn from the election promises, the government insisted that the result would be much fairer than the existing system and small businesses were also granted exemption from VAT. According to estimates by a group of economists, the tax-reform package was likely to benefit those with incomes over Y6 million a year, while the effect on those below that level was thought to be less clear.[16] However, the proposal for VAT came under strong criticism from both business and consumer groups. It was argued that it would complicate accounting procedures and consumers were unhappy that the government had reneged on its earlier promises. It also did not help that the government had acted too hastily without allowing proper and adequate public debate on the proposal. Confronted with this strong reaction, the government was forced to withdraw the proposal for VAT, although the tax-reduction scheme was approved despite some controversy over the elimination of tax-free savings. As such, by sheer coincidence, it appeared that the government would be forced to delay its objective of balancing the fiscal budget and at the same time it lost whatever rationalizations there were not to introduce fiscal demand expansionary measures. Indeed, shortly after the defeat on VAT, the government did announce a large-scale fiscal package to stimulate domestic demand.

The removal of tax incentives to save will, no doubt, affect the future savings rate of the Japanese. Tax-free savings (*Maruyu*) were to be abolished on 1 October 1987 and interest earned thereafter subject to a flat-rate tax of 20 per cent. As well, we could expect future savings to decline as the result of on-going demographic trends. Japan, at present, has a relatively young population structure, meaning a high ratio of the working population to the total population. Since it was the working population that saved, a large work-force would naturally result in high total savings. The last 'baby boom' in Japan was in the early 1950s and since then the birth rate has declined drastically to where the current birth rate is around one of the lowest in the world. As a result, the population is ageing rapidly and this trend would be vastly accelerated as the 'baby boom' generation moved out of the work-force. The future demographic changes of the Japanese population are shown in figure 6.2

Figure 6.2 Japan's population structure

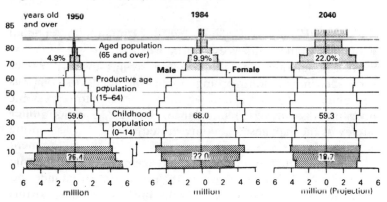

Source: *Statistical Handbook of Japan, 1986*, Statistics Bureau, Management and Co-ordination Agency, Tokyo, p.19.

For comparative purposes, figure 6.3 shows the trend in Japan relative to some Western countries. It is expected that by the turn of the century Japan will have a larger percentage of

Figure 6.3 Ratio of people 65 years and above to population

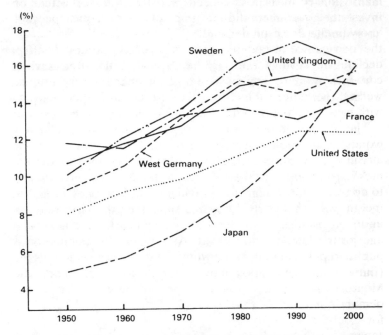

Source: *Nihon Keizai no Genko, 1985*, Tokyo; Keizai Kikakucho, p.193.

the population above 65 years than the United States, United Kingdom, France, and West Germany.

As a population ages, the absolute savings level will necessarily decline (a non-working population tends to comprise consumers, not savers), and we can expect this to redress the investment–savings (IS) imbalance. The EPA, in its annual survey of the Japanese economy, noted,

> It is anticipated that with the rapid ageing of our population, and provided that investment levels are sustained, the savings–investment balance will move from the existing surplus of savings to where savings are inadequate. Together with this, our international balance of payments structure and the current account structure as well will change from the existing surplus to deficits.[17]

The surplus of capital, which increased from 3 per cent of

GNP in the late 1970s to about 5 per cent in recent years, mainly flowed to the United States, attracted by a shortage of investment capital resulting from the fiscal expansion and 'crowding out' of capital from the private sector. Within Japan, the decline in investment demand resulted, first, from the decline in economic growth, but also from increases in corporate tax rates and reduction of tax-reserve provisions, as well as a low rate of inflation (below 2 per cent in recent years, with a few exceptions).[18]

The alternative to private sector investment demand was to expand fiscal expenditure. However, the Japanese government, already burdened by a high debt ratio, was unwilling to add more to it, and nor did Japan's trading partners push hard for it to do so. At the G-5 meeting and again at the Baker–Miyazawa meeting of October 1986, the Japanese government agreed to undertake demand expansion but through measures to encourage private sector consumption without necessarily spending public money. It should be emphasized that on neither occasion (the G-5 agreement or at the meeting between Baker and Miyazawa) did Japan agree on specific fiscal measures to boost demand. At the Baker–Miyazawa meeting in September 1986, for example, Treasury Secretary Baker simply requested the Japanese Finance Minister to do only as much as he could.[19] Also, at the G-5 meeting of September 1985, Japan agreed only to use monetary policy and other measures to enhance private sector consumption. Japan did follow through on this commitment with three successive rate cuts by the Bank of Japan that lowered the discount rate to 3.5 per cent.

Throughout this period, the priority for the Japanese government was to balance its budget. According to a self-imposed timetable, the government was committed to eliminate the practice of financing the budget deficits through deficit bond issues and to lower the overall dependence on government bonds by FY1990.[20] The reason for fiscal austerity and budget balancing was that this was essential to meet future contingencies. The fact that the population was ageing and that industrial restructuring was likely to result in structural unemployment meant that there would be additional demands on the government to provide better social services in the future. The government, therefore, had to be prepared, financially, to respond to these demands and improve social capital. The social welfare system in Japan was still rather rudimentary by

Western standards and the government anticipated having to make considerable financial outlays in the future which would necessitate strict austerity to bring the present fiscal crisis under control.

At the end of FY1975, total outstanding bond issue was Y15 trillion, but it increased rapidly thereafter, rising to Y70 trillion in FY1980 and up to Y110 trillion by the end of FY1983.[21] Several factors could be noted as having contributed to the deteriorating fiscal condition:

1. decline in tax revenue as the economy slowed down following the oil crisis of 1973;
2. fiscal expansion to combat deflationary tendencies after the oil crisis;
3. increased government expenditure in the 1970s to improve the social welfare system.[22]

Table 6.2 gives an indication of the Japanese fiscal crisis as compared to other countries.

As measured by the indicators above, the Japanese fiscal condition was considerably worse than in other countries and it is easy to understand why the government felt compelled to take remedial steps. At its peak, in FY1979, the government's dependence on bond issue to finance the general accounts

Table 6.2 State of public finances

	Percentage of bond issue in total revenue	Per capita outstanding long-term govt debt (Y10,000)	Interest payment as percentage of total budget spending	National tax revenue as percentage of total budget spending
Japan	22.2 (FY1985)	126 (FY1985)	18.8 (FY1985)	73.4 (FY1985)
United States	19.4 (FY1985)	120 (FY1983)	14.4 (FY1985)	77.3 (FY1983)
United Kingdom	5.2 (FY1984)	96 (FY1982)	6.6 (FY1984)	83.7 (FY1983)
West Germany	9.8 (FY1985)	52 (FY1983)	11.4 (FY1985)	78.5 (FY1984)
France	14.0 (FY1985)	16 (FY1980)	8.4 (FY1985)	84.7 (FY1984)

Source: Matsuzawa, T. (1985) 'Keidanren's Viewpoint on Government Spending and Future Administrative and Fiscal Reform', *Keidanren Review* no. 195, p. 3.

budget had reached a high of about 35 per cent. Since then, a concerted campaign to hold down fiscal spending succeeded in reducing this dependence to about 22 per cent in FY1985 and to 20 per cent in the initial budget for FY1986.[23] Until recently, the belt-tightening measures had been relatively painless because the economy had performed fairly well, especially since 1983. But the economy had performed well precisely because of its close articulation with the American economy through a constant stream of exports. This practice, obviously, could not be continued if Japan was to play a positive role in the trading system and the government, instead, had to create conditions that would increase the share of domestic consumption in GNP growth and lead to expanded imports.

Despite the fact that fiscal measures are generally considered more effective in demand expansion, the government, unable to overcome opposition from the conservative Ministry of Finance, concentrated initially on non-spending programmes. The government tried to keep the issue of demand expansion separate from fiscal expansion, arguing that non-fiscal measures were sufficient to boost private consumption and overall domestic demand. At the same time, with declining oil prices, it felt that fiscal expansion was not urgently required. The Economic Planning Agency, weighing up the positive (import) and negative (export) aspects of the rise in the yen, concluded that they virtually cancelled each other out. However, if the lower oil prices were taken into consideration, the results, according to the EPA, were, on the whole, beneficial to the Japanese economy.[24] Even so, fiscal expansion became increasingly more difficult to avoid as private forecasts indicated growth rates substantially below the official target rate of 4 per cent GNP growth. Conflicts within the official bureaucracy also became more pronounced, especially that between the internationalist MITI and the conservative MOF. Commenting on the rivalry between the MITI and the MOF, the *International Currency Review* noted that

in an unprecedented dispute between the major pillars of Japan's bureaucratic establishment, MITI is carrying its campaign for aggressive reflationary action into the open, even to the extent of giving press briefings warning of the severe consequences which would ensue in the event of fiscal inaction.[25]

The intrabureaucratic friction created a dilemma for the Prime Minister. For much of his term in office, he had strongly backed the MOF and its objective of balancing the budget, but that was before the international circumstances had changed. Still, he found it difficult to break away sharply from his past policies and also found himself caught between the contradictory pressures to adhere to his past policy objective, on the one hand, and to adapt to the international circumstances, on the other. At a news conference in March 1986, he definitely appeared to be leaning in favour of fiscal expansion when he commented that he had a 'free hand' on fiscal spending, only that he had not felt it necessary to exercise that option in the past.

DEMAND EXPANSION MEASURES

As a first step, the Japanese government on 15 October 1985 announced a set of demand expansion measures aimed at stimulating consumption patterns. The government claimed it to be the largest demand expansion package, at Y3.12 trillion, but it was not particularly well received because it contained no public works component. In principle, since aggregate demand was composed of personal consumption, private housing investment, private capital spending, and fiscal outlays, the government could have targeted any of these to achieve the results. Naturally, we would expect the effects to vary depending on the particular set of measures adopted. According to an analysis prepared by MITI of the potential effects of a Y1 trillion demand expansion package composed of either investment/income-tax cuts or expanded public works, the net effect on the trade balance would be significantly different, as table 6.3 shows.

From the estimates, it would appear that an investment-tax cut held the greatest promise, but the problem was that it was

Table 6.3 Demand expansion and trade surplus (Y million)

Effect of Y1	1st year	2nd year
Trillion income-tax cut	− 580m	− 1,340m
Public works expenditure	− 450m	− 790m
Investment-tax cut	− 2,010m	− 730m

Source: *Asahi Shinbun* (Chokan), 11 October 1985, p. 8.

also most likely to lead to an export growth over the longer run as increased private investment was related to higher productivity. On the other hand, neither an income-tax cut nor an expanded public works programme was acceptable at the time because of the budgetry constraints. The actual package agreed upon (Y4.1 trillion, including the multiplier effect) was composed of the following measures:

1. promotion of public housing investment and urban development;
2. promotion of private investment in plant and equipment;
3. activation of private consumption.[26]

The package also included relaxation of regulations on various aspects, although only a very small number of the 150-odd regulations governing housing investment were thus affected. To promote housing construction, the government announced that it would expand both the amount and the number of housing loans approved by the Housing Loan Corporation (HLC). The amount of individual loan was to be raised by Y1.5–2.5 million per borrower and the number of these loans was to be increased by 20,000 from the existing 490,000 units. The HLC loans are made at interest rates slightly lower than private banks, involving a monthly saving of between Y3,000–6,000. But these loans were not very popular and in the two application periods in FY1985 there were only 165,000 applications as opposed to 191,000 for the same period the year before. There were several factors behind the unattractiveness of HLC loans, but the one that figured prominently was, no doubt, the application fee of Y40,000 introduced in 1985.[27] Because an application did not guarantee that a loan would be approved, the fee had become a deterrent to potential applicants despite the fact that such loans, when approved, inevitably lowered the repayment burden. Even the Construction Ministry admitted that, at best, the new measure would only raise housing investments to the levels of the year before.[28] The government's focus on stimulating housing construction was justified with the explanation that it was least likely to contribute to an increase in exports which might result if the emphasis had been on stimulating private sector capital spending.

On the second item on the list of demand expansion measures, the government stated that it would encourage utilities companies to undertake investment in plant and facilities and in such areas as laying underground electric cables, etc.

The last item contained mainly guidelines for banks and financial institutions to make credit more readily available for consumption purposes and to operate cash-dispensing machines on those Saturdays when the banks were closed. Cash-dispensing machines were normally operated from 9.00 a.m. to 6.00 p.m. on weekdays, 9.00 a.m. to 3.00 p.m. on those Saturdays when the banks were open, and no service was provided on Sundays. Whether extending the hours of operation would raise consumption was not certain, but in so far as this would be an improvement in services, it was certainly worthwhile. In appendix 2 of the measures, the government also outlined the desirability of implementing a five-day working week. In March 1987 the government submitted a bill to shift gradually to a five-day working week, which according to one estimate could expand consumption expenditures by Y3 trillion.[29]

From the gist of the package, it was obvious that the government had chosen to stimulate private consumption with indirect measures not necessitating the expenditure of public funds. A spokesman for the EPA explained the absence of fiscal measures in the following words, 'With respect to personal consumption, we really wanted to include tax reduction or lowering of interest rates, but both are difficult which resulted in the small steps taken'.[30] Also, there was less of an urgency to do more as the appreciation of the yen had still not reached a critical stage. Deflation was not yet a serious threat as the yen had risen only by 10 per cent. Thus, while the potential value of the package was not insignificant, the EPA estimated that it would lead to an increase in imports of only about $2 billion,[31] primarily in the form of lumber imports for housing construction. The total trade effect was indeed small and unlikely to make more than a minor dent in the total balance of payments.

However, as the yen continued to appreciate, the need for anti-deflationary measures was more clearly obvious. Accordingly, the government announced a second demand expansion programme on 28 December 1985. Although the total sum of the package was smaller than that of the first, it did contain some public works expenditure which was to be implemented in FY1986. The scale of the package was only Y1.6 trillion, including the multiplier. This time, however, the government did not provide any estimate of how much the measures would contribute to import growth, which was deemed to be only marginal, according to one EPA official who was interviewed. The increased general expenditure was to be financed through the Fiscal Investment and Loan Programme (FILP) which is regarded as Japan's second budget and which used the postal savings as the source of funding for investments by special corporations and public companies. The December package contained the following measures:

1. promotion of housing construction and urban development;
2. promotion of plant and equipment investment and technical development;
3. expansion of public investment.[32]

Since the public works projects were to be funded in the FILP, the government could continue with its austere fiscal policies. Furthermore, when we look at public works expenditure in the general accounts budget, there was a noticeable 2.3 per cent decline in FY1986 compared to the year before. There was some improvement, however, if we combined both the FILP and the general accounts budget. In that case, the total public works expenditure in FY1986 showed a 4.3 per cent increase over the previous year as compared to a 3.7 per cent increase in FY1985.[33]

The two major projects taken up in the December package, to be constructed as third sector projects (i.e. involving public as well as private sector funding), were the construction of a tunnel across Tokyo Bay to facilitate traffic flow between Tokyo and Chiba, and a bridge over the Akashi straits separating the main island of Honshu from the southern island of Shikoku. With these two large projects, to be taken up in FY1986, the government hoped to impress upon the leaders of the advanced countries the seriousness with which Japan was fulfilling its international obligations.

The two demand expansion packages were formulated within the framework of restructuring the Japanese economy, to make it less dependent upon exports by raising levels of domestic consumption. Prime Minister Nakasone, eager to project the right image, expressed his determination to press ahead on this front: 'To any country, restructuring its economy is no easy task, but I am determined to rise to the challenges'.[34] Economic restructuring, unlike industrial restructuring, is something new for Japan. It could involve encouraging direct foreign investment by Japanese companies, but if this was not to result in a downturn in domestic economic activity, there had to be some emphasis on raising the level of domestic consumption.

To raise domestic consumption levels and restructure the economy, the MITI, in its annual white paper on international trade (1985), observed that it was necessary to do the following:

1. increase private consumption and housing investment;
2. encourage continued and steady addition of social capital;
3. increase levels of private domestic investment.[35]

In the field of social capital, there is general consensus that Japan should put a lot more emphasis on improving the quality of life to bring it up to a level comparable to that prevailing in the West. Housing and living conditions in Japan were lagging well behind the West, and Westerners often compared Japanese housing conditions to 'rabbit hutches'. Figure 6.4 gives an indication of the poor state of Japanese social capital development.

To stimulate personal consumption, government and EPA officials openly expressed their desire for substantial wage increases in the Spring 1986 wage offensive (*Shunto*). According to EPA estimates, the rate of wage increase had lagged about one percentage point behind annual productivity growth rates over the period 1980–4 and it felt, therefore, that employers could afford a larger-than-usual wage increase.[36] The problem was that in the annual wage negotiations, the trendsetters were usually the unions in the large exports industries, like steel and autos, and it was unlikely that these industries would be willing to make major wage concessions when growth prospects were bleak and since they all hoped to overcome the impact of the high yen by taking advantage of productivity gains. Thus, as the Chairman of Nikkeiren, a business organization, stated, it was unreasonable to anticipate a 7 per cent wage increase when economic growth was expected to be only about 3 per cent.[37]

To raise private investment levels and achieve IS balance,

Figure 6.4 Level of capital stock in selected countries

	Housing	Sewage	Roads	Parks
Japan				
United States				
United Kingdom				
West Germany				
France				
Sweden				

Source: *Tsusho Hyakusho, 1985*, Tokyo: Tsusho Sangyo sho, p.238.
Notes: Housing: average number of people per room.
      Sewage: percentage of population with access to sewage.
      Roads: paved roads/total road length.
      Parks: area of park space (square metre) per person. The broken
      line gives the average for the six countries.

domestic consumption had to increase and by some significant measure to compensate for the expected decline in foreign demand. It was expected that the corporate-tax reduction, when implemented, would have some effect in stimulating private investment. In the past, domestic investment decisions were often determined by factors relating to foreign demand. This is illustrated in figure 6.5.

In the meantime, in September 1986 the government announced an eight-point demand expansion package that promised to boost GNP growth by about $23 billion for the fiscal year. The package, part of the supplementary fiscal budget for the year, contained a $15 billion increase in public works expenditure and the government also decided to raise additional revenue by issuing new Construction Bonds to the tune of $3.4 billion. As a result of this additional public works spending, the government's dependence on deficit financing was predicted to increase beyond the originally proposed levels for FY1986. According to estimates of the Nomura Research Institute, this latest demand expansion package was likely to add 0.5 per cent to GNP growth for the year.[38] It would appear, therefore, that the Japanese government had finally decided to de-emphasize fiscal austerity in favour of fiscal expansion. It was, however,

157

Figure 6.5 Share of foreign and domestic demand in private investment

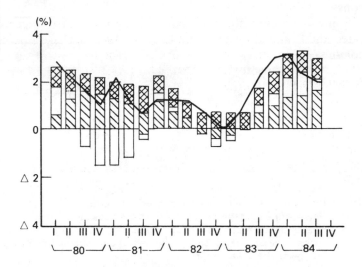

Source: *Tsusho Hyakusho, 1985,* Tokyo: Tsusho Sangyo sho, p.241.
Notes: Diagonally ruled area is foreign demand component.
White areas represent the domestic demand component.
Hatched area is the residual.
Trend line is the real private investment growth over the previous period.

only after the government failed to introduce indirect taxation, in 1987, that the budget-balancing target was perceived to have been seriously jeopardized. Shortly thereafter, the government introduced a Y6 trillion (about $40 billion at Y150=$1) economic stimulation package including a total of Y5 trillion in public spending. This was a major new initiative and it was estimated that it would add 1.5 percentage points to GNP growth and help to reduce the trade imbalance significantly. According to Okumura Ariyoshi, this package was 'a bold decision on the part of the government, given the enormous budget deficit. Japan has indeed made a clear-cut policy change in favor of expansion led by domestic demand'.[39]

However we look at it, a key component in the economic restructuring of Japan is related to the expansion of domestic consumption and efforts to raise levels of consumer spending have had some positive effect. Consumer spending in August

1986 rose by 3.5 per cent, in real terms, over the year before, marking the fifth consecutive monthly increase in private consumption.[40]

Some time after the G-5 agreement to readjust currency rates, the Prime Minister, on 31 October 1985, set up a private commission to study the problem of economic restructuring. The seventeen-member advisory group on Economic Structural Adjustment for International Harmony, commonly known as the Maekawa Commission, after its Chairman Haruo Maekawa, former Governor of the Bank of Japan, became much talked about in both domestic and foreign circles, as the beginning of a long-awaited process. Hopes were high because of reports in the press that an overall consensus had been achieved within the Commission on 'various "new" ideas, such as a target year for Japan to bring its trade surplus to zero, or boosting government spending to stimulate the economy'.[41]

When, however, the Commission reported its findings on 7 April 1986, many analysts immediately pounced on the report as a prime example of bureaucratic inconsistency and regurgitation of old and established ideas. The critics argued that the report was simply a compilation of various bureaucratic interests, garnished with a plethora of high-sounding noble declarations, with no mention of the means to be used to achieve those objectives. The respected vernacular *Nihon Keizai Shinbun*, in its editorial the following day, summed it up simply as a report that displayed all the pettiness of a typical bureaucratic undertaking. Critics also charged that the whole notion of industrial restructuring which the report emphasized contained nothing new or revolutionary. All this, however, missed the point that the report was not meant to lay down a concrete guide to action, but rather to elaborate on the more fundamental philosophic issue of reorienting the economy with a view to promoting international harmony. The report, observing that the time had come for a 'historical transformation' of the economy, recommended that the government reduce current account imbalance in the medium term and initiate as soon as possible steps to restructure the economy. The fact that the report did not propose any specific measures should not be seen as detracting from its utility. One of its main objectives was to help lay the groundwork for a new domestic consensus that would support a more positive role by Japan in the international system. The reaction outside Japan to the

159

Maekawa report was much more favourable than the domestic reaction. The *Far Eastern Economic Review*, for example, observed,

> for the first time in the history of such efforts, the focus is almost entirely on what Japan needs to do to set things right by way of domestic economic reforms and not on the need for foreigners to 'try harder' to penetrate the Japanese market.

It added that the report made a potentially major change in the 'psychological climate' surrounding the 'Japan problem', meaning the position of Japan within the system.[42]

As specific steps, the report suggested these should focus on housing development, consumption increase, and, significantly, gradual withdrawal of protection of the domestic coal-mining industry so as to stimulate imports.[43] More specifically, the report made the following recommendations:

1. Expand domestic demand.
   (a) Promote housing construction by easing regulations and expanding tax deductions.
   (b) Stimulate private consumption through wage increases, tax cuts, and reduced working hours.
   (c) Increase the role of local government in public works.
2. Transform Japan's industrial structure.
   (a) Encourage investment in manufacturing overseas.
   (b) Rationalize depressed industries.
   (c) Ease restrictions on agricultural imports.
3. Continue to improve market access.
   (a) Streamline distribution network.
   (b) Implement Action Programme.
4. Liberalize capital and financial markets.
5. Expand Japan's overseas co-operation.
   (a) Promote ODA.
   (b) Promote GATT New Round.
   (c) Expand imports from the LDCs.[44]

Although not mentioned in the final report, at a press conference the same day Maekawa suggested that the committee also favoured removing protection from two other 'sunset' industries – aluminium and shipbuilding.[45] That this was not contained in the text of the report reflected the pressure to harmonize bureaucratic interests. This was also evident from the position taken on fiscal spending and fiscal austerity. The Commission, mindful of MOF interests, somehow managed to support each of the two goals of fiscal expansion and budget balancing, and it was only at the news conference that Maekawa candidly revealed that his group did 'not favor the fundamental governmental goal to balance the national budget by 1990'.[46]

The American reaction to the Maekawa report was also very favourable. The Undersecretary of State for Economic Affairs, Allen Wallis, termed the Maekawa report a 'watershed in Japan's post-war economic history'.[47] And the Deputy Assistant Secretary of State, Gaston Sigur, expressed his view that the Maekawa report could not simply be attributed to foreign pressure, but rather represented a recognition of Japan's own national interest.[48] The Japanese Prime Minister, following two days of talks with President Reagan, remarked as follows:

> I believe that Japan must tackle the epoch-making task of structural adjustment and transform its economic structure into one dependent on domestic demand, rather than exports leading to a significant increase in imports, particularly of manufactured products. Recently, my private advisory group produced a report containing many variable recommendations in this regard. In order to translate the recommendations into policies, the government will set up a promotion headquarters which will formulate the work schedule very shortly.[49]

In the period after the above US–Japan Summit and prior to the Tokyo Summit in early May 1986, it was widely reported in Japan that the two countries had come to an agreement to stabilize exchange rates and on Japan's commitment to economic restructuring, as per the Maekawa recommendations. Later events, however, showed that the nature of the agreement had been blown well out of proportion.

Concerning the alleged agreement on economic restructuring, Nakasone, upon his return from the United States, was subject to considerable criticism from within and outside the party for allegedly having made a commitment to upgrade the Maekawa report as government policy. Party members questioned the wisdom of raising economic restructuring as an issue in an election year and at a time when the business sector was still reeling under the impact of the high yen. In fact, however, Nakasone had made no formal or official commitment. In the dynamics of the Japanese political system this was politics as usual. By making bold public statements, Nakasone was only trying to force the existing domestic consensus in a particular direction. He was not only trying to dictate the direction of change, but also trying to force the pace rather than allow the new consensus to congeal in the usual time-consuming fashion. His political style was to declare a position that was so far removed from the existing consensus that the eventual compromise somewhere in the middle was still a significant achievement. His public statement in the United States clearly implied a personal commitment to do his best, which he later reconfirmed at a news conference on 28 April. He stated that the Maekawa report did not constitute an international agreement, but went on to add that, 'We will formulate policy in line with the report'.[50] This was not the first time Nakasone's bold remarks had landed him in trouble domestically following a visit to the United States. The most noteworthy occasion was when he allegedly pledged to transform Japan into an 'unsinkable aircraft carrier.'

The Prime Minister had not transformed Japan into an 'unsinkable aircraft carrier', but he did try to implement a number of major steps, including a secrecy bill which was rightly rejected by the diet as being too draconian. But he did achieve his other important goal of removing the 1 per cent ceiling on defence expenditures. The 1976 cabinet-level agreement to contain defence spending to under 1 per cent of GNP was finally lifted by another cabinet-level agreement in December 1986. The Prime Minister might not be able to achieve transformation of the economy as readily as the United States might hope, but this would not be for lack of effort, rather because it was necessarily a more long-term undertaking. But some improvement was already evident.

Japan's exports have declined in recent years, particularly in areas such as steel, textiles, colour TVs, and VTRs. Although the dollar-denominated exports had gone up because of the rise in the yen, the yen-denominated exports declined by about 15 per cent in FY1986 over the previous year.[51] In due course the dollar-denominated exports were also expected to go down. In terms of overall trade balance, Japan's surplus was expected to decline by $20 billion in FY1987 and a further $10 billion in FY1988.[52] Trade statistics for the month of August 1987 were also very encouraging. In that month exports posted a mere 4.4 per cent gain while imports went up 32.9 per cent over the same month the year before. More significant was the success achieved in reorienting economic growth toward domestic demand. FY1986 GNP growth was only 2.6 per cent and below the official target of 3.5 per cent, but the main thrust of the growth came from domestic demand which expanded by 4.3 per cent.[53] The micro-level statistics showed a similar reduction in export dependence of the leading sectors of the industry. For example, according to the Bank of Japan, the export dependence (ratio of exports to total sales) of 386 leading manufacturers was likely to decline to 21.5 per cent in the fourth quarter of 1987 compared to 26.3 per cent in the second quarter of 1985. Over the same period, the export dependence of auto and electronics manufacturers was expected to decline from 48.7 per cent to 39.9 per cent and from 37.7 per cent to 27.8 per cent respectively.[54] As is evident from the above statistics, the Japanese economy was rapidly being transformed to rely more on domestic demand and consumption.

This transformation was also reflected in the GNP growth figures for the third quarter of 1987. According to provisional estimates released by the EPA, GNP growth in the third quarter of 1987 was 2 per cent compared to the previous quarter. Of this, the domestic demand component was 1.8 per cent and foreign demand only 0.2 per cent (see figure 6.6).

The 2 per cent growth in GNP was also the largest such increase in about 10 years. The biggest boost to domestic demand came from private housing construction, which pushed up the GNP by 0.6 per cent, followed by private investment (0.5 per cent), private consumption (0.4 per cent), and public investment (0.2 per cent). Unlike other advanced countries, Japan's economy was performing well and due largely to the revitalization of domestic demand.

The effect on imports resulting from demand expansion and appreciation of the yen was equally dramatic. Imports of steel, cement, and chemical products, in particular, have shown rapid increase. The *Nihon Keizai Shinbun* in late November 1987 reported that steel imports in 1987 were expected to rise by 40 per cent over the previous year, while the imports of cement

Figure 6.6 Real GNP growth

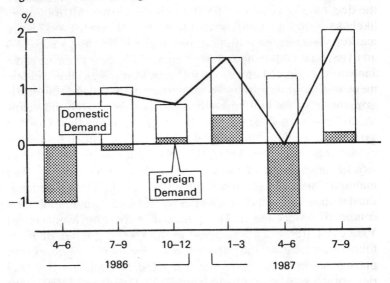

Source: *Nihon Keizai Shinbun* (Chokan), 5 December 1987, p.1.
Note: The trend line is real GNP growth over previous quarter.

and aluminium were likely to double and increase by 60 per cent, respectively. Although these imports still had only a small market share domestically (steel 8 per cent, cement 4 per cent, and aluminium 3 per cent), industry sources anticipated that their market share was likely to rise to about 10 per cent of domestic demand.[55]

With respect to exchange-rate adjustments, it was reported after the US–Japan Summit that the two countries had reached an agreement to stabilize the yen, an issue of considerable concern to Japanese business. The United States, especially the Treasury Department, did not concur with the Japanese analysis that currency adjustments had gone far enough. Thus, in late April, the Treasury Department sent a formal note of protest to the MOF asking it to desist from spreading the false impression to reporters that Japan and the United States had an agreement on exchange rates.[56] Indeed, after the Tokyo Summit, when Japan could not squeeze out a commitment to stabilize the dollar, it was quickly perceived to mean an American desire to see the yen rise further, which is exactly what happened.

164

Returning to the issue of economic restructuring, apart from the declining reliance on export sales, Japanese firms were also likely to undertake more foreign investment to consolidate their market shares in foreign countries. Only a few years ago, the analysis would have been considerably more pessimistic, as was James Abegglen in his discussion of Japanese foreign investment in the United States. In 1984, he wrote that production investment in the United States was 'likely to remain small and to have little impact on the trade balance'.[57] Since then the G-5 agreement and the sharp revaluation of the yen had created newer opportunities and a positive incentive to locate production facilities in the major markets overseas. In the case of car manufacture, local production was expected to make up over a third of total Japanese car sales in the United States by 1990, compared to less than 7 per cent in 1984. In this instance the VER had a major effect, but other industries were likely to follow suit given the stronger yen and in the interest of preserving their market share in the United States. Certainly, the initial establishment costs were now much lower. Mr Nukazawa of the Keidanren, in a recent interview with the *New York Times*, said that, 'So far investment overseas has been political . . . Now it will be more of an economic response'.[58] And overseas investment will have an impact on export statistics. In a report prepared by the MITI, it was suggested that if overseas investment increased at the annual rate of 12 per cent, there would be a reduction in the trade surplus by about $53 billion by the year 2000.[59] An annual growth of 12 per cent may seem a tall order, but there had been rapid growth of foreign investment in recent years and Japan had already become the largest source of foreign investment on an annual basis.

Table 6.4 shows Japan's direct investment overseas on an

Table 6.4 Japan's direct overseas investment

	Amount ($ million)	Growth (%)
FY1980	4,693	
FY1981	8,931	90
FY1982	7,703	− 13
FY1983	8,145	5.7
FY1984	10,155	24.6

Source: *Japan 1985*, Keizai Koho Center, Tokyo, p. 56.

annual basis. The growth in foreign investment has continued and in the calendar years 1985 and 1986 total direct investment overseas was $12.2 billion and $22.4 billion, respectively.[60] Of course, the decision to invest will be determined by conditions in the host country. At present, a number of states in the United States maintain a unitary tax system where taxes are levied not just on the profits of the foreign subsidiary, but rather on a percentage of global earnings. The intention of the unitary tax system is to prevent foreign operations from evading tax payments by creative accounting procedures to show losses, but this can also deter investment as it results in double taxation for some. Since 1980, there have been four attempts to repeal the law in California, but each time this was unsuccessful.[61] Despite the unitary tax, however, California is the largest recipient of Japanese investment in the United States. It is possible though that this is keeping out investments at the margin. A survey conducted by Keidanren of its 866 member companies, of which 348 submitted valid responses, concluded that for some companies a decision to invest in California would be contingent on the future course of the unitary tax.[62]

CONCLUSION

In this chapter we have looked primarily at the issue of demand expansion in Japan. As mentioned, the importance of stimulating domestic demand was in the potential not only to expand imports, but also to reduce the export dependence of the Japanese economy. In the early to mid-1980s, the foreign demand component in annual GNP growth in Japan had deepened considerably, and in this chapter we looked at some of the steps taken by the Japanese government, like eliminating the tax incentives on small savings and fiscal expansion, to dampen the export-push growth pattern. This was partly responsible for the burgeoning Japanese trade surplus during this period, and we argued that rectifying this would allow the Japanese economy to play a role commensurate to that envisioned in the concept of system supporter by removing one of the sources of the trade imbalance, which might thereby lower the protectionist threat to the system.

We might note that the task of demand expansion proved rather difficult for the Japanese government because it conflicted with the objective to balance the budget and because there was no overwhelming pressure from outside Japan to expand fiscal spending. Nevertheless, the government did implement a number of measures, including fiscal expansion, albeit at a later date. Because the earlier demand expansion packages contained no fiscal spending on public works, analysts were generally sceptical about the efficacy of these packages. But even then, the measures aimed at stimulating housing construction did have a better-than-anticipated result. Reviewing the effects of these measures, the Chief Economist for the Nomura Research Institute, Kagami Nobumitsu, stated that, if we looked at construction figures for the period following the adoption of the measures, we could see that they 'had very favorable effects'.[63]

It might be worthwhile here to review briefly how the task of consensus building on Japan's international role had progressed over the period when the Japanese government was engaged in reflating its economy to meet with foreign expectations. Unlike in 1977, when the Japanese government was forced to abandon its international commitment due to pressure from the MOF, this time at least, a number of expansionary measures were taken and, later, the MOF even acquiesced to fiscal expansion. This may be taken as an indication that there had been some progress in overcoming the obstacles that stood in the way of the realization of Japan's international role. While the MOF did agree to expand fiscal spending and while the new expenditures meant that the government was not likely to remain within the originally scheduled deficit-financing ratio, the objective of balancing the budget had not entirely been discarded. Even with the additional spending in 1987, the MOF still maintained that the budget remained the top priority. Indeed, later reports suggested that the government could still achieve the 1990 target for balancing the budget through economic revitalization and increased tax revenues.[64]

Consensus building, at the best of times, is a slow process, but in times of economic uncertainty, the problems are compounded. For a country like Japan, the lack of full consensus rendered decision making all the more difficult. Finally, given the state of the fiscal condition in Japan, one may conclude that the government had done rather well in responding to international expectations. We do not assert, however, that the measures adopted by the Japanese government had

167

transformed the Japanese economy to a point where it could play a supportive role in the liberal trade system, but the direction of change was clearly consistent with such a role in the future.

7

Japan and Asia–Pacific

THE REGIONAL-GLOBAL DIVIDE IN JAPANESE FOREIGN POLICY

In the previous chapters we focused our attention primarily on the US–Japan nexus. The reason for doing so was that the main challenge to the stability of the trading system could be located in the dynamics of their bilateral trade relations. We argued that if Japan was to emerge as a system supporter, there had to be an easing of trade tensions between the two countries, arising from the perception that unfair Japanese trade practices were to blame for their trade imbalances. Accordingly, the earlier chapters concentrated on how Japan, in recent years, had attempted to manage its relations with the United States and defuse the protectionist threat to liberal trade. In the case of the auto dispute, an important consideration of the Japanese government was to assist in the revitalization of the American auto industry. Similarly, in the case of their trading imbalance, Japan took the initiative to phase out many of the non-tariff barriers to imports and to restructure its economy to make it less dependent on export demand. These were important because the large, and growing, trade imbalance between the two countries had become the main vehicle for the protectionists demanding trade retaliation.

This is not to suggest, however, that the hegemon always had to enjoy a trade surplus for it to remain interested in liberal trade, but obviously a large structural deficit was not conducive to long-term regime stability. Theoretically, a surplus or deficit on bilateral trade should not be given too much importance, but when a deficit on bilateral trade makes up an inordinate share of total deficit, it may become politically impossible to ignore it as inconsequential. Many people in the United States seriously believed that Japan was the problem and that the cure to the American economic malaise was in the resolution of trade problems with Japan. Because of the systemic salience of US–Japan relations, it was natural, therefore, that our analysis focused on their economic interactions.

In this chapter we wish to identify a potential problem area that, given present trends, may probably emerge as a major destabilizing force in the trade regime. For many analysts, it is not merely a potential threat, but rather a very distinct possibility. The challenge that they refer to is the export dependence of the Asian newly industrializing countries (ANICs) and the member countries of the Association of South East Asian Nations (ASEAN) on the United States. Convinced that this was inevitable, Robert Wescott of the Wharton Econometric Forecasting Institute warned that 'The Pacific Rim is the next trade battleground'.[1]

Most of the ASEAN–ANIC grouping had consciously implemented an export-oriented growth strategy and, like Japan, they too relied on the United States as their main export market. Japan, as we saw, was trying to restructure its economy and economic growth away from dependence on foreign demand to domestic demand, but for most of these other regional countries, this is much more difficult. Their development strategy will continue to require a steady growth of export trade, given the difficulty of finding the dynamics of growth within their own limited domestic markets. Given this constraint, the challenge would be to devise new mechanisms to accommodate their legitimate developmental interests with the necessity of avoiding disruptions in any one foreign market resulting from excessive dependence. Yamazawa *et al.*, noting that much of ANIC exports had gone to the United States and Western Europe, suggested that it was time 'to search for possibilities for more active *intra*-Pacific trade'.[2] If we include ASEAN exports with those of the ANICs, the trade picture is more evenly balanced, but only because Japan is an important market for such raw-material-exporting countries like Indonesia and Malaysia. However, even within ASEAN, there is a growing emphasis on the development of manufactured exports, and in so far as trade in manufactures is concerned, the direction of ASEAN trade again is very lop-sided. In this chapter we will consider how the potential problems associated with this skewed export pattern can be averted. Dependence on the United States, as noted, is already high, but perhaps not yet of critical proportions. It was fortuitous for the ANIC–ASEAN grouping that the United States, so far, has been largely pre-occupied with the trade problems with Japan. However, if the analysis in the earlier chapter is correct, the 'problem' of the ASEAN–ANIC grouping is likely to become increasingly salient. Fortunately, Japan can also be expected to rectify the 'neglect' of the regional countries that had resulted from its preoccupation with managing relations with the United States. Presumably, that would allow for a greater degree of trade diversification.

In the post-war period, Japanese foreign policy emphasized friendly relations with the United States, partly because the United States was important as a trading partner and partly because Japan was dependent on American security guarantees. As such, the attention of the Japanese government was largely taken up by the various issues in their bilateral relations. Regional concerns, although not completely ignored, were not accorded a high priority.

According to Watanabe Akio, the historical development of Japanese foreign policy contained a dual emphasis on the themes of regionalism and globalism. However, he observed that Japan 'never succeeded in inventing a satisfactory formula for blending the two different concepts together'.[3] For example, although the Anglo–Japanese alliance of the 1920s was based on the delicate balance of collaboration with a global power (Britain) and the recognition of Japan's 'special interests' in Asia, the later Washington Treaty refused to acknowledge Japan's regional ambitions as valid. The American objective, under the 'Open Doors' policy, was to guarantee and protect the independence of China. This frustrated Japan's desire to combine its global and regional interests, and it could be argued that it was this inability to combine the two objectives that eventually pushed Japan to seek a military solution.

After the war, Japan's regional ambition remained rather subdued. Priority was given to economic growth and to establishing an identity as an industrial power. The Japanese withdrawal from the region was due largely to the lingering pre-war and wartime legacies. The crudity of the short-lived Japanese colonialism in the region made sure that there was not going to be a Japanese 'commonwealth' after the liberation of these countries, and the vivid memories of Japanese atrocities helped to sustain a strong feeling of antagonism toward Japan. At the same time, from a regional perspective, apart from reparations payments, these countries could expect little from Japan. Thus, not only was there no desire, but also no incentive to allow Japan a greater role in the region.

Japan's isolation was further entrenched by the policies pursued by the occupation forces, which sought to purge all Japanese influence from the region. The method used was repatriation of Japanese to Japan, a task that was undertaken with thorough-going and ruthless efficiency. Reischauer explained that, in the interest of rooting out all Japanese influence from the neighbouring countries, the repatriation programme included not only soldiers, but all Japanese,

> regardless of humanitarian considerations and the long-range interests of the countries in which they resided. Civilians and their families who had been legitimate, permanent residents in overseas areas for decades and sometimes for their whole lives were deported on essentially the same terms as soldiers and camp followers.[4]

This must have been a traumatic experience for the Japanese nation, making it more difficult for them to identify with the region. Another factor behind Japan's isolation was the US–Japan Security Treaty, signed in 1951, which barred relations with the communist regime on mainland China, a country with which Japan would, otherwise, have had a closer relationship after independence.

During this period, however, Japan's globalist vision was brought to full bloom, beginning with its admission to the Organization for Economic Co-operation and Development (OECD) in the mid 1960s. It was only after Japan had finally joined the ranks of advanced industrial countries that it began to reconsider the regional role. Although as far back as 1957, the Diplomatic Blue Book, published yearly by the Ministry of Foreign Affairs, declared that Japan's foreign-policy orientations ought to be determined partly in consideration of the fact that Japan was an Asian country, this essentially remained a verbal exhortation and an agenda for future consideration. Throughout the 1960s, there continued to be similar calls for Japan to establish a regional role, by Prime Minister Kishi, who emphasized the idea that 'Japan [was] a member of the Asian Community', and later by Prime Minister Sato, who forthrightly remarked that Japan would play 'a leading role' in Asia.[5] Regardless, however, Japan kept a low profile. It chose, instead, to rely mainly on the American presence in the region to protect and safeguard its interests. Perhaps the only exception to this was in Japanese relations with Indonesia. Indonesia was important because of its vast oil resources and because the Indonesian archipelago straddled the Malacca Straits, through which Japan's imports of oil from the Middle East had to pass. The economic and geographic significance of Indonesia explains why Japan persevered to maintain friendly relations even through the turbulent years when Indonesia swerved back and forth between pro-Washington, pro-Moscow, and pro-Beijing policies. Indonesia's volatile foreign-policy posture through the mid-1960s made it risky for Japan to rely solely on the United States, to protect Japanese interests and these early years have been characterized as 'special' years of Japanese–Indonesian relations.[6] The Japanese task was made easier by the influence wielded by President Sukarno's Japanese wife, Ratna Devi. Below the surface, however, hostility toward Japan remained and welled over in 1974.

The early Japanese regional overtures were, understandably, couched in globalist terms. The two most prominent ideas that were floated around this time were the Pacific Free Trade Area (PAFTA) and the Pacific Basin Economic Co-operation (PBEC), the former by a group of academics and the latter by private businesses. Professor Kojima of Hitotsubashi University, Tokyo, initiated the concept of PAFTA in 1966, but at that stage it was only marginally regional. The membership that he envisaged was to include only the five developed economies in the region – the United States, Japan, Canada, Australia and New Zealand. Even with a restricted membership, he realized that the prospect of establishing a regional free trade system was not likely, considering that the gains would accrue mainly to Japan. As originally intended, and if brought to fruition, a PAFTA scheme could have been potentially harmful to the developing countries of Asia because of the trade diversion effects.[7] With modifications, the two concepts of PAFTA and PBEC have since been institutionalized as a series of conferences, the former as PAFTAD – Pacific Area Free Trade and Development.

These were private-level initiatives – which was understandable since the Japanese government still felt insecure about how an official initiative would be received by the South East Asian countries. Hostility toward Japan was still high and manifested itself in a rather ugly manner when Prime Minister Tanaka's visit to the region, in 1974, prompted riots and demonstrations in Thailand and Indonesia.

Apart from the psychological gap between Japan and the regional countries, there also emerged an economic and trade gap. Although Japan's resource dependence ensured a persistent Japanese trade deficit *vis-à-vis* the raw-material-exporting countries, Japan was criticized for shutting out the manufactured exports of the regional countries. This, however, was a common complaint of the less developed countries against the developed countries in general, which maintained high trade-restricting tariff barriers against developing countries' exports of semi-processed and manufactured products. It was not particularly unusual, therefore, that the Japanese tariff structure, for example, gave preferential treatment to lumber in the form of logs than to processed lumber like plywood. However, what made matters worse was that Japanese tariffs also discriminated unfairly against exports from less developed countries over those from developed countries in the same product categories, despite the fact that GATT prohibited such overt discrimination. For example, the differential tariff structure in Japan for softwood and hardwood plywood made the regional exports of hardwood plywood less competitive than the softwood plywood exports of North America. Finally, in 1985, after years of protest from the Asian exporters of plywood, the tariff schedule was revised as part of the MOSS agreement with the United States. The softwood–hardwood categorization was removed and the tariff rates, too, were lowered. However, a differential, and discriminatory, tariff structure remained in place as plywood exceeding a certain thickness was given a lower tariff rate. The consequence, like before, continued to disadvantage exporters of hardwood plywood which was usually thinner than softwood plywood.

The above was symptomatic of some of the problems that confronted Japan in reconciling its regional and global interests. It is almost certain that without a differential, and discriminatory, tariff structure on plywood, lumber trade would be diverted to the Asian countries, causing displeasure in the

United States and making the task of reducing the trade surplus with the United States all the more difficult. And with the surplus, seemingly out of control, Japan was pressed to show some improvement even if this had to be at the expense of the regional countries of Asia. Japan's first and foremost priority was to maintain harmonious relations with the United States, but, as will be argued below, the regional and global concerns may not necessarily be a part of a zero-sum game, although it would appear to have been treated as such by Japanese policy makers.

DEVELOPMENT STRATEGIES OF ANICs AND ASEAN

To assess the nature of the potential threat to the existing trade regime, it is necessary to consider the development strategies of the regional countries of Asia and the role of manufactured exports. The countries that we will be concerned with are the six members of ASEAN (Brunei, Indonesia, Malaysia, Philippines, Singapore, and Thailand), Hong Kong and the newly industrializing countries of Taiwan and Korea. Although Singapore's primary affiliation is with ASEAN, it is also included within the ANIC grouping and, depending on the context, we will do the same.

As a bloc, these countries displayed a robust economic growth through the 1970s, even when other countries were fighting off recession. The pace of economic growth was so rapid, especially for the ANICs, that they were dubbed 'mini Japans', partly because their development pattern resembled that of Japan. Growth in the region was phenomenal and with economic growth trade also expanded rapidly, both within and outside the region. Total American trade with the countries of the Western Pacific (including Japan) now exceeds its transatlantic trade.

Behind the common feature of high growth rates there was a richness of diversity, not only as collectives between ASEAN and the ANICs, but also amongst the six ASEAN countries. This diversity could be measured not only in terms of ethnicity or language, but also in the levels of economic development and industrialization. Within ASEAN, the two poles were represented by Singapore and Indonesia, the latter almost entirely dependent on oil exports (Brunei was in a class by itself, having

175

the second highest *per capita* income in the world). About 84 per cent of Indonesian exports in 1983 were in the SITC (Standard International Trade Classification) categories 2 and 3, that is, crude materials excluding fuels, and minerals and fuels, respectively. For Singapore, the ratio of manufactured goods to total export was 46 per cent in 1984 (SITC categories 6, 7, and 8), although if we include petroleum products (SITC category 3) the ratio increases to 72 per cent. Although Singapore did not have any oil resources itself, it developed a large refining capacity, taking advantage of its strategic geographic location.

As we would expect from their development strategies, the export dependence of the ANICs, in particular, was high. To give an example, whereas in 1960 the export value to GNP for South Korea and Taiwan was only 0.9 per cent and 9.6 per cent, respectively, in 1980 this had jumped to 30 per cent and 49 per cent, respectively. The ASEAN countries were somewhat less dependent on exports than the ANICs and there was a wide spread ranging from 16 per cent to 54 per cent in 1980.[8] For most of the countries in these two groups, export growth was due mainly to the growth of the manufacturing sector and industrialization. According to Hofheinz and Calder, the export drive for the four ANICs (Hong Kong, Singapore, Taiwan, and Korea) derived from motivations similar to that behind the Japanese export drive, that is, the lack of available raw materials internally, notably food. Of the four, only Taiwan could boast self-sufficiency in food.[9]

Exports became a top national priority in South Korea in the early 1960s after the early emphasis on industrialization through import substitution had more or less run its course. Easy import substitution had been completed by the 1960s and at that time the state planners were confronted with three alternative growth-promoting strategies:

1. agricultural exports;
2. advanced import substitution; and
3. manufactured exports.

The first alternative was rejected because of poor prospects for primary commodities, and the second alternative, too, had to be dismissed because of unfavourable factor endowments and the difficulties of achieving economies of scale in a small market. The size of the Korean market in the early 1960s was estimated to be only about $1 billion (production plus imports minus exports) compared to $23 billion for India and $14 billion for Brazil.[10] This narrowed the choice to the third option of fostering advanced industrialization based on an outward-looking export-oriented strategy.

In 1962 Korea established the Korean Organization for Trade Advancement (KOTRA), modelled on the Japanese External Trade Organization (JETRO), to promote exports, conduct market surveys overseas, and provide information to domestic manufacturers to enable them to expand into foreign markets. The Korean counterpart of MITI, the Ministry of Commerce and Industry (MCI), was also instrumental in pushing exports, even when export sales were less profitable than domestic sales. MCI, through its control over the granting of export licenses, encouraged exports by setting minimum targets ($200,000 in 1970) which had to be met if a firm was to retain its import permit. Thus, even though export sales had a profitability of 2.12 per cent in 1968, compared to 9.49 per cent for domestic sales, there was a steady growth in export volume.[11]

In 1965, President Park Chung-hee initiated the monthly sessions of the National Expanded Trade Promotion Meeting to discuss and assess progress toward meeting national export targets.[12] Trade promotion naturally took the form of promoting manufactured exports and the development of export-oriented industrialization. The success of this policy was so remarkable that from a low of 14 per cent in 1960, manufactured exports rose to constitute almost 90 per cent in 1980.[13] South Korea has, in recent years, moved ahead to diversify its industrial and export base and entered the market for shipbuilding, steel, and high-technology industries. Both Korea and Taiwan also established a strong services export trade, concentrated in the construction business, with the oil-producing countries of the Middle East. Manufactured exports, however, remained the main foreign-exchange earner.

Taiwan, another major trading country in the region, also witnessed a dramatic shift in its trade composition. As mentioned above, it was the only ANIC to have achieved a measure of self-sufficiency in food, and agricultural products were its principle export commodities in the early 1950s. In 1952, rice and sugar, for example, constituted 78 per cent of its total exports, but by 1970 this had declined to only 3 per cent, to be replaced by manufactured products.[14] The changeover occurred as a direct shift in government policy in the late 1950s to move away from an emphasis on industrialization based on import substitution to export-based industrialization. This was necessitated by increased domestic demand and consumption of rice, which consequently reduced the available surplus for export. Other factors that influenced the change in government policy were the low foreign demand elasticity for primary products and the fact that a small domestic market constrained the viability of continuing with import-substitution industrialization. Although not the first export-promotion measure, the government in 1957 implemented a programme of low-cost export loans which could be repaid at the low rate of 6 per cent per annum, if repayment was in foreign currency.[15] There was thus a clear incentive for manufacturers to export and earn foreign exchange so that they could take advantage of the low-interest loan repayment scheme.

Later, in the 1960s, the government announced plans to establish special 'export processing zones' (EPZ) and the first one, the Koasiung EPZ, was set up in July 1965. As a result of these policies and currency devaluation, the Taiwan government successfully transformed the economic landscape of the country. In 1960, agriculture constituted 33 per cent of GNP, but by 1980 this had declined to 9 per cent, while in the meantime, the share of the secondary, industrial, sector went up from 25 to 45 per cent.

The export growth of the ASEAN countries, as well, followed on the heels of industrial expansion. The early impetus to industrialization came from import substitution and this received a further boost with the adoption of an outward-looking policy, although import-substitution policies were not completely abandoned. The reorientation toward exports in Malaysia, Thailand, and the Philippines started in the early 1970s and, according to Ariff and Hill, owed partly to the disappointment with their own import-substitution policies as well as to the 'spectacular demonstration effect of the four Asian newly industrializing countries [Singapore, Hong Kong, Taiwan, and Korea]'.[16] Industrial exports began initially with consumer goods. 60 per cent of these two countries' exports were in the SITC category 7 (machinery, communications equipment, etc.).[17] Only Indonesia, a late starter in import-substitution industrialization, lagged behind the other ASEAN countries and this was, perhaps, due to the fact that Indonesia, with its vast oil resources, did not experience the same difficulties in earning foreign exchange. The transformation of the various economies of this region can be seen in table 7.1

Table 7.1 Output by sector (%)

Country	Agriculture 1960	1980	Industry 1960	1980	Services 1960	1980
Korea	37	16	20 (14)	41 (28)	43	43
Taiwan	33	9	25 (17)	45 (34)	42	46
Hong Kong	4	1	39 (26)	32 (24)	57	67
Singapore	4	1	18 (12)	37 (28)	78	62
Malaysia	37	24	18 (09)	37 (23)	45	39
Thailand	40	25	19 (13)	29 (20)	41	46
Indonesia	54	26	14 (08)	42 (09)	32	32
Philippines	26	23	28 (20)	37 (26)	46	40

Source: EPA (1985) *Taiheiyo Jidai no Tenbo*, p. 10.
Note: Figures in parentheses represent the share of manufacturing output.

The pace of manufacturing export was high in all of the Asian countries except for Hong Kong, which had traditionally been a service-oriented economy, specializing in banking and international finance. To foster manufacturing growth, most of these countries also set high tariff barriers to protect the nascent domestic industries from foreign competition. In the case of Taiwan, the effective tariff rate (total tariff revenue as a percentage of total imports) in 1985 was 7.89 per cent, considerably higher than for the United States (3.6 per cent), Canada (4.3 per cent), and Japan (2.6 per cent). Effective tariff rates, however, do not tell us much about the protective function of tariffs since it is possible to set tariffs at such high levels as to bar imports completely, in which case the effective tariff rate would be zero. To obtain an idea of the protective

179

function of tariffs, it is necessary to consider both the effective rates as well as the average nominal tariffs. Taiwan's average nominal rate in 1985 was 26.5 per cent, more than three times the effective tariff rates. As a concession to Western criticisms, however, the government of Taiwan recently announced its decision to lower average nominal and effective rates to 22.18 per cent and 5 per cent, respectively, over the next five years.[18]

The success of the industrialization policies of ASEAN and the ANICs was due largely to the growth of export trade. Reliance on foreign demand to propel industrialization was a natural outcome of the low *per capita* GNP. Even for the middle-income countries, in general, domestic demand and consumption levels had been kept low by the government so as to generate high levels of domestic savings, which were necessary to meet investment demands. Both South Korea and Taiwan successfully achieved a very high savings rate, reaching almost 35 per cent of GNP in the case of Taiwan. As a group, the savings rate in ASEAN and the ANICs was, in all cases, above the level of 20 per cent of GDP in the period 1978–80. The high savings rate provided investment financing and made possible the rapid growth in these countries. It was crucial in ensuring a continuous and steady increase in the capital output ratio to overcome the downward pressure caused by a relatively high population growth rate.[19]

A 1970 United Nations Conference on Trade and Development (UNCTAD) publication, *The Measurement of Development Effort*, made a comparison of domestic savings rate to GNP for a group of fifty less developed countries and ranked Korea forty-ninth in 1950. By the mid-1960s, however, according to a separate United Nations study, Korea's high savings to GNP ratio had placed it at the top of the thirty-nine countries included in that study.[20] It is creditable that much of Korean private investment was financed through domestic capital formation, although in the initial stages of industrialization the government had anticipated considerable reliance on foreign capital sources to supplement low domestic savings. To raise domestic capital available, the government, following the election of President Park Chung-hee, raised interest rates on deposits to encourage savings. In the late 1970s, national savings was about 28 per cent of GNP. According to Salleh and Osman, this could be attributed to the following factors.

1. An uneven income distribution favouring the very rich, who also have a high savings rate.
2. The value system of the economically dominant Chinese community which favoured low consumption and high savings.
3. A relatively advanced social security system (public) involving long-term forced savings for a large portion of wage and salary earners.
4. High savings by the corporate sector.[21]

In Taiwan, in the 1950s, investment finance came mainly from overseas sources, but starting in the 1960s the domestic savings ratio began to exceed 10 per cent of GNP and 'this higher savings rate constituted the main source of domestic investment in that decade'.[22] The higher savings, generated by a hidden rice tax, allowed for low taxes on the industrial sector of the economy.

The constraints of a small domestic economy and the lack of resources, as mentioned, were the main reasons for the adoption of an outward-looking growth strategy. In terms of securing export markets, the focus of the ASEAN and the ANICs was largely restricted to the Asia–Pacific region. The EC, a potentially important market for these countries, was relatively difficult to penetrate because of protectionist policies. Another factor restricting the growth of exports to the EC was its slow average growth rate, even when compared to the United States.

Within the Asia–Pacific region, although Australia and New Zealand were advanced developed economies, their market for imports was rather limited. The governments of both countries had adopted protectionist policies aimed at fostering import-substitution policies. As such, the main export destinations for the goods of these countries were the United States and Japan. Table 7.2 gives the export figures for five of the regional countries, broken down for the ten (0–9) SITC categories. As can be seen, Japan was an important market for crude and raw-material exports of Indonesia and Malaysia, but with the emphasis shifting increasingly to the export of manufactures, these countries had come to rely mainly on the United States. The United States, for example, took about a third of Hong Kong's and Singapore's manufactured exports, whereas Japan imported less than 4 per cent. Malaysia, Indonesia, Singa-

Table 7.2 Export breakdown for selected Asian countries ($1000)

	SITC 0 Food and live animals			SITC 1 Beverage and tobacco			SITC 2 Crude materials excluding fuels			SITC 3 Minerals and fuels			SITC 4 Animal and vegetable oil, fats		
	Total	USA	Japan	Total	USA	Japan	Total	USA	Japan	Total	USA	Japan	Total	USA	Japan
Hong Kong (1984)	175,000	58,061 (33.1%)	48,159 (27.4%)	83,810	1,606 (2%)	120 (0.1%)	245,507	4,361 (1.8%)	52,616 (21.4%)	39,942	–	–	1,353	128 (9.4%)	–
Malaysia (1983)	493,333	52,790 (5.2%)	61,885 (12.5%)	9,477	–	–	3,245,906	133,576 (4.1%)	1,072,004 (33.0%)	3,447,978	118,367 (3.4%)	916,880 (26.6%)	1,393,597	76,649 (5.5%)	71,873 (5.1%)
Singapore (1984)	1,359,616	178,125 (13.1%)	83,550 (6.1%)	98,517	1,581 (1.6%)	5,096 (5.2%)	1,601,411	209,330 (13.1%)	124,347 (7.8%)	6,191,313	334,225 (5.4%)	1,364,728 (22.0%)	723,381	46,900 (6.5%)	15,270 (2.1%)
Indonesia (1983)	109,133	213,232	287,013 (26.2%)	47,837	9,653 (5.3%)	–	1,649,580	353,474 (21.4%)	518,840 (31.3%)	16,152,952	3,394,831 (21.0%)	8,642,240 (53.5%)	148,647	9,632 (4.6%)	4,441 (3.0%)

	SITC 5 Chemicals and related products			SITC 6 Basic manufactures			SITC 7 Machines and transport equipment			SITC 8 Miscellaneous manufactured goods			SITC 9 Goods not classified		
	Total	USA	Japan	Total	USA	Japan	Total	USA	Japan	Total	USA	Japan	Total	USA	Japan
Hong Kong (1984)	167,835	7,595 (4.5%)	33,187 (19.8%)	1,775,429	365,534 (20.6%)	34,398 (1.9%)	4,258,394	2,181,295 (51.2%)	59,724 (1.4%)	10,746,944	5,219,322 (48.6%)	429,281 (4.0%)	144,325	16,993 (11.8%)	1,176 (0.81%)
Malaysia (1983)	100,935	15,477 (15.3%)	5,334 (5.2%)	1,124,010	42,862 (3.8%)	209,051 (18.6%)	1,855,531	880,252 (47.4%)	91,684 (4.9%)	322,661	83,320 (25.8%)	19,671 (6.1%)	38,019	3,576 (9.4%)	2,653 (7.0%)
Singapore (1984)	1,156,897	22,695 (2.0%)	81,939 (7.1%)	1,702,052	141,845 (8.3%)	111,700 (6.6%)	7,919,331	3,205,361 (40.5%)	244,961 (3.1%)	1,600,321	575,361 (35.9%)	49,231 (3.1%)	1,755,059	117,285 (6.7%)	176,268 (10.0%)
Indonesia (1983)	118,978	9,584 (8.0%)	5,481 (4.6%)	1,349,724	186,881 (13.8%)	208,778 (15.8%)	133,341	–	145 (0.1%)	213,240	86,416 (40.5%)	6,663 (3.1%)	238,423	5,655 (2.4%)	4,619 (1.9%)

Source: Compiled from *Commodity Trade Statistics* (UN), 1982, 1983, 1984, series D, vol. 32, no. 21; vol. 34 no. 1 and no. 10.

pore, Hong Kong, and Korea together exported about 8.4 per cent of their total manufactured exports to Japan (SITC 6–8), whereas Japan imported 14 per cent of its SITC 6–8 imports from these five countries. The figures are not strictly comparable because import statistics are based on CIF prices, but as a rough measure it would suggest that the weight of these countries for Japan was much greater than vice versa. But this has to be qualified by the low levels of manufactured imports for Japan and the high level of manufactures to total exports for three of the above five countries – Singapore, Hong Kong, and Korea.

JAPAN'S REGIONAL ROLE AND SYSTEM STABILITY

Throughout their growth period, it was exceedingly difficult for the regional countries to penetrate the Japanese market for manufactures, although the Japanese government insisted that there were no systemic biases against the export of these countries. This, however, appeared not to be the case as we saw in the case of processed lumber trade. Apart from this, a major obstacle to market penetration was, again, the Japanese distribution system. If the Japanese distribution network was frustrating for Western countries to overcome, it had a much more negative effect on the manufactured exports of ASEAN and the ANICs. Given the initial condition of low levels of manufactured imports in Japan, imports from the less developed countries also suffered from the traditional marketing practice of surrounding imported products with a brand image. This was certainly not an easy task to accomplish in the case of Third World manufactures. Rightly or wrongly, goods produced in the developing countries had acquired the image of shoddy workmanship and poor quality. This made it difficult for Japanese distributors to market Third World exports as high-quality, exclusive products. Since brand image was a major selling point for imported goods in Japan, allowing the local importer to sell at a high unit price and profitability to compensate for low sales volume, it disadvantaged the manufactured exports of the regional countries which promised moderate quality at low prices. The fact that the Japanese market minimized price competitiveness between domestic and imported products meant that exporters from the developing countries were handicapped in their ability to secure a niche for their products.

This feature of the Japanese market made it substantially different from the American market which absorbed a large quantity of cheap, low-quality products.[23] Recently, however, exporters in some of the regional countries have expressed optimism that the quality of their products has improved sufficiently to allow them to take advantage of the opportunities provided by the appreciation of the Japanese yen. According to S. K. Chung, Deputy General Manager of Daewoo Japan (the Japanese branch of the South Korean conglomerate), 'We're at a point now that our product quality is good enough to sell in Japan. If the yen had risen five or six years ago, we wouldn't have been ready, and price competitiveness wouldn't have made a difference'.[24] Others were making serious efforts to improve their product quality. Thus, in Singapore, manufacturers were actively implementing Japanese-style quality control circles in the workplace.

Besides the Japanese distribution system, the maze of government-established standards and certification procedures also proved difficult for Third World exporters to master and overcome. These standards, too, tended to minimize price competition in favour of uniform quality and prevented Third World exporters from exploiting their cost advantages.

Because of these handicaps confronting regional exporters trying to penetrate the Japanese market, as their industrialization programmes gathered speed, so did their dependence on the United States. It is not particularly relevant, for our purposes, to determine how easy the access to the American market was or the number of obstacles that had to be overcome, but the important point is that not only were these smaller countries successful, but they were in fact very successful. For example, until the late 1950s, two-thirds of Taiwanese exports constituted agricultural products, rice, and sugar, and for much of that time Japan was the principal export and import partner of Taiwan, accounting for one-half of its total exports and one-third of its imports. The United States replaced Japan only after 1967, and in 1971 the share of exports to the United States peaked at almost 42 per cent.[25] Hong Kong's traditional export markets were the Commonwealth countries, which together accounted for about 40 per cent of total exports in 1955. The United States, in that year, accounted for only 2 per cent of Hong Kong exports, but later became the main destination of its exports. In the mid-1970s, West Germany also overtook the United Kingdom to take second place.[26] The growth of the regional countries' export to Japan was not insignificant, but this growth took place mainly in primary commodities and industrial raw materials. Japan's import of manufactures, however, remained low. Thus, although over 50 per cent of all Indonesian exports went to Japan, only about 13 per cent of its manufactures were exported to Japan. Kershner, in his study of Japanese trade patterns, found that during the decade of the 1960s there was very little change in the composition of exports to Japan by the regional countries. He wrote that

> The principal change is that some increase in manufactures was recorded by a few countries in the region; in no sense was the export diversity widely shared throughout all the countries of Pacific Asia. Even for these countries moreover, their manufactured goods export to Japan simply did not account for major market shares. . . . In view of the world export data . . . what results is the finding that the region's exports to Japan centered around a set of commodities that when taken together formed a pattern that differed significantly from these countries' exports to the rest of the world. In addition, the comparable world export growth rates for these commodities were on balance rising sluggishly.[27]

As an indicator of the trade dependence on the United States, it is worth noting that it alone accounted for almost half of the total OECD imports from the ASEAN and ANICs. Table 7.3 gives the total OECD imports as well as the American share in the export of a select group of the regional countries.

The export growth stagnation in the early 1980s was due to global recession, but the strong American economic recovery starting in 1983 and weaker growth rates in other countries meant that the export drive of the regional countries was concentrated in meeting import demand in the United States.

So far, we have tried to explain the factors behind the export drive of the regional countries and the existing patterns of trade in the Asia–Pacific region. It should be clear from the discussion above why this had become a destabilizing influence in the international trading regime. With the economic decline of the

185

Table 7.3 OECD imports from Asian countries ($ billion)

	1979	1980	1981	1982	1983	1984[a]
Singapore	5.1	7.0	6.6	6.6	6.9	8.6
Korea	10.8	11.1	12.5	12.7	14.6	18.1
Taiwan	11.9	13.8	15.2	15.6	18.4	23.7
Hong Kong	10.2	12.3	12.6	12.2	13.3	15.5
Malaysia	8.3	9.2	7.7	7.2	7.7	10.1
Total	46.2	53.4	54.6	54.2	60.9	75.9
Of which USA	17.6	20.4	23.0	24.1	29.7	39.8
Annual rate of change in real terms[b]						
Total		6.3	2.2	11.6	17.5	29.4

Source: OECD (1985) *Costs and Benefits of Protection*, Paris, p. 173.
Notes: [a] Based on data for the first three quarters.
[b] Volume of imports: values deflated by export price index of manufactures.

United States, its ability to serve as the principal vent for *sustained* external supply and demand imbalance had become politically difficult. Thus, unless there emerged a measure of trade diversification, it was likely to continue to fan the protectionist movement in the United States.

In response to growing American criticisms of the trade practices of the ANICs, the government of Singapore tried to dissociate itself from the remaining three ANICs on the grounds that Singapore was a free port and that its trade surplus with the United States was only slightly more than 1 per cent of the total American trade imbalance.[28] No doubt this was an accurate portrayal of their trade relations, but it should be pointed out that American concerns, in so far as these focused on the level of the trade imbalance, were also seen as reflecting the high trade dependence of the ANICs on the US market. To the extent that this was true, however, it would be practically impossible to resolve the problem of trade structure on the basis of ANIC–US relations alone. What is necessary is a multilateral arrangement between the United States, Japan and the ANICs.

In terms of the balance of payments position, the American deficit had increased rapidly in recent years. Table 7.4 outlines the American trading imbalance *vis-à-vis* the ASEAN–ANIC grouping. Between 1980 and 1984, the American trade deficit with these countries increased from around $8 billion in 1980 to nearly $28 billion in 1984 and $32 in billion in 1986. The reason that this large deficit had not yet aroused the same sort of sentiments as those against Japan was perhaps due to the fact that this deficit was incurred against a group of countries. This, however, appeared to be changing and trade problems were likely to intensify as American deficits against Japan start to decline.

Table 7.4 US trade balance with ASEAN–ANIC ($ million)

	1980	*1982*	*1984*	*1986*
Korea	252	−482	−4,044	−7,142
Taiwan	−1,800[a]		−11,000[b]	−13,000[c]
Malaysia	−1,351	−223	−969	−804
Hong Kong	−2,341	−3,442	−5,837	−6,444
Singapore	1,048	940	−446	−1,504
Indonesia	−3,994	−2,484	−4,650	−2,729
Philippines	86	−102	−856	−787
Total	−8,100	−5,793	−27,902	−32,410

Source: IMF (1985) *Direction of Trade Statistics Yearbook*, pp. 404–5.
Notes: [a] *Far Eastern Economic Review Yearbook (FEER)* 1981, p. 254.
[b] *The Economist*, 13 July 1986, p. 69.
[c] *FEER*, 1987, p. 253.

Since these countries' export dependence on the United States was partly a function of a lack of alternative markets, it could be argued that the creation of a greater horizontal division of labour within the region might be one possible mechanism for systemic stability. Essentially, this would require Japan to provide greater market access to the regional countries. In chapter 5, we noted the argument made by Matsuda Manabu of the Ministry of Finance that the reason Japan had a low ratio of manufactured imports was the absence of industrialized countries in the region to allow for a horizontal division of labour as had merged on the European continent. This may have been true in the past, but it was no longer a credible explanation. To the extent that Japanese manufactured imports increased, it would help to relieve pressures that might otherwise build up in the United States. It would also be beneficial to the regional countries since it would provide them with a large market close to home. For such a burden sharing to take place, Japan would have to alter its import preference and give easier access to those processed and manufactured products

187

that were of primary concern to the regional countries. To the extent that we can extrapolate from Japan's recent decision to allow the import of refined petroleum, optimism may not be too unreasonable.

Japan's dependence on foreign sources of raw materials is particularly acute in the case of petroleum. Like most of the other industrial countries, Japan had a tariff structure biased in favour of primary products over processed goods. Increasingly, however, developing countries were trying to expand their export shares of value-added products and this was true also of the oil-exporting countries. Many of these countries established large petroleum-refining capacity to increase the share of refined petroleum in total exports. In July 1985, the Japanese government, for the first time, agreed in principle to import refined petroleum from the Middle East, instead of only crude oil. Accordingly, the first purchase of refined petroleum from the Middle East was made in January 1986. The *Economist* (London), commenting on this departure from past practice, observed that this should,

> take some pressure off the community [EC], which otherwise would have to import the bulk of 50m [million] tonnes of refined petroleum that the oil producing states of the Middle East and North Africa are expected to produce between now and 1990. Without extra purchases from Japan, the Ten would feel obliged to protect themselves against the quite legitimate desire of the third-world oil producers to increase their exports of refined products.[29]

As mentioned, we cannot expect the ASEAN–ANIC grouping to deviate much from their export-oriented development strategy, and if this was to be prevented from becoming a destabilizing force within the trading system, other markets had to be made available to them, such that the cost of balancing the excess of domestic supply to domestic demand was not imposed on one country. It is for this reason that Japan had to provide easier access, to the regional countries, to its large domestic market. In our earlier examples of the US–Japan auto dispute and market liberalization, it was obvious that regime stability had been defined, by the Japanese government, largely in terms of its bilateral trade relations with the United States. This may not be adequate in the future, particularly if the ASEAN countries are successful in speeding up their industrialization programmes and become more reliant on export trade.

The currency realignment that followed the G-5 agreement of 1985 might be expected to promote a more balanced trading position. Unfortunately for the United States, however, many of the regional countries, like Singapore, South Korea, Taiwan, and Hong Kong, maintained their currencies linked to the American dollar, and with the decline of the dollar, their own competitiveness received a strong boost. Thus, their exports to the United States increased, making it even more difficult for the United States to reduce its trade deficit through reliance on exchange rates. Nevertheless, on the positive side, the regional countries also increased their exports to Japan, taking advantage of the surge in the Japanese yen. In the period April–October 1985, Japanese imports from the four ANICs (Singapore, Taiwan, South Korea, and Hong Kong) had declined 4.8 per cent over the same period a year before, but since then their imports had increased, led by manufactured products. In March 1986, South Korea and Taiwan boosted their exports of manufactures to Japan by 31.3 per cent and 23.4 per cent, respectively, over the same period in 1985.[30]

A JETRO report issued in September 1987 noted that the exports of the four ANICs to Japan in the first six months of 1987 had increased by 66 per cent, largely in the category of manufactured goods. The report noted that

The rise in Japan's manufactured imports is directly connected to changes in the country's industrial structure. Major contributors to the increase in Japan's imports of manufactured goods were the Asian NICs (40.5 per cent) and the European Community (37.4 per cent).[31]

The rapid growth in manufactured imports, *albeit* from a low base, was a distinct move away from past patterns and could be attributed to a recognition of the importance of fostering a regional horizontal division of labour, as the Maekawa report had proposed. The Japanese concern reflected not merely a desire to forestall protectionism in the United States, but also to ensure a favourable economic climate in the region, a precondition to regional stability. Reflecting the rapid increase in the regional countries' exports to Japan, there was growing optimism that dependence on the United States could be reduced to less critical levels. Taiwan, for instance, officially announced a new policy that would seek to lower its export dependence on the United States from 45 per cent to 33 per cent over the next five years.[32] This was, of course, predicated on the belief that other export destinations would become more easily accessible. To ensure this, the government of Taiwan, in late November 1987, demanded that Japanese companies operating in Taiwan submit firm proposals outlining the plans to import more Taiwanese products. It even threatened that non-co-operating Japanese firms would be denied visa extensions for Japanese personnel based in Taiwan.[33]

In the past, the various market-opening measures adopted by Japan had been geared to promoting imports from the United States and European countries to the neglect of the regional NICs. Watanabe and Kajiwara wrote that

It is one of the first priorities for Japan to rectify this oversight. . . . Most urgently required of Japan is a policy review reformulating its current stance on international trade and investment, development aid, and structural adjustments to facilitate the horizontal ties to the ANICs, ASEAN-4, and other Asian neighbours.[34]

In recent reports released by the Japanese government on the future of the domestic economic structure, the term 'softization' of the economy has been taken up as an indicator of the future direction of the economy. This is not meant to imply a weakening of economic resilience, but rather a concentration of economic activity in the upper levels of the technological spectrum. To the extent that the 'softization' of the economy progressed as envisioned, there should be new opportunities for the regional countries to fill the vacuum created at the lower ends of the technology spectrum leading the development of a genuine horizontal division of labour.

Throughout much of the post-war period, Japan relied on a multilateral approach to the region. This was a convenient way for it to combine regional and global interests. Thus, concepts like the Organization of Pacific Trade, Aid, and Development (OPTAD), floated by Foreign Minister Miki in 1967 and fleshed out by Peter Drysdale and Hugh Patrick in 1979, and Prime Minister Ohira's Pacific Basin proposal envisaged a wide membership and no special role for Japan. It might be necessary, in the future, for Japan to take a greater initiative on its own. So far, this had been lacking. In a press conference broadcast at midnight on 31 December 1984, Prime Minister Nakasone, touching on the theme of Pacific Co-operation said, 'As I have said all along, Japan and the United States should avoid taking the lead and becoming conspicuous'. Instead, he expressed his hope that, 'the ASEAN foreign ministers conference will take the front seat and things will be handled with ASEAN leadership'.[35] Commenting on this and the explanation given for a Japanese Pacific non-policy, the *Far Eastern Economic Review* stated, 'Japan has taken Asean doubts over its intentions too seriously, as if the doubts were a genuine expression of concern than the political hyperbole of Asean leaders that is an era out of date'.[36]

That wartime legacies continue to influence interactions within the region may be an irrational manifestation, but was true not only for Japan but also for the other Asian countries. Given the importance of 'not losing face' in Japan, it was understandable that the Japanese approach had been cautious and subdued for fear of stirring up latent hostilities. The regional countries also, at least in their public statements, displayed an aversion to a larger Japanese role in the region. The persistence of this negative attitude and ill-feeling could, perhaps, be attributed to the relative neglect of regional concerns in post-war Japanese foreign policies and the fact that there was little positive in their relationship to purge the negative perceptions. Japanese development assistance, into the 1970s, remained tied and, in general, the economic linkages were seen to result in asymmetrical benefits. Recent events, however, suggest that that could be changing. Confidence about each other is growing as trade linkages expand and as the ASEAN–ANIC grouping increases its penetration of the Japanese market. The Japanese government has also, recently, announced its intention to establish a $2 billion fund to aid in the development of the ASEAN countries, and if successfully implemented it could help to restore regional relationships to a more even level.

The exchange-rate adjustments have led to major flows of manufacturing investment from Japan to the regional countries of Asia. The *Business Week* in late 1986, however, expressed the concern that much of this direct investment could be geared towards 'triangular trade' and part of a Japanese strategy to

191

retain their market shares in the United States, using the Asian countries as a manufacturing base. However, while triangular trade cannot be completely ruled out, Kitada Yoshiharu observed that Japanese firms were unlikely to ignore the advantages of production in third countries to satisfy domestic demand in Japan, much as had been done earlier by American TV manufacturers.[37] Honda, for example, announced that it planned to import, into Japan, cars manufactured at its Ohio plant in the United States. Other Japanese car manufacturers in the United States were expected to do the same by 1990.[38]

CONCLUSION

In this chapter we identified a potential problem area for the stability of the trading system and an area in which Japan could do considerably more to relieve a build-up of stress. Japanese foreign economic measures have so far been geared to smoothing out trade frictions with other industrialized countries to the relative neglect of the developmental aspirations of the regional countries. It was only in the mid-1970s that Japan, according to Akaha Tsuneo, began to take a 'visibly active' interest in South East Asia. The occasion was the explication of the Fukuda Doctrine of December 1976 in which the Japanese Prime Minister stated that 'the area for which Japan is responsible in the international society is Southeast Asia, particular ASEAN'.[39]

The reason for the low profile of Japanese regional diplomacy was that, besides the wartime legacies, none of these countries were as important to Japan as was the West, which essentially meant that these countries had very little influence over Japanese policy making. At the same time, these countries were less than successful in overcoming their individual weaknesses through a collective effort. It is necessary to overcome this handicap, and according to one Filipino analyst,

> ASEAN would be well-advised to mount its own political lobbying for the lowering of import barriers in Japan involving products of export interest to them. Joint efforts of ASEAN countries in seeking trade concessions from Japan would, of course, be more effective than individual country efforts.[40]

However, while political lobbying and external pressure was important in earlier attempts to liberalize the Japanese economy, our thesis of Japan as a system supporter should enable us to predict a shift toward interest-based market liberalization. Japanese concern for regional stability can be seen in the $2 billion fund for the promotion of development in the ASEAN countries, but obviously a lot more is needed. A former Japanese foreign minister, Okita Saburo, suggested that Japan implement an Asian version of the Marshall Plan which would increase the purchasing power of these countries and provide additional markets for the products of advanced countries, in what he envisioned as a 'virtuous cycle' of growth. These proposals are not without merit, but it should not be forgotten that the American Marshall Plan was accompanied with easy access to the American market for European products and other trade advantages. A Japanese Marshall Plan that did not ease access to the Japanese market would not have the same beneficial effect. Okita Saburo did not overlook this in making his proposal and stated that, 'At the same time, Japan must continue its efforts to import more primary products and, more important, more internationally competitive manufactured products from other Asian countries'.[41]

Although Japan was an important trading partner for these countries, the bulk of Japanese imports, from ASEAN in particular, was in the category of primary products. Indonesia, with its oil, alone provided over half of total ASEAN exports to Japan. However, with the ongoing industrialization, first of the ANICs and presently in the ASEAN countries, it will be necessary for Japan to increase imports of manufactured products to prevent an asymmetric, destabilizing dependence on the United States. For many years, Japanese economists attributed the country's low ratio of manufactured imports to the absence of industrialized countries in the region to allow for a horizontal division of labour. With the emergence of the ANICs and the increased emphasis on manufactured exports in the ASEAN countries, this rationalization can no longer be given much weight. The continued stability of the liberal trading system requires the development of a horizontal division of labour in the region.

8

Conclusion

This study was an attempt to analyse, in theoretical and practical terms, the role of the supporter in the liberal economic system. In Part I we provided the theoretical framework for this dissertation and argued that, contrary to the opinion that a liberal order could be sustained on the basis of system-wide co-operation, a leader was necessary for system stability in the long run. However, given that the relative decline of the United States had weakened its leadership capability, we argued that a system supporter was essential to the continued stability of the world trading system. We tried to apply this concept to Japanese foreign economic policies and assess the extent to which Japan was likely to adjust its policies and take on a larger burden within the system commensurate with its economic capabilities. The analysis of recent Japanese economic policies would suggest that Japan was in the process of readjusting its position within the liberal trading system with particular concern to contribute to system stability. One corollary of this transformation would be to give Japan a greater say in the system. We noted the various obstacles, in Japan, to this change, but it should be pointed out that the problems of adjustment, in the United States, may not be any easier, since it would have to take greater account of specific Japanese interests even if there was a basic congruence of interests. The potential for instability, however, was likely to be low as long as the military alliances remained strong.

The role of the supporter, we argued, could be deduced from an analysis of its interests. We emphasized that a distinction be made between a system supporter and a leader supporter and that total congruence may not always be possible. At the same time, we should not forget that Japan's interests in the preservation of the liberal economic order were primarily defined in terms of economic gains, given its vertical trade structure and trade dependence. American interests, in addition to the economic ones, also had a political dimension in that the liberal order was set up as an alternative to the Soviet system of domination. The addition of a supporter to the leadership principle need not necessarily undermine the influence of the leader in the system, particularly as the leader of the system – the United States – is also the provider of military security for Western Europe and Japan through NATO and the US–Japan Security Treaty. Instability, however, could creep in if Japan acquired a vastly enhanced defence potential. That would reduce Japan's dependence on the United States and enable it to define its political interests in ways not totally coincident with those of the United States. Instability, therefore, may take the form of a greater divergence of political interests, resulting in conflict. Thus far, Japan's military build-up has been kept to within narrow limits, the parameters being defined by the domestic consensus and the regional setting. However, apart from a nationalist reawakening in recent years, Japan has also been subject to American pressure to expand its defence potential, and these two factors together could lead to a future redefinition of the long-term Japanese defence goals. This clearly points to a dilemma for American policy makers, whether recognized as such or not, who must either temper their demands on Japan or be willing to accept and accommodate a more independent and assertive Japan. Although the latter is by no means a foregone conclusion, it cannot be ruled out either. A politically independent Japan might be more willing to come to some sort of agreement with the Soviet Union, considering that Japan is unlikely to be able to enhance its security through military measures alone. Depending on how American and Soviet relations developed in the future, this could be an undesirable state of affairs from the American point of view. However, we do not expect a major change in Japan's defence potential in the near future.

The system of joint leader and supporter was also not visualized as having a formal institutional framework and required only that the interests of the supporter not be totally ignored within the system. It was argued here that the supporter had a vested interest in ensuring the stability of the liberal trade system, but that it lacked the potential to take over the leadership function. This discrepancy between interest and power was postulated to be the basis of system support and this condition applied well to the case of Japan. As supporter, Japan was likely to supplement the United States as a 'vent for surplus' within the system and undertake to shoulder some of the costs of system maintenance. Apart from this, and during periods of systemic crises, we may also witness the kind of policy co-ordination that was agreed upon regarding exchange-rate adjustments. However, unlike the views of Nakatani Iwao, who argued that the September 1985 agreement was a formal admission by the United States of its inability to lead and the onset of *pax consultica*, the position taken here was less radical. It was, after all, the United States that held up currency adjustments at an earlier date – an exercise of negative leadership. It may be premature to declare the end of *pax americana*, although the relative changes in the post-war period necessitated a relative restructuring of the cost matrix.[1]

Our analysis found sufficient evidence to support the view that Japan was actively striving to develop a role that would strengthen the liberal economic system. We argued that Japanese decision makers were aware of the responsibilities that accompanied economic power, but we also suggested that the ability to translate political will into action requires, as a precondition, the creation of a national consensus, a consensus of the kind Prime Minister Ikeda had achieved in the early 1960s concerning the doubling of national income within a decade. The somewhat paralyzing effect of the lack of consensus could be discerned in our discussion of demand expansion in Japan.

While we postulated that system support could be understood in terms of interest, it should be emphasized that, theoretically, there was no inevitability of interest-based system support. Just as the presence of a hegemon could not be automatically correlated to the creation of a liberal trading order, system-supportive behaviour may not follow automatically from identification of interests. It was this absence of a direct relationship between interests and support that made the study of system support interesting and worthwhile. Our case studies also illustrated the importance of strong leadership in Japan for the purpose of reorienting policy directions. Both Amaya and Nakasone were strong personalities and their strong leadership was essential for their policy initiatives. Whether Japan would have achieved the same degree of success under a more traditional leadership is uncertain and an interesting topic for speculation.

Significant progress was made under Nakasone to correct trade imbalance and facilitate market access, but the task is by no means complete. If strong political leadership was, indeed, essential, then one could be excused for pessimism about the future and with the replacement of Nakasone by Takeshita Noboru. If Nakasone represented the 'bold' politician, Takeshita was more in the traditional mould of Japanese politicians, that is, low key and emphasizing above all the importance of achieving consensus prior to action. In terms of Japan's international responsibilities therefore, Miyazawa, the Finance Minister, would have been the logical successor to Nakasone. But the selection of Takeshita as the President of the LDP and the next Prime Minister was necessary to maintain the unity of the Tanaka faction within the ruling LDP, the largest such factional grouping. The inability of former Prime Minister Tanaka to exercise effective leadership of his faction, due to failing health, had caused a leadership struggle between Takeshita and Nikaido Susumu. Takeshita's credibility was seen to depend on his ability to win the party leadership and should he have failed, the Tanaka faction would probably have split into separate factions led by Nikaido and Takeshita, resulting in a loss of factional position within the party. In the end, however, the faction did split, but only an insignificant minority defected to join Nikaido. If, however, party politics appear to have triumphed over present-day imperatives, this may not necessarily be altogether correct. Takeshita was closely allied to Nakasone and, given the popular belief that Nakasone was likely to continue to influence politics from the sidelines, the selection of Takeshita as the Prime Minister may ensure continuity. Since the selection of the Prime Minister was left to Nakasone, it was understandable that he chose Takeshita, whom he could more easily influence and dominate than someone more independently minded, like Miyazawa.

In the discussion of the specific case studies, we found that there was a clearly manifested awareness within the ranks of Japan's political leadership for a more supportive and active role in the trading system. Outside the political leadership, this awareness was also shared by certain segments of the bureaucratic structure. In this latter group, we could identify the Ministry of Foreign Affairs and the Ministry of International Trade and Industry, the former because of its functional responsibilities and the latter because of a dramatic reorientation away from protectionism and towards internationalism. The process of MITI's internationalization was studied in considerable detail by Chalmers Johnson and explained partly in terms of the rise of a younger and more liberal-minded crop of officials and partly in terms of the changes in the international environment in the 1970s. The oil crisis of 1973 had a tremendous impact on the policy reorientation of MITI officials, since it highlighted the difficulties of regime maintenance (the oil regime) in the face of hegemonic decline. As far as the trading regime was concerned, there was no reason to assume that things would work out differently, which made it imperative that both the leadership function be strengthened and Japan's own position within the system be modified to ensure and enhance regime stability.

Nevertheless, it was also true that the main opposition to this line of reasoning also came from within certain segments of the bureaucracy which remained relatively steeped in the conservative tradition of protecting domestic interests, as in the case of the Ministry of Health and Welfare. And, given the fact that, in Japan, political leaders have less effective control over the bureaucracy, progress may be, and has been, relatively slow. In Japan, the particular relationship between the political leadership and the bureaucracy predates the Second World War and would suggest that the post-war democratic reforms instituted by the occupation authorities to establish party government along Western lines were less than completely successful. In the inter-war years, it was the relative weakness of political control over the bureaucracy that made the outbreak of hostilities inevitable.

As stated above, the political leadership in Japan was trying to build a more constructive consensus, but consensus building was a time-consuming process even at the best of times and more problematic when economic conditions were adverse. Similarly, economic restructuring in Japan could have been undertaken relatively smoothly if the economy had been performing well, but became exceedingly difficult for the government to promote actively, given the economic gloom caused by the appreciation of the yen. Still, the government did take it up, as evidenced in the Maekawa report, even as many political analysts predicted that it would lead to electoral set-backs for the ruling LDP.

We suggested that Western pressure had been useful in the past and remained a functionally useful tool, but indiscriminate use of pressure could be dysfunctional, just as it was in the period leading up to the Japanese attack on Pearl Harbor. Pressure, when used injudiciously, could be used by the intransigent forces in Japan to highlight the futility of Japanese 'concessions' on the grounds that the West was engaged in unfair 'Japan bashing' to divert attention away from its own internal problems. Thus, while pressure was useful, the exercise of pressure had to be cautions and, in particular, crude retaliatory measures had to be avoided. In this latter category, we can include the $300 million retaliatory tariff imposed by the United States on 17 April 1987 on Japanese electronic exports. This measure was taken in retaliation for the failure on the part of the Japanese government to implement an agreement reached the year before that would guarantee US manufac-turers a 20 per cent market share in Japan and bar Japanese manufacturers from selling in the United States at prices below production costs outside Japan. On top of the fact that the agreement itself was badly conceived, *Fortune* magazine noted that blame was being unfairly assigned to Japan since many US buyers, apparently convinced of Japanese sincerity to imple-ment the agreement and cut production, rushed to get their orders in before prices went up.[2] This retaliatory action also could not have been more ill-timed. In chapter 6 we mentioned the tax-reform package drawn up and approved by the LDP as part of a measure designed to reduce savings and expand levels of consumption. Prime Minister Nakasone and the LDP were faced with a serious political crisis in the shape of popular and opposition parties' opposition to the tax-reform package. With-in the deteriorating political climate, the American retaliatory tariff only served to undermine further the position of the Naka-sone administration and strengthened the voice of those who felt that Japan had already gone too far in its 'appeasement' policies. If anything, this will make it even harder to develop the domestic consensus that the government has been trying to achieve.

To recapitulate on some of the main findings of this study, we have argued that, in practical terms, system support implied both a broadly shared responsibility for system maintenance and a greater degree of policy co-ordination. A major portion of this study dealt with the former issue, although we did note the G-5 agreement as a clear example of policy co-ordination. The G-5 agreement revealed both the principle of interest aggregation as well as the centrality of the American position, since it could hardly have been achieved without American consent. In terms of Japan's role as the system supporter, we identified the auto dispute and its resolution as a prime indicator. MITI's positive attitude toward restricting Japanese car exports to the United States was largely motivated by its concern to help in the restructuring of the US auto industry, in recognition of the fact that it was a key component of the American economy and that successful revitalization of that sector was likely to dampen protectionism in the United States. As far as the macro-level trade imbalance was concerned, specific steps recently implemented to open further the market in Japan were identified as evidence showing Japan's readiness to help control the destabilizing influences within the system. However, the macro-economic policy imbalance between the United States and Japan cannot be ignored either. To tackle the investment–savings imbalance in both countries, it was not sufficient that Japan increase its fiscal spending. There had to be a similar attempt in the United States to bring the federal budget deficit under control. The impact of the budget deficit on trade imbalance was clearly stated by Bergsten and Cline, who wrote that

> The difference between the US financial balance and that of Japan rose from +1 per cent of GNP in 1980 to −5 per cent in 1984. The same large reversal occurred (by accounting definition) in the difference between the two countries' external balances. This growing divergence was the underlying factor driving the sharp rise in bilateral trade imbalance.[3]

In so far as Japan's market opening was concerned, the Japanese pointed out that market opening by itself cannot achieve anything unless there was a greater concomitant effort by foreign manufacturers to penetrate the market. The Japanese complained that the Americans and others had made inadequate efforts to respond to specific Japanese demand patterns and had, therefore, not been rewarded with market success (with exceptions, of course).

Furthermore, while the focus of this study was on Japanese attempts to resolve the trade friction with the United States and the West, this should not be interpreted as implying an admission of guilt by Japan. Certainly there were a large number of people in Japan and overseas who, correctly I believe, saw the trade problem as involving blame on both sides. Both Shimomura Osamu, Advisor to the Japan Development Bank, and Shinohara Myohei, Director of the International Development Institute, felt that the United States was largely responsible for its trade deficit. Shimomura, for example, wrote that

In 1982 the United States ran a current account deficit of only $9 billion, but by 1985, that had swollen to $118 billion. During this time Japan's current account surplus rose from $7 billion to $49 billion. Something happened to trigger this abnormal phenomenon, and the question is whether the change occurred on the Japanese side or the American side.

Confident that the problem was on the American side, he continued, 'President Reagan must face up to the fact his tax-cutting and fiscal expansion policies have gone haywire'.[4] Even if we disagree that this was an accurate statement of the entire problem, it cannot be denied that there was at least some truth in it.

In recent years, the pace of liberalization of the Japanese economy has quickened markedly and we can expect this process to be continued. However, as we have emphasized at several points in the text, total liberalization cannot be achieved overnight because of the difficulty of altering the underlying social problems. The direction of change, however, is unmistaken, but it will take time, even though Japan, on more than one occasion in the past, has displayed the remarkable ability to transform itself very rapidly.

One such occasion was in the mid-nineteenth century when the Meiji Restoration ended the 250 years of isolation imposed at the start of the Tokugawa era. Although the rest of the country bitterly opposed the opening of Japan and rallied to the popular cry of 'revere the emperor; expel the barbarian', they quickly adjusted to the new conditions. Edwin Reischauer wrote that

The young aristocrats of Satsuma and Choshu [two outer *hans* in southern Japan] saw how hopeless their fiefs were against Western naval strength. They learnt their lesson at once, and demonstrating an amazing ability to reorient their thinking, they dropped all thought of a narrow policy of isolation and immediately began to study the techniques of warfare that had made the West so strong.[5]

Almost a century later, Japan demonstrated this same ability to reorient itself when it quickly adopted a democratic form of government after the Second World War and under American occupation. The Allied Powers, expecting strong resistance to their programme of change, were pleasantly surprised at the ease with which Japan adapted itself to the new form of government. However, it would be unreasonable to expect this same sort of transformation today. In the past two instances, the transformation followed cataclysmic events – the bombardment of Kagoshima (Satsuma) and Shimonoseki (Choshu) by American, British, French, and Dutch warships which demonstrated superior Western military strength, as well as the distinct threat of colonization; and in the latter instance defeat in the Pacific War. It could be argued that a crisis exists today as well, but analysts differ as to the meaning of the crisis. Unlike in the mid-nineteenth and twentieth centuries when the crisis was physically visible, the present crisis is open to various interpretations.

The Action Programme for market liberalization did not constitute the third opening of Japan, but it did represent a major new initiative as well as an attempt to build a national consensus on the role and responsibilities of Japan in the international system. The culmination of the process may take time, but at least it is underway. In chapter 7, we identified the potential future threat to the system resulting from the excessive dependence of the ANICs and ASEAN on the United States as export market and suggested that Japan could help to defuse this potential threat by facilitating export diversification of the regional countries and by allowing greater access to its own market.

In this respect, a number of authors have suggested that Japan should provide ASEAN and other regional exporters special help and training to overcome their biggest obstacle to selling in Japan – the Japanese distribution system. For

Narongchai Akrasanee, this could best be carried out in the private sector by the Japanese Keidanren and other business organizations,[6] but the task force set up by the Pacific Economic Cooperation Conference (PECC) in October 1982 also envisaged a public sector role. According to the report of the task force

> since positive actions are the most attractive, high priority should be given to the recommendation that governments and business provide marketing help to firms in the Pacific Basin. In reality, Japan would be called upon to be the major provider of such help since the Japanese market appears to be particularly difficult for foreigners to penetrate.[7]

Although the role of supporters was likely to gain in significance in the future, it should be emphasized that regime stability would still require a strong and healthy economy in the leading country as well as a rebuilding of the domestic consensus on free trade. The latter, however, will be determined to a large extent by the objective economic indicators, since it is quite obvious that protectionism becomes a rallying cry during periods of economic decline. Below, we will discuss each of these two points.

Taking the last point first, one striking feature of post-war developments in the United States was the erosion of domestic support for liberal trade, especially within the ranks of organized labour groups. As our case study of the US–Japan auto dispute revealed, it was the UAW that triggered the dispute and continued to have a significant influence over the course of the dispute. It will be important for the future stability of the system that labour did not perceive itself to be the sacrificial lamb at the altar of liberal trade, as well as to avoid those conditions that, in fact, brought this about. To rebuild the domestic consensus it is imperative that acceptable mechanisms be found to make it easy for labour to make the transition from depressed industries to industries that display growth or the potential of growth.

In 1962, as part of the Trade Expansion Act, President Kennedy proposed the establishment of trade adjustment assistance (TAA) comprised of three main parts – income maintenance (TRA); relocation benefits; and training. This was instrumental in securing the support of organized labour for the

Trade Expansion Act, but the actual implementation of TAA was disappointing and succeeded only in antagonizing labour interests. As Steve Charnovitz wrote, 'From 1962 to 1969, not a single TAA petition was approved. . . . [Starting in late 1969 and] . . . over the next several years, only about 35,000 workers received TRA and very few received training.'[8] Since then, the costs of TRA continued to mount, but the programme remained ineffective because it was misused to provide an additional unemployment compensation rather than for job retraining and adjustment. It was not surprising, therefore, that American labour had swiftly transformed itself into a vocal champion of protectionism as a means of ensuring job security.

With respect to the other point, it should be noted that while exchange-rate adjustments could restore external balance to a country's trade position, they were no substitutes for flagging productivity and lack of industrial dynamism. For the United States this is an important pending issue. Even though, under the projected new round of GATT multilateral trade negotiations, the United States placed particular emphasis on the liberalization of the services trade, an area where it has an edge over its competitors (though not in all sectors), the future of the American economy cannot be built around the service industry alone. As R. Reich writes, 'The nation's service exports depend on the vigor of its future manufacturing base. Approximately 90 per cent of American's income from services consists of the investment income of its manufacturing firms . . .'.[9] Not only was the growth in services dependent upon the state of the manufacturing sector, this particular sector of the economy was important for other reasons as well. Thus, even though the manufacturing sector accounted for only a fifth of the total employment in the United States, 'it is often considered the fulcrum of a modern economy, an important source of jobs and high wages, the major locus of productivity growth, the center of vital regional economies, and a crucial contributor to national defense'.[10]

The authors of the Brookings study, however, found no evidence that the United States was deindustrializing or that 'structural change is accelerating, or that the country is suffering from some fundamental disadvantage in world trade'.[11], They concluded that the changes that affected the US manufacturing sector over the past decade were normal and to be expected, given the global recession and a strong currency.

Others, like B. Scott, found a declining ability of the United States to produce, distribute, and service goods in the international economy in competition with others. One of the factors behind this, he suggested, was the low ratio of net fixed investment to the GNP. The share of the GNP devoted to net fixed investment during the last decade in the United States was only 34 per cent of the comparable share in Japan and 56 per cent of the comparable share in West Germany.[12] Scott suggests four factors that have contributed to the relative decline of the United States:

1. an overvalued dollar;
2. mismanagement and complacency in the private sector;
3. incoherent, non-competitive government policy and the lack of an industrial policy, unlike the case of competing countries;
4. failure to learn from its competitors.[13]

The problem of an overvalued dollar appears to have been resolved through the G-5 agreement. As of late 1987, the dollar had declined by approximately 70 per cent against the yen, and there was a similar decline against the major European currencies. The most critical weakness of the American economy was that structural adjustments tended not to keep pace with changes in the international division of labour. Instead of adjusting to global structural changes, much energy was devoted to fighting the current of change through protection, and in the process the American economy did only marginally better than stand still. Part of the blame for this was in the nature of the American political system. The US Constitution gives Congress the final authority to make trade policy, and trade matters have thus become hostage to the narrow electoral interests of individual Congressmen.

The emphasis in the private sector has been to preserve and protect an existing line of products through the protection of the domestic market rather than evolve new product lines. The latter, of course, is both more risky and costly and structural adjustment, therefore, has been avoided to the extent possible. To a large degree, this was possible because the US economy is large and it was clearly understood that if it could be protected from the foreign onslaught, it was sufficient to ensure profitability for the domestic industries. While acknowledging exceptions to the rule, industries in the United States have not been as internationalist in their outlook as their counterparts in competing countries.

In contrast, Japanese industries have been more successful in adapting to international conditions. For example, when the regional countries emerged as textiles exporters, Japan gradually moved out of basic textiles manufacturing and into synthetics. Later, when the ANICs surged ahead with steel production, 'Japan reduced its domestic steel making capacity and became a major exporter of steel technology – engineering services and equipment'.[14] The American solution to structural decline has been to diversify into other unrelated areas. Reich argued that the solution to the American malaise was not 'paper entrepreneurship' – diversification through corporate take-overs and acquisition – but rather the adoption of 'flexible system of production'. Standardized production should be left to those NICs and developing countries that had a comparative advantage in the production of these goods and American firms should continuously attempt to upscale their existing product lines. Flexible system production would not require abdication from the traditional sectors – steel, autos, etc. – which were the gateway to new products and processes, but rather required learning from the other industrialized countries which were 'seeking to restructure them toward higher value-added and technologically more sophisticated businesses'.[15] There is no certainty, however, that this can be achieved through market forces and particularly where Congress cannot help but be responsive to pressure from industry for protection.

This, however, is a negative function of government and it has been argued that what is required now is a more positive governmental role in the economy. It has been argued that the government should develop an industrial policy to provide a blueprint for industrial development and for industrial restructuring. Of course, most countries do have an industrial policy, but it is also true that success is by no means guaranteed, as in the case of the United Kingdom, where industrial policy had been based on the regional concept as opposed to the sectoral concept that Japan and France adopted. The United States too, had an industrial policy, but it was, wrote Muller and Moore, of 'the worst sort – implicit, ad hoc, uncoordinated, and poorly administered'.[16]

Thus, it is not simply a question of having an industrial

policy. What is important is that the industrial policy be intended to promote international competitiveness. If anything, American industrial policy has been inward looking and protectionist, as opposed to the outward-looking and export-oriented model adopted by Japan and the NICs of Asia. For protectionism in America to abate, it will be necessary to reinvigorate the industrial sector such that it can withstand foreign competition.

In the case of autos, as we saw, Japan's primary concern was to see the American auto industry rehabilitated. The VER was intended to facilitate this, but its success can be attributed to the structure of the American auto industry and the domination of GM. At the time of the auto dispute, the call for restricting Japanese imports came mainly from Ford, Chrysler, and the UAW, but not from GM, which was more afraid that restrictions on Japanese car imports would cause its market share to climb, which might then increase its vulnerability to anti-trust action. However, GM did take advantage of the VER to modernize its plants and facilities, and in doing so, forced Ford and Chrysler to follow suit, resulting in an overall improvement in the state of the auto industry.

However, the auto industry is just one sector of the economy, and just as one swallow does not herald the onset of summer, revitalization of the American economy, too, will require a more broadly based improvement. This demands a concerted effort by industry, labour, and the government to raise domestic productivity and international competitiveness. Only then will the threat to the liberal trading regime subside.

Notes

2 POLITICAL REALISM AND INTERNATIONAL REGIMES

1 Krause, L. B. and Sekiguchi, S. (1976) 'Japan and the World Economy', in H. Patrick and H. Rosovsky (eds) *Asia's New Giant: How the Japanese Economy Works*, Washington, DC: The Brookings Institution.
2 Keohane, R. O., 1980, 'The Theory of Hegemonic Stability and Changes in International Economic Regimes, 1967–1977', in O. R. Holsti, R. M. Siverson and A. L. George (eds) *Change in the International System*, Boulder CO: Westview Press, p.136.
3 See, Ashley, R. K. (1984) 'The Poverty of Neorealism', *International Organization* (IO) 38:232.
4 Keohane, R. O. (1984) *After Hegemony: Cooperation and Discord in the World Political Economy*, Princeton, NJ: Princeton University Press. See chapter 4, especially pp.50–1.
5 Ruggie, J. G. (1982) 'International Regimes, Transactions and Change: Embedded Liberalism in the Postwar Economic Order', *IO* 36: no. 2; and Stein, A. A. (1982) 'Coordination and Collaboration: Regimes in an Anarchic World', *IO* 36: no. 2.
6 Kratochwil, F. (1984) 'The Force of Prescriptions', *IO* 38:687.
7 ibid., passim.
8 Cited in Stein, A. A. (1984) 'The Hegemon's Dilemma: Great Britain, The United States and the International Economic Order', *IO* 38:357.
9 Kamijo, T. (1985) *Beikoku no Ude: Nihon no te – Nichi-Bei Keizai Masatsu: Joho no koyo*, Tokyo: Nihon Keizai Shinbun sha, p.150.
10 Keohane, R. O. (1984) op. cit., p.32.
11 *New York Times*, 15 November 1985, section IV, p.2.
12 Kratochwil, F. (1984) op. cit., p.693.
13 Keohane, R. O. (1984) op. cit., p.137.
14 Kissinger, H. A. (1982) *Years of Upheaval*, London: Weidenfeld and Nicolson and Michael Joseph, p.916.
15 Keohane, R. O. (1984) op. cit., p.136.
16 Kindleberger, C. P. (1973) *The World in Depression, 1929–1939*, Harmondsworth: Allen Lane, The Penguin Press.
17 Ruggie, J. G. (1984) 'Another Round, Another Requiem? Prospects for the Global Negotiations', in J. G. Ruggie and J. N. Bhagwati (eds) *Power, Passions and Purpose: Prospects for North-South Negotiations*, Cambridge, MA: The MIT Press, p.35.
18 Kindleberger, C. P. (1973) op. cit., p.235.
19 Buzan, B. (1984) 'Economic Structures and International Security: The Limits of the liberal Case', *IO* 38:618.
20 Lake, D. A. (1984) 'Beneath the Commerce of Nations: A Theory of International Economic Structures', *International Studies Quarterly* (ISQ) 28:143.

21 ibid. p.156.
22 Russet, B. (1985) 'The Mysterious Case of Vanishing Hegemony', *IO* 39:226–7.
23 Carr, E. H. (1962) *The Twenty Years' Crisis, 1919–1939*, London: Macmillan, p.75.
24 Kindleberger, C. P. (1976) 'Systems of International Economic Organization', in D. P. Calleo (ed.) *Money and the Coming World Order*, New York: New York University Press, pp.23–4.
25 Lake, D. A. (1984) op. cit., pp.156–7.
26 Schmidt, H. (1983) 'The World Economy at Stake: The Inevitable Need for American Leadership', *The Economist* (London), 26 February–4 March, p.30. A few years later, however, Schmidt had apparently modified his views arguing that every country had to rid itself of petty national interest and adopt policies of international co-operation. See, *Economist* (Tokyo), 18 February 1986. p.13.
27 Keohane, R. O. (1984) op. cit., p.9.
28 ibid.
29 ibid., p.244.
30 Gilpin, R. (1981) *War and Change in World Politics*, Cambridge: Cambridge University Press, p.9.
31 Keohane, R. O. (1984) op. cit., p.244.
32 ibid., pp.245–6.
33 See, Jervis, R. (1976) *Perception and Misperception in International Politics*, Princeton, NJ: Princeton University Press; and Steinbruner, J. D. (1974) *Cybernetic Theory of Decision: A New Dimension of Political Analysis*.
34 Keohane, R. O. (1984) op. cit., p.115.
35 Snidal, D. (1985) 'The Limits of Hegemonic-Stability Theory', *IO*, vol. 39, no. 4. Both quotations taken from p.593 (emphasis in original).
36 Stoga, A. J. (1986) 'If America Won't Lead', *Foreign Policy*, Fall, p.91.
37 Ministry of Foreign Affairs (1985) 'Bonn kara Tokyo e: Dai 11 kai Shuyo Koku Shuno Kaidan o Oete', *Sekai no Ugoki*, no. 432, p.20.
38 Sakamoto, M. (1981) *Keizai Taikoku no Chosen*, Tokyo: Nihon Seisansei Honbu, p.178.
39 Lake, D. A. (1983) 'International Economic Structures and American Foreign Economic Policy, 1887–1934', *World Politics* 35: no. 4. p.523.
40 ibid. p.523.
41 Krasner, S. D. (1976) 'State Power and the Structure of International Trade', *World Politics* 28:341.
42 Goldstein, J. (1986) 'The Political Economy of Trade: Institutions of Protection', *American Political Science Review* (APSR) 80:162.
43 Waltz, K. N. (1979) *Theory of International Politics*, Philippines: Addison–Wesley, p.74.
44 Stoga, A. J. (1986) op. cit., p.89.
45 Mikdashi, Z. (1986) *Transnational Oil: Issues, Policies and Perspectives*, London: Frances Pinter, p.98.

46 *Economic Report of the President to the Congress* February 1984, Washington, DC: United States Government Printing Office, p.5.

3 THE POST-WAR LIBERAL INTERNATIONAL ECONOMIC ORDER

1 Mack, A. (1986) 'The Political Economy of Global Decline: America in the 1980s', *Australian Outlook* 40:11.
2 ibid., p.15.
3 Stein, A. A. (1984) 'The Hegemon's Dilemma: Great Britain, the United States and the International Economic Order', *International Organization* (IO) 38:384, 386.
4 See Newton, C. C. S. (1984) 'The Sterling Crisis of 1947 and the British Response to the Marshall Plan', *The Economic History Review* 37:397.
5 Sakamoto, M. (1985) 'Pax Amerikana ni Okeru Kokusai Kokyo Zai no Futan', *Sekai Keizai Hyoron* 29: no. 9. See also Sakamoto, M. (1986) 'Shihyō kara mita Pax Amerikana no tokushoku: Pax Britanika ni hikaku shite', *Sekai Keizai Hyōron* 30: no. 4.
6 Newton, C. C. S. (1984) op. cit., p.394.
7 Bhagwati, J. N. and Irwin, D. A. (1987) 'The Return of Reciprocitarians – US Trade Policy Today', *The World Economy* 10:122.
8 See (1986) *Forbes* 137:440.
9 Keohane, R. P. (1984) *After Hegemony: Cooperation and Discord in the World Political Economy*, Princeton, NJ: Princeton University Press, p.139.
10 Amaya, N. (1986) 'When Fair is Unfair', *Journal of Japanese Trade and Industry* 5:6.
11 Johnson, H. G. (1965) 'An Economic Theory of Protectionism', *Journal of Political Economy* 73:272–3. See also Bhagwati, J. N. and Irwin, D. A. (1987) op. cit., p.124.
12 Whitman, M. V. N. (1979) *Reflections of Interdependence: Issues for Economic Theory and U.S. Policy*, Pittsburg, PA: University of Pittsburg Press, p.195.
13 *U.S. Trade Policy*, Hearings before the Subcommittee on Trade of the Committee on Ways and Means, House of Representatives, 96th Congress, 2nd Session, 26 June and 21 July 1980, p.98.
14 Golt, S. (1974) *The GATT Negotiations: A Guide to the Issues*, British North American Committee, p.5.
15 Murakami, Y. (1982) 'Toward a Socioinstitutional Explanation of Japan's Economic Performance' in K. Yamamura (ed.) *Policy and Trade Issues of the Japanese Economy: American and Japanese Perspectives*, Seattle, WA: University of Washington Press, p.16.
16 Johnson, C. (1982) *MITI and the Japanese Miracle: The Growth of Industrial Policy, 1925–1975*, Stanford, CA: Stanford University Press, pp.268–71.
17 Stein, A. A. (1984) op. cit., p.383 (emphasis in original).

18 Wolf, M. (1984) 'Two Edged Sword: Demand of Developing Countries and the Trading System', in J. G. Ruggie and J. N. Bhagwati (eds) *Power, Passions and Purpose: Prospects for North-South Negotiations*, Cambridge, MA: The MIT Press, pp.205–6.

19 Bernstein, E. M. (1980) 'Structural Problems and Economic Policy: The U.S. Experience', in I. Leveson and J. W. Wheeler (eds) *Western Economies in Transition: Structural Change and Adjustment in Industrial Countries*, Boulder, CO: Westview Press, p.178.

20 Bergsten, C. F. (1980) 'The Future of U.S.–Japan Economic Relations', in C. F. Bergsten *The International Economic Policy of the United States: Selected Papers of C. Fred Bergsten, 1971–1979*, Lexington, MA: Lexington Books, p.310. Similarly, at a speech given at Cornell University on 27 March 1985, Lionel Olmer, Undersecretary of Commerce, said that of the new employment created in the United States during the previous five years in the manufacturing sector, 80 per cent was export oriented.

21 *Asahi Shinbun* (Chokan), 10 September 1985, p.5.

22 Statement of Prime Minister Nakasone on External Economic Measures, 9 April 1985. Translation provided by the Ministry of Foreign Affairs, Tokyo, Japan.

23 Morley, J. W. (1985) 'Japan and America – The Dynamics of Partnership', Presidential Address, *Journal of Asian Affairs* 45:19.

24 Johnson, C. (1982) op. cit., p.301.

25 ibid., p.279.

26 Amaya, N. (1985) 'Nichi-Bei kankei: setogiwa no sentaku', in *'Saka no ue no kumo' to 'saka no shita no numa'*, Tokyo: Tsusho Sangyo Chosa Kai, p.60.

27 Destler, I. M., Fukui, H., and Sato, H. (1979) *The Textile Wrangle: Conflict in Japanese American Relations, 1969–1971*, Ithaca, NY: Cornell University Press, p.316.

28 ibid. p.205. However, Chalmers Johnson writes that MITI's intransigence during the textiles dispute was largely intended to refute the accusations of foreign appeasement and that MITI had gone soft trying to 'placate foreigners'. See, Johnson, C. (1982) op. cit., pp.280–1.

29 Amaya, N. (1985) 'Nihon wa tsuyoi Amerika o nozomu' op. cit., pp.119–20.

4 THE US–JAPAN AUTO DISPUTE

1 Winham, G. R. and Kabashima, I. (1982) 'The Politics of U.S.–Japan Auto Trade', in I. M. Destler and H. Sato (eds) *Coping with U.S.–Japanese Economic Conflicts* Lexington, MA: Lexington Books, Heath and Co., pp.73–119.

2 Riegle, D. R. (1981) 'The Legislative Response to Unemployment in the U.S. Auto Industry', in R. E. Cole (ed.) *The Japanese Automobile Industry: Model and Challenge for the Future?*, Michigan Papers in Japanese Studies, no. 3, p.72.

3 'The Automobile Crisis and Public Policy', an interview with P. Caldwell, Chairman, Ford Motor Co., *Harvard Business Review*, January–February 1981, p.78.

4 *U.S. Trade and Investment Policy: Imports and the Future of the American Automobile Industry*, Hearings Before the Joint Economic Committee, Congress of the United States, 96th Congress, 2nd Session, March 19, 1980, p.12.

5 Kamijo, T. (1985) *Beikoku no ude: Nihon no te – Nichi-Bei keizai masatsu: jōhō no kōyō*, Tokyo: Nihon Keizai Shinbun Sha, p.151.

6 *Issues Relating to the Domestic Auto Industry*, Hearings before the Subcommittee on International Trade of the Committee of Finance, US Senate, 97th Congress, 1st Session on S-396, 9 March 1981, p.90.

7 *Nihon Keizai Shinbun* (Chōkan), 2 May 1981, p.1.

8 Higashi, C. (1983) *Japanese Trade Policy Formulation*, New York: Praeger Publishers, p.70.

9 Craig, A. M. (1975) 'Functional and Dysfunctional Aspects of Government Bureaucracy', in E. Vogel (ed.) *Modern Japanese Organization and Decision Making*, Berkeley and Los Angeles: University of California Press, p.22.

10 The 1974 Trade Act is a revision of the 1962 Trade Expansion Act, and as the change in name suggests, the 1974 Trade Act makes it considerably easier for domestic manufacturers to apply for protection from imports.

11 Ogura, K. (1984) *Nichi-Bei keizai masatsu: omoto no jijo, ura no jijo*, Tokyo: Nihon Keizai Shinbun Sha, p.173.

12 Patrick, H. and Sato, H. (1982) 'The Political Economy of Unites States–Japan Trade in Steel', in K. Yamamura (ed.) *Policy and Trade Issues of the Japanese Economy: American and Japanese Perspectives*, Seattle, WA: University of Washington Press, p.208.

13 'Joyōsha jiyuka ron ni hantai suru', Interview with K. Kawamata, Chairman, Japan Automobile Industry Association (1968) *Asahi Journal* 10:88.

14 Allen, G. C. (1968) *Japan's Place in Trade Strategy: Larger Role in Pacific Region*, London: The Atlantic Trade Study, p.29.

15 Bain, J. S. (1968) *Industrial Organization*, New York: Wiley, p.177.

16 Cusumano, M. A. (1985) *The Japanese Automobile Industry: Technology and Management at Nissan and Toyota*, Cambridge, MA: Harvard East Asian Monographs, 12, p.190.

17 Boorstein, E. (1984) *What's Ahead? . . . The U.S. Economy* New York: International Publishers Co., p.98.

18 *Jidosha Sangyo Handbook*, Nissan Motor Co. Ltd, 1985 edn, p.108.

19 Sobel, R. (1984) *Car Wars: The Untold Story*, New York: Dutton, 224–60.

20 *New York Times* (NYT) 6 November 1975, p.66.

21 Shimokawa, K. (1985) *Jidōsha sangyō datsu seijuku jidai*, Tokyo: Yūhikaku Sensho, pp.17–18.

22 'Funman uzumaku jidosha hanbai sai zensen', *Shūkan Tōyō Keizai*, 28 March 1981, p.76.

23 According to Cohen, Japan's market share of the US compact car market was 40 per cent in 1980. See, Cohen, R. B. (1983) 'The Prospects for Trade and Protectionism in the Auto Industry', in W. R. Cline (ed.) *Trade Policy in the 1980s*, Washington, DC: Institute for International Economics, p.538.

24 *U.S. Trade and Investment Policy.* . . (1980) op. cit. In January 1980, when Honda announced that it would set up an auto assembly plant in Marysville, Ohio, producing 100,000 cars a year, doubts were raised about the viability of such a small-scale operation. Honda, however, was confident of the correctness of its decision. Later, the local Content Bill, introduced in the US Congress in 1981 and 1982, proposed local content requirements on manufacturers selling more than 100,000 units in one model year, running from October to September.

25 *Nichi-Bei jidōsha mondai no sui-i*, Prepared by Nissan Motor Co. Ltd, (undated internal document). See also *Mainichi Shinbun* (Yukan), 2 May 1980, p.1.

26 Muto, H. (1984) 'Jidosha sangyō', in R. Komiya, M. Okuno, and K. Suzumura (eds) *Nihon no sangyo seisaku*, Tokyo: Tokyo Daigaku Shuppan Kai. Japan abolished auto tariffs in March 1978. Prior to that auto tariffs were at the level of 10 per cent since 1971.

27 See, Cole, R. and Yakushiji, T. (1984) *The American and Japanese Auto Industries in Transition*, University of Michigan, Ann Arbor: Center of Japanese Studies, p.57.

28 *U.S. Trade and Investment Policy.* . . (1980) op. cit., p.79.

29 Amaya, N. (1982) *Nihon kabushiki kaisha: nokosareta sentaku*, Tokyo: PHP Research Institute, p.67.

30 Kumei, Y., and Shimokawa, K. (1981) 'Kyōsō shitsutsu kyōsō kyōzon o', *Tsūsan Journal* October.

31 Shimokawa, K. (1985) op. cit., p.49.

32 In this regard, this report differed quite markedly from the report presented to President Ronald Reagan in March 1981, recommending relief to the auto industry. There was division within the Reagan administration as well, but the report of the Transportation Secretary, Lewis, was only presented once consensus had been reached.

33 *NYT* 9 July, 1980, section IV, p.4.

34 ibid.

35 *Nihon Keizai Shinbun* (NKS) (Yukan), 19 September 1980, p.1.

36 *NYT* 28 February 1980, p.22.

37 *NKS* (Chōkan), 20 September 1980, p.1. See also Kusano, A. (1984) *Nichi-Bei keizai masatsu no kōzō*, Tokyo, p.137.

38 Patrick, H. and Sato, H. (1982) op. cit., p.200.

39 The United States has three pieces of anti-trust legislation on the books: the Sherman Act of 1890, the Federal Trade Commission Act of 1914 (amended 1937), and the Clayton Act of 1914 (amended 1936 and 1950). Section 1 of the Sherman Act very specifically states that 'every contract, combination . . . or conspiracy in restraint of trade or commerce among several States, or with foreign nations, is hereby declared to be illegal', The Federal

Trade Commission Act is somewhat less clear-cut, but the result is still the same.

40 *NKS* (Chokan), 23 September 1980, p.2.
41 By law, a decision must be handed down within six months of a petition, in this case by 12 December 1980. However, the ITC had already made known its intention to submit its decision to the President in early November, in order to stay clear of election politics.
42 *NYT* 11 November 1980, p.1. The Chairman of the Commission voted against the petition but also criticized Japan. See Yano, T. (1980) *Tsusan Seisaku no saikin no Juyo Kadai: Boeki Masatsu o Chushin to shite*, Nihon Keizai Chosa Kyogi Kai, p.15.
43 Obi, T. (1981) ' "Nihon sha shimedase" wa shosu iken da', *Shūkan Tōyō Keizai*, 4 April.
44 'O katame no Nichi-Bei tsūshō senso-Suzuki hō Bei mae ni osuji ketchaku e', *Shūkan Tōyō Keizai*, 4 April 1981.
45 ibid., p.24. See also *NKS* (Yūkan), 25 March 1981, and Amaya, N. (1984) *Tsūsho masatsu to Nichi-Bei kankei*, Tokyo: Nihon Keizai Chosa Kyogi Kai, pp.9–10.
46 *NKS* (Chōkan), 9 April 1981, p.1.
47 *NKS* (Yūkan), 21 April 1981, p.1.
48 *NKS* (Yūkan), 25 March 1981.
49 Amaya, N. (1982) op. cit., pp.103–4.
50 ibid., p.106.
51 ibid., pp.107–8.
52 ibid., p.109.
53 Patrick, H. and Sato, H. (1982) op. cit., p.235.
54 *NKS* (Chōkan), 29 March 1981, p.3.
55 Hargrave, E. C. and Morley, S. A. (eds) (1984) *The President and the Council of Economic Advisors: Interviews with CEA Chairmen*, Boulder, CO: Westview Press. The two quotations are taken from pages 474 and 481, respectively.
56 *Far Eastern Economic Review* 27 February 1981, p.48.
57 Kusano, A. (1983) '1980 nen 7 gatsu: Maboroshi no Jidosha Jishu Kisei,' *Chuo Koron*, November, pp.130–2.
58 Amaya, N. (1981) 'Soap-nationalism o Osu', *Bungei Shunju*, July.
59 Amaya discusses the Chōnin no kokka ron in *Nihon kabushiki kaisha* (1981) op. cit., pp.35–44.
60 Halberstam, D. (1986) *The Reckoning*, New York: William Morrow, pp.31–2.
61 Amaya, N. (1981) *Tsūshō masatsu to Nichi-Bei kankei*, op. cit., p.10.
62 *NKS* (Chōkan), 21 March 1986, p.4.
63 *The U.S. Automobile Industry*, Report to the Congress from the Secretary of Commerce, December 1984, p.28.
64 Interview with Mr S. Kawaharada, Nissan Motor Co. Ltd, Tokyo. Prior to the VER, it was estimated that the cost advantage of Japanese manufacturers of subcompacts was about $2000 compared to the US manufactures. See *The US Automobile Industry, 1981*, Report to the Congress from the Secretary of Transportation; and

Kawaharada, S. (1985) *Jidōsha sangyo ron* (unpublished), p.30. According to the report of the Secretary of Transportation, the cost advantage of Japanese subcompacts landed in the United States was about $1700.

5 TRADE IMBALANCE AND IMPORT PROMOTION

1 According to one unofficial, but reliable, source, despite the public pronouncements, the US government had informally indicated to Japan the need to restrict the total quota to under 2.2 million units.

2 *Yomiuri Shinbun* (Chokan), 18 January 1986, p.7.

3 *Asahi Shinbun* 26 January 1986, p.9.

4 'Foreign Barriers to US Trade: Part II – Merchandise Exports', US Senate, Committee on Banking, Housing, and Urban Affairs, Subcommittee on Finance, 4 March 1982, p.7.

5 Curran, T. J. (1983) 'The Politics of Trade Liberalization in Japan', in J. D. Katz, and Friedman-Lichtschein, T.C. (eds) *Japan's New World Role*, Boulder, CO: Westview Press, p.113.

6 *The Japan Times*, 29 January 1986, p.11. At a press conference on the 13th at the Foreign Correspondents' Club, Tokyo, Senator Danforth stated that the trade problem was no longer issue specific but one of a general nature. See *Asahi Shinbun* (Chokan), 14 January 1986, p.9.

7 Hofheinz, R. and Calder, K. E. (1982) *The Eastasia Edge*, New York: Basic Books, p.175.

8 The two sets of statistics are taken from (1985) *OECD Economic Outlook*, December, no. 38; and (1985) *World Economic Outlook*, Washington, DC: IMF, April, p.131.

9 Ogura, K. (1984) *Nichi-Bei keizai masatsu*, Tokyo: Nihon Keizai Shinbun Sha, p.100.

10 Matsuda, M. (1986) 'Ō-Bei shokoku to no boeki mondai no ichi shiten: seihin yunyū hiritsu hijyō yōso no Datōsei no tsuite', *Bōeki to Kanzei*, Japan Tariff Association, 34:3:36, p.36.

11 ibid., p.38.

12 'Foreign Barriers to U.S. Trade. . .' (1982) op. cit., p.5ff.

13 About forty years ago, when the Bretton–Woods system was being put together, the United States insisted that trade adjustment was the responsibility of the deficit, not the surplus country.

14 *The Japan Times*, 29 January 1986, p.11 (emphasis added).

15 Higashi, C. (1983) *Japanese Trade Policy Formulation*, New York: Praeger Special Studies, p.122. See also Kitamura, H., Okazaki, H., and Murata, R. (1983) *Nichi-Bei kankei o toitsumeru*, Tokyo: Sekai no Ugoki Sha, p.163.

16 Olsen, E. (1985) '"Cheap rider" e no Fuman', *Chuo Koron*, December, p.51.

17 To rectify the perception gap, the Ministry of Foreign Affairs, in February 1986, announced an Action Programme to promote

better understanding between Japan and the United States. The programme calls for a campaign of speeches by Japanese Embassy and Consular personnel in the United States to disseminate proper information to the general public as well as to members of Congress. See *Yomiuri Shinbun* (Chokan), 4 February 1986, p.2.

18 Higashi, C. (1983) op. cit., p.122.

19 Interview with JETRO official (Overseas Research Dept), Tokyo, January 1986.

20 Kitamura, H. *et al.*, (1983) op. cit., p.177.

21 'Foreign barriers to U.S. Trade . . .' (1982) op. cit.

22 *Asahi Shinbun* (Chokan), 28 September 1985.

23 Writing in the early 1970s, the period of high economic growth, James Morley suggested that a 1 per cent increase in defence spendings would reduce annual GNP growth by only about 0.4 per cent. See Morley, J.W. (1972) 'Economism and Balanced Defence', in *Forecast For Japan: Security in the 1970s*, Princeton, NJ: Princeton University Press.

24 Kamijo, T. (1985) *Beikoku no ude; Nihon no te*, Tokyo: Nihon Keizai Shinbun Sha, p.181.

25 Koganei, Y. (1987) 'Shijō kaihō e no mukete no shinario', *Chuo Koron*, July, pp.97–8.

26 'Multilateral Trade Negotiations; International Codes Agreed to in Geneva, Switzerland, April 12, 1979', House of Representatives, Committee on Ways and Means, 96th Congress, Washington, DC, 23 April 1979, p.245.

27 'Foreign Barriers to U.S. Trade. . .' (1982) op. cit., p.18.

28 Japan Economic Research Institute (1984) *Analysis of the Degree of Openness of the Japanese Market*, Tokyo, August, p.18.

29 *Mainichi Shinbun* (Yukan), 13 Janaury 1983, p.1.

30 *The Japan Times* 3 March 1983, Editorial.

31 *Standards and Certification System in Japan: Measures for Improving Market Access*, The Intra-Governmental Council on Standards and Certification Systems, (no date), p.3.

32 Matsushita, K. (1983) *Nichi-Bei tsūshō masatsu no hōteki sō ten*, Tokyo: Yūhikaku, p.280.

33 The full text of the law appears in the annual compilation of laws, *Roppo Zensho*. The original appears in pre-1983 editions and the revised text in later editions. The Japanese title of the law is 'Shohi Seikatsu yo Seihin Anzen Ho'.

34 'Progress in Implementing the Action Program for Improved Access', *News from MITI*, NR-317 (86–2), February 1986.

35 Matsushita, K. (1983) op. cit., p.278.

36 'Report of the Advisory Committee for External Economic Issues', 9 April 1985, p.2.

37 'The Outline of the Action Program for Improved Market Access', Government-Ruling Parties Joint Headquarters for the Promotion of External Economic Measures, 30 July 1985, p.7.

38 ibid., p.13.

39 Ministry of Foreign Affairs (1985) 'Explanatory Note of "Outline of Action Program for Improved Market Access"' July, pp.2–3.

40 *New York Times* 20 October 1986, p.A26.
41 In so far as industrial policy in Japan is concerned, it is worth noting that, over time, the government has become less interventionist as the success of past policies made it less important to intervene actively at the micro level.
42 Keizai Kikakuchō (EPA) (1984) *Nihon keizai no genkyo: naiju chūshin no antei seichō o mezashite*, 1985 ed., pp.140–1.
43 Rapp, W. C. (1980) 'Japan's Invisible Barriers to Trade', in T. A. Pugel (ed.) *Fragile Interdependence: Economic Issues in U.S.– Japanese Trade and Investment*, Lexington, MA: Lexington Books, p.26.
44 'The Outline of the Action Program. . .' (1985) op. cit., p.3.
45 Memo on Japan–US Economic Relations, MITI, January 1986, p.2.
46 *Asahi Shinbun* (Chokan), 10 April, 1985, p.3.
47 *Toki no Ugoki* 15 October 1985. See also *Asahi Shinbun* (Yukan), 12 April 1985, p.1.
48 Memo on Japan–US Economic Relations, MITI, January 1986.
49 *Yomiuri Shinbun* (Chokan), 28 March 1986, p.6.
50 Asahi Shinbun (Chokan, 20 October 1985, p.9.
51 Higashi, C. (1983) op. cit., p.107.
52 'The Outline of the Action Program. . .' (1985) op. cit., pp.1–2.
53 *Amakudari* is literally translated as 'descent from Heaven', which refers to the practice of senior bureaucrats retiring to top-level corporate positions. This has ensured a close relationship between the government and corporate sector.
54 Keidanren, 'Toward World Economic Stability and Prosperity – Japan's Contribution to the International Community', 25 February 1986, p.3.
55 Yoshino, M. (1971) *The Japanese Marketing System: Adaptations and Innovations*, Cambridge, MA: MIT Press, p.272. MITI's 'closeness' has been with big business, in general, not the traditional sector of the economy.
56 *The Economist* (London), 20 February 1982, p.80.
57 'Japanese Industrial Collusion and Trade', US Congress, Joint Economic Committee, Subcommittee on Economic Goals and Intergovernmental Policy, 31 January 1986, 2nd Session, p.10.
58 'Yunyū Hin ryūtsū oyobi sho kankō no tsuite', *Bukka Antei Seisaku Kaigi Seisaku Bukai*, 28 March 1986, p.16.
59 EPA (1985) 'Yunyū hin ryūtsū Jittai chōsa kekka no matome', November, p.253.
60 *The Wall Street Journal* 14 July 1986, p.2.
61 MITI, 80 nendai no ryūtsū sangyo bijion, 30 December 1985, passim. See, especially, pages 5ff and 86ff.
62 'O.T.O. no saikin no kujō shori jōkyō ni tsuite', Shijō Kaihō Mondai Kujō Shori Suishin Honbu, 17 January 1986, p.2.
63 Ōkita, S. 'Role of the Trade Ombudsman in Liberalizing Japan's Market', *The World Economy*, vol. 7, no. 3, September 1984, p.250. Some of the members of the OTO advisory council include Sony's Akio Morita, Honda's Soichiro Honda, MFA Advisor

Y. Ogawara, etc. The total membership is eight, together with the establishment of the Advisory Council; the full name of the OTO was changed to the Office of Trade and Investment Ombudsman. The acronym remains OTO.

64 Interview with Economic Planning Agency official (Coordination Division), Tokyo, February 1986.
65 Okita, S. (1984) op. cit., p.250.
66 *Asahi Shinbun* (Yukan), 23 October 1985, p.2. Also *Asahi Shinbun* (Chokan), 25 October 1985, p.9.
67 Interview with Ministry of Foreign Affairs official (Second North American Division), Tokyo, September 1985.
68 EPA (1984) op. cit., p.8.
69 See (1985) 'Beikoku no kokusai kyōsōryoku', *Chosa Geppo* 74:50.
70 *Far Eastern Economic Review* Annual 1986.
71 See Komiya, R. (1987) 'The U.S.–Japan Trade Conflict: An Economist's View from Japan', in D. I. Okimoto, (ed.) *Japan's Economy: Coping with Change in the International Environment*, Boulder, CO: Westview Press, p.204.
72 See (1986) *The Federal Reserve Bulletin* 72:17.
73 *Asahi Evening News* 13 March 1986, p.1.
74 *Fortune*, 28 October 1986, p.26.
75 *International Herald Tribute* 11 September 1987, p.1.
76 Yoshitomi, M. (1987) 'Taigai fukinkō no nidankai chōsei', *Chūō Kōron*, April.
77 *International Herald Tribune* 5 October 1987, p.7.
78 Imlah, A. H. (1958) *Economic Elements in Pax Britannica: Studies in British Foreign Trade in the Nineteenth Century*, Cambridge, MA: Harvard University Press, p.14.

6 INDUSTRIAL RESTRUCTURING AND DEMAND EXPANSION

1 Inoguchi, K., Amaya, N., and Kurosawa, Y. (1987) 'Hasha naki jidai Nihon no Yakuwari', *Chūō Kōron*, August, p.76.
2 Curtis, G. L. (1986) 'Trade, Yen, and Politics: Comments on the Political Implications of U.S–Japan Economic Relations', in H. T. Patrick, and R. Tachi (eds) *Japan and the United States Today: Exchange Rates, Macroeconomic Policies and Financial Market Innovations*, New York: Columbia University Press, p.200.
3 Destler, I. M. and Mitsuyu, H. (1982) 'Locomotives On Different Tracks: Macroeconomic Diplomacy, 1977–1979' in I. M. Destler and H. Sato (eds) *Coping with U.S.–Japanese Economic Conflicts*, Lexington, MA: Lexington Books, Heath and Co., p.245.
4 ibid., p.254.
5 ibid., p.245.
6 *Wall Street Journal* 2 September 1986, p.26.
7 Kitada, Y. (1983) 'Bōeki masatsu to Nihon no sangyō', in *Bōeki masatsu to keizai seisaku*, Tokyo: Daitsuki, p.14.

8 Kanamori, H. (ed.) *Nihon keizai: dai Hendō no jidai*, Tokyo: Nihon Keizai Kenkyū Center, p.188.
9 Aoki, T. (1985) *Taiheiyo no seiki to Nihon*, Tokyo: Yūhikaku, p.193.
10 See Kitamura, H. (1974) 'The End of an Economic "Miracle"? Domestic Implications of Japan's Growth', *Asian Affairs* 5: no. 3.
11 Honma, M. (1986) 'Zeisei kaikaku no kadai to hōkō', *The Keizai Seminar*, no. 376, May.
12 *Far Eastern Economic Review* (FEER), 9 October 1986, p.59.
13 'Kongo no zeisei no arikata ni tsuite no tōshin', Zeisei Chōsa Kai, November 1983, p.9–10.
14 Sakaiya, T. (1986) '5 cho yen de Nihon o sukue', *Bungei Shunju* April, p.116.
15 *FEER* 18 December 1986, pp.93–4.
16 Kaeda, B. (1987) 'Zeisei kaikaku haya wakari 20 mon', *Bungei Shunju*, February.
17 Keizai Kikakucho Chosa Kyoku (EPA), 'Nihon keizai nō genkyo: naiju chūshin no antei seichō o mezashite', Tokyo: MOF Publications Dept, 1985 edn, p.232. According to Ōkita Saburō, by the year 2000 the population will have aged enough to eliminate excess savings. See *FEER* 13 June 1985, p.65.
18 Noguchi, Y. (1985) 'Tax Structure and the Saving–Investment Balance', *Hitotsubashi Journal of Economics* 26: no. 1.
19 *New York Times* (NYT) 9 September 1986, section IV, p.20.
20 The government issues two types of bonds: deficit bonds and construction bonds.
21 'Kongo no zeisei no arikata. . .' (1983) op. cit., p.2.
22 ibid.
23 EPA (1986) *Economic Outlook, Japan*, p.17.
24 Aso, Y. (1986) 'Cheaper Oil, Stronger Yen: Not All Good News', *The daily Yomiuri* 25 March, p.5.
25 (1986) *International Currency Review* 17:33.
26 Naiju kakudai ni kansuru taisaku, *Keizai Taisaku Kakuryo Kaigi*, 15 October 1985.
27 *Asahi Shinbun* (Chokan), 16 October 1985, p.4.
28 Nishida, S. (1985) 'Boost in Domestic Demand Won't End Trade Friction', *The Daily Yomiuri* 18 October, p.5.
29 *Journal of Japanese Trade and Industry* September/October 1987, p.23.
30 *Asahi Shinbun* (Chokan), 16 October 1985, p.4.
31 Interview with Economic Planning Agency official (Coordination Division), Tokyo, February 1986.
32 'Measures for Domestic Demand Expansion', Ministerial Conference for Economic Measures, 28 December 1985.
33 *Shukan Toyo Keizai* 29 March 1986, no. 4649, p.20.
34 *The Daily Yomiuri* 16 April 1986, Editorial, p.2.
35 MITI (1985) *Tsusho Hyakusho, so-ron, 1985* Tokyo: MOF Publishing Dept, June, p.236.
36 Ninomiya, A. (1986) 'shinnen no keizai roncho', *Keizai*, no. 262, February, p.31.

37 Tsuruta, M. (1986) 'En daka ka no Nihon Keizai – sono genjo to kōhō', *Keizai*, no. 262, February, p.92.
38 *NYT* 20 September 1986, section I, p.33.
39 Okumura, A. (1987) 'Japan's Changing Economic Structure', *Journal of Japanese Trade and Industry*, no. 5, September/October, p.13.
40 *Wall Street Journal*, 20 October 1986, p.59.
41 *The Japan Times* 8 April 1986, p.1.
42 *FEER*, 17 April 1986, pp.130–1.
43 Coal is one of the products that is covered by quota restrictions and the government requires that steel mills and utility companies purchase at least 20 per cent of their coal requirement from the domestic mines. The rise of the yen since last year and the cost pressures on the domestic industries prompted the steel mills unilaterally to refuse to pay higher prices from domestic coal. The coal industry responded with the decision to stop the production of coking coal. The government, it is reported, is considering closing down eight of the eleven big mines and reducing total production to half the 1985 level of 18 million tons. See *The Economist* 9 August 1986, pp.56–7.
44 See (1986) *Dept. of State Bulletin' vol. 86, no. 2112. Speech by Allen Wallis, Undersecretary of State for Economic Affairs, before the U.S.–Japan Economic Agenda Meeting, 23 April 1986, p.70.*
45 *The Japan Times* 8 April 1986, p.5.
46 ibid.
47 Wallis, A. (1986), op. cit., p.70.
48 See 'Nihon no katsuro wa "Mackawa Report" ni ari', Interview with G. Sigur, *Chūō Kōron*, July 1986, p.113.
49 (1986) *Dept of State Bulletin*, vol. 86, no. 2112, p.54.
50 *NYT*, 29 April 1986, sectoin 4, p.4.
51 Okumura, A. (1987) op. cit., p.11.
52 *Asian Wall Street Journal* 29 October 1987, p.8.
53 Okumura, A. (1987) op. cit., p.11.
54 *Nihon Keizai Shinbun* (Chokan), 7 December 1987, p.1.
55 *NKS* 24 November 1987, p.1.
56 *Wall Street Journal* 21 April 1986, p.26.
57 Abegglen, J. C. (1984) *The Strategy of Japanese Business*, Cambridge, MA: Ballinger Publishing Co., p.21.
58 *NYT* 5 June 1985, section D, p.7.
59 MITI (1986) 'Interim Report by the Industrial Structure Council Focusing on International Perspective', NR 319 (86–4), February, p.7.
60 Okumura, A. (1987) op. cit., p.11.
61 *The Economist* (London), 2 August 1986, p.65.
62 'Report of Survey on Japanese Investment Trends in the United States', December 1985. Keidanren, International Economic Affairs Department. The unitary tax in California was finally repealed in 1986.
63 *NYT* 20 September 1986, section I, p.33.
64 *NKS* (Chōkan), 6 December 1987, p.1.

7 JAPAN AND ASIA–PACIFIC

1 Wescott, R. (1986) 'The Pacific Rim is the Next Battleground', *The Wall Street Journal*, 31 October, p.18.
2 Cited in Berlin, D. L. (1986) 'New Situations Facing the NICs in East Asia', *Intereconomics* 21:267.
3 Watanabe, A. (1985) 'The United States, Japan and the Asia/ Pacific: A Japanese Perspective with Special Reference to the Pacific Cooperation Concept', Prepared for the Colloquium on Japan and the United States in a Changing World Setting, Georgetown University, Center for Strategic and International Studies, Washington, DC, 26–27 March 1985, p.8. A Japanese version of the paper was published under the title 'Kan taiheiyō kōzō no uta to shinjitsu', *Chūō Kōron*, November 1985.
4 Reischauer, E. O. (1961) *The United States and Japan*, Cambridge, MA: Harvard University Press, pp.241–2.
5 Nishihara, M. (1976) *The Japanese and Sukarno's Indonesia: Tokyo–Jakarta Relations, 1951–1966*, Honolulu, HI: The University of Hawaii Press, p.7 and p.9.
6 ibid., p.212.
7 Allen, G. C. (1968) *Japan's Place in Trade Strategy: Larger Role in the Pacific Region*, Atlantic Trade Study Group paper no. 9.
8 EPA (1985) *Taiheiyō jidai no tenbō*, p.6.
9 Hofheinz, R. and Calder, K. E. (1982) *The Eastasia Edge*, New York: Basic Books, p.175.
10 Kuznets, P. W. (1977) *Economic Growth and Structure in the Republic of Korea*, New Haven, CT: Yale University Press, p.155.
11 ibid., p.159.
12 Hofheinz, R. and Calder, K. E. (1982) op. cit., p.178.
13 EPA (1985) op. cit., p.11.
14 Lin, Chin-Yuan (1973) *Industrialization in Taiwan: Trade and Import Substitution; Policies for Developing Countries*, New York: Praeger, p.116.
15 ibid., p.105.
16 Ariff, A. and Hill, H. (1986) 'Industrial Policies and Performance in ASEAN's "Big Four"', in H. Mutoh, S. Sekiguchi, K. Suzumura and I. Yamazawa (eds) *Industrial Policies for Pacific Economic Growth*, Sydney: Allen & Unwin, p.90.
17 'ASEAN shokoku no kōgyō seihin bōeki to kokusai bungyō', *Tokyo Ginkō Geppō*, March 1984, p.11.
18 Cheng, Chu-yuan (1986) 'United States–Taiwan Economic Relations: Trade and Investment', *The Columbia Journal of World Business*, 21:81.
19 According to W. A. Lewis, ensuring a continuous increase in the capital output ratio requires at least a 12 per cent private savings rate, if we assume a population growth of 3 per cent a year and a capital output ratio of between 3 and 4 per cent. See Tsiang, S. C. and Wu, Rong-I. (1985) 'The Experience of the Four Asian Newly Industrializing Countries', in W. Galenson (ed.) *Foreign Trade and Investment: Economic Development in the Newly Industrializing*

Asian Countries, Madison, Wisconsin: University of Wisconsin Press, pp.301–2. Also, according to a report of the Asian Development Bank, a 6 per cent economic growth rate requires a gross domestic savings of at least 18 per cent of GDP, assuming an output capital ratio of 0.33 per cent. See (1981) *Development Issues and Strategies*, Manila: ADB, pp.54–5. Of course, a high savings rate does not automatically guarantee a high economic growth. India, too, has a high savings rate, but economic growth has not been particularly high because of underutilization of available domestic capital.

20 See Wade, L. L. and Kim, B. S. (1978) *Economic Development of South Korea: The Political Economy of Success*, New York: Praeger Publishers, p.94.

21 Salleh, M. Z. and Osman, Z. (1982) 'The Economic Structure', in E. K. Fisk and H. Osman-Rani (eds) *The Political Economy of Malaysia*, Kuala Lumpur: Oxford University Press, p.127.

22 Kuo, Shirley W. Y. and Fei, John C. H. (1985) 'Causes and Role of Export Expansion in the Republic of China', in W. Galenson (ed.) (1985) op. cit., p.55. In recent years, the savings rate in Taiwan has been about 33 per cent of GNP. See *Far Eastern Economic Review* (FEER), 15 May 1986, p.82.

23 *FEER* 12 June 1986, p.89.

24 ibid., p.63.

25 Kuo, Shirley W. Y. and Fei, John, C. H. (1985) op. cit., p.59.

26 Lin, T. B. and Ho, Y. P. (1981) 'Export-Oriented Growth and Industrial Diversification in Hong Kong', in W. Hong and L. B. Krause (eds) *Trade and Growth of the Advanced Developing Countries in the Pacific Basin: Papers and Proceedings of the Eleventh Pacific Trade and Development Conference*, Seoul: Korea Development Institute, p.92.

27 Kershner, T. R. (1975) *Japanese Foreign Trade*, Lexington, MA: Lexington Books, Heath and Co., p.107 and p.110. Similarly, in the report of a task force set up by the Pacific Economic Cooperation Conference in October 1982, it was noted that throughout the 1970s, Japanese imports of manufactured goods from ASEAN–ANIC was from 75–80 per cent less than the figure for the United States. See the report of the task force in *Issues for Pacific Economic Cooperation: A Report of the Third Pacific Economic Cooperation Conference*, Jakarta, March 1984, p.67.

28 See the speech of Dr Richard Hu, Minister of Finance, Singapore, to the Insead Club, the Harvard Club, and the Oxford and Cambridge Society in early December 1987. *The Straits Times* 14 December 1987, p.20.

29 *The Economist* (London), 13 July 1985, p.50.

30 *FEER* 12 June 1986, p.59. The classification of manufactured goods is somewhat different from the one used in this book and includes SITC category 5 – chemicals and related products.

31 *The Straits Times* (Singapore), 12 September 1987, p.3.

32 *The Straits Times* (Singapore), 27 October 1987, p.4.

33 *Nihon Keizai Shinbun* (Chōkan), 28 November 1987, p.1.

34 Watanabe, T. and Kajiwara, H. (1983) 'Pacific Manufactured Trade and Japan's Options', *The Developing Economies* 21:337.
35 Cited in Watanabe A. (1985) op. cit., pp.24–5.
36 ibid., p.27.
37 Kitada, Y. (1986) 'Taigai shinshutsu de henka suru Nihon no sangyō kōzō', *Keizai*, no. 262, February, p.104.
38 *The Straits Times* (Singapore), 3 December 1987, p.27.
39 Akaha, T. (1986) 'Japan's Response to Threats of Shipping Disruptions in Southeast Asia and the Middle East', *Pacific Affairs* 59:265.
40 Bautista, R. M. (1985) 'The Recent Recession and Rising Protectionism in Developed Countries: Some Thoughts on the ASEAN Economies', *Journal of Philippine Development* 12:249–50.
41 Okita, S. (1987) 'The Outlook for Pacific Co-operation and the Role of Japan', *The Indonesian Quarterly* 15:501.

CONCLUSION

1 Nakatani, I. (1986) 'Policy Coordination: An Idea Whose Time has Come', *Japan Echo* 13: no. 3.
2 *Fortune* 27 April 1987,pp.175–6.
3 Bergsten, C. F. and Cline, W. R. (1985) *The United States–Japan Economic Problem*, Policy Analyses in International Economics, no. 13, Washington, DC: Institute for International Economics, p.31.
4 Ito, M. and Shimomura, D. (1986) 'The Folly of Structural Adjustment', *Japan Echo* 13:34–5.
5 Reischauer, E. O. (1984) *Japan: Past and Present*, New York, p.116.
6 See Akrasanee, N. (1983) 'ASEAN–Japan Trade and Development: A Synthesis', in *ASEAN–Japan Relations: Trade and Development*, Singapore: Institute of South East Asian Studies, pp.28–9.
7 See 'Report of the Task Force', in *Issues for Pacific Economic Cooperation: A Report of the Third Pacific Economic Cooperation Conference, Jakarta, 1984, p.71. Bali, 1983,* Centre for Strategic and International Studies.
8 Charnovitz, S. (1986) 'Worker Adjustment: The Missing Ingredient in Trade Policy', *California Management Review* 28:159.
9 Reich, R. B. (1983) 'The Next American Frontier', *The Atlantic* 251:45.
10 Rivlin, A. M. (ed.) (1984) *Economic Choices, 1984*, Washington, DC: The Brookings Institution, p.120.
11 ibid., pp.119–20.
12 Scott, B. R. (1985) 'U.S. Competitiveness: Concepts, Performance and Implications', in B. R. Scott and G. C. Lodge (eds) *U.S. Competitiveness in World Economy*, Boston, MA: Harvard Business School Press, p.32.

13 ibid., pp.41–3.
14 Reich, R. B. (1983) op. cit., p.45.
15 ibid., p.148.
16 Muller, R. E. and Moore, D. H. (1982) 'America's Blind Spot',
    Challenge, January/February, p.11.

Bibliography

BOOKS

Abegglen, J. C. (1984) *The Strategy of Japanese Business*, Cambridge, Mass: Ballinger Publishing Co.

Aggarwal, V. K. (1985) *Liberal Protectionism: The International Politics of Organized Textile Trade*, Los Angeles: University of California Press.

Akrasanee, N. (1983) *ASEAN-Japan Relations: Trade and Development*, Singapore: Institute of Southeast Asian Studies.

Allen, G. C. (1968) *Japan's Place in Trade Strategy: Larger Role in the Pacific Region*, London: Atlantic Trade Study Group Paper No. 9.

Amaya, N. (1982) *Nihon Kabushiki Kaisha: Nokosareta Sentaku*, Tokyo: PHP Research Institute.

Amaya, N. (1985) *'Saka no Ue no Kumo' to 'Saka no Shita no Numa': Nihon Keizai no Shinro'* Tokyo: Tsushu Sangyo Chosa Kai.

Analysis of the Degree of Openness of the Japanese Market (1984), Tokyo: Japan Economic Research Institute.

Avery, W. P., and Rapkin, D. P. (eds) (1982) *America in a Changing World Economy*, New York: Longman.

Bain, J. S., *Industrial Organization* (1968) New York: John Wiley.

Barfield, C. E. and Schambra, W. A. (eds), (1986) *The Politics of Industrial Policy*, Washington, DC: American Enterprise Institute.

Blaker, M. (1977) *Japanese International Negotiating Style*, New York: Columbia University Press.

Bergsten, C. F. (1975) *Toward a New World Trade Policy: The Maidenhead Papers*, Lexington, Mass: Lexington Books, D. C. Heath.

Bergsten, C. F. (1980) *The International Economic Policy of the United States: Selected Papers of C. Fred Bergsten*, Lexington, Mass: Lexington Books, D. C. Heath.

Bergsten, C. F. and Cline, W. R. (1985) *The United States–Japan Economic Problem*, Policy Analyses in International Economics, no. 13, Washington, DC: Institute for International Economics.

Calleo, D. P. (ed.) (1976) *Money and the Coming World Order*, New York: New York University Press.

Carr, E. H. (1962) *The Twenty Years' Crisis, 1919–1939*, London: Macmillan.

Caves, R. E. and Uekusa, M. (1976) *Industrial Organization in Japan*, Washington, DC: The Brookings Institute.

Chang, C. S. (1981) *The Japanese Auto Industry and the U.S. Market*, New York: Praeger Special Studies.

Cole, R. E. (ed.) (1981) *The Japanese Automobile Industry: Model and Challenge for the Future?* Ann Arbor, Mich: Michigan Papers in Japanese Studies, No. 3.

Cole, R. E. and Yakushiji, T. (1984) *The American and Japanese Auto*

Industries in Transition, Ann Arbor, Mich: Center of Japanese Studies, University of Michigan.

Corbo, V., Krueger, A. O., and Ossa, F. (eds) (1985) *Export-Oriented Development Strategies: The Success of Five Newly Industrializing Countries*, Boulder, Colo: Westview Press.

Cusumano, M. A. (1985) *The Japanese Automobile Industry: Technology and Management at Nissan and Toyota*, Cambridge, Mass: Harvard East Asian Monographs No. 122, The Council on East Asian Studies.

Davenport, M. (1986) *Trade Policy, Protectionism and the Third World*, London: Croom Helm.

Destler, I. M. and Sato, H. (eds) (1982) *Coping with U.S.–Japanese Economic Conflict*, Lexington, Mass: Lexington Books, D. C. Heath.

Development Issues and Strategies (1981) Manila: Asian Development Bank, Economic Office.

Downen, R. L. and Dickson, B. J. (eds) (1984) *The Emerging Pacific Community: A Regional Perspective*, Boulder, Colo: Westview Press.

Ebinger, C. K. and Morse, R. A. (eds) (1984) *U.S.–Japanese Energy Relations: Cooperation and Competition* Boulder, Colo: Westview Press.

Fisk, E. K. and Osman-Rani, H. (eds) (1982) *The Political Economy of Malaysia*, Kuala Lumpur: Oxford University Press.

Fried, E. B., Trezise, P. II. and Yoshida, S. (eds) (1983) *The Future Course of U.S.–Japan Economic Relations*, Washington, DC: The Brookings Institution.

Galenson, W. (ed.) (1985) *Foreign Trade and Investment: Economic Development in the Newly Industrializing Asian Countries*, Wisconsin: University of Wisconsin Press.

Golt, S. (1974) *The GATT Negotiations, 1973–75: A Guide to the Issues*, London: British North American Committee.

Halberstam, D. (1986) *The Reckoning*, New York: William Morrow.

Hargrave, E. C. and Morley, S. A. (eds) (1984) *The President and the Council of Economic Advisors: Interviews with CEA Chairmen*, Boulder, Colo: Westview Press.

Higashi, C. (1983) *The Japanese Trade Policy Formulation*, New York: Praeger Special Studies.

Hofheinz, R. and Calder, K. E., (1982) *The Eastasia Edge*, New York: Basic Books Inc.

Hollerman, L. (ed.) (1984) *Japan and the United States: Economic and Political Adversaries*, Boulder, Colo: Westview Press.

Holsti, O. R., Siverson, R. M. and George, A. L. (eds) (1980) *Change in the International System*, Boulder, Colo: Westview Press.

Hong, W. and Krause, L. B. (eds) (1981) *Trade and Growth of the Advanced Developing Countries in the Pacific Basin: Papers Proceedings of the Eleventh Pacific Trade and Development Conference*, Seoul: Korea Development Institute.

Hunker, J. A. (1983) *Structural Change in the US Automobile Industry*, Lexington, Mass: Lexington Books, D. C. Heath.

227

Imlah, A. H. (1958) *Economic Elements in 'Pax Britannica': Studies in British Foreign Trade in the Nineteenth Century*, Cambridge, Mass: Harvard University Press.

Ishizaki, T. (1985) *Shin Keizai Nationalism*, Tokyo: Tokyo Daigaku Shuppan Kai.

Issues for Pacific Economic Cooperation, A Report of the Third Pacific Economic Cooperation Conference, Bali, 1983 (1984), Jakarta: Centre for Strategic and International Studies.

Johnson, C. (1982) *MITI and the Japanese Miracle: The Growth of Industrial Policy, 1925–1975*, Stanford, Calif: Stanford University Press.

Kamijo, T. (1985) *Beikoku no Ude: Nihon no Te – Nichi-Bei Keizai Masatsu: Joho no Koyo*, Tokyo: Nihon Keizai Shinbun Sha.

Kaoru, M., *Tsusansho no Chosen* (1986) Tokyo: Tokyo Keizai Shinpo Sha.

Katz, J. D. and Friedman-Lichtschein, T. C. (eds) (1983) *Japan's New World Role*, Boulder, Colo: Westview Press.

Keohane, R. O. (1984) *After Hegemony: Cooperation and Discord in the World Political Economy*, Princeton, New Jersey: Princeton University Press.

Kershner, T. R. (1975) *Japanese Foreign Trade*, Lexington, Mass: Lexington Books, D. C. Heath.

Kindleberger, C. P. *The World in Depression, 1929 1939*, London: Allen Lane.

Kissinger, H. A. (1982) *Years of Upheaval*, London: Weidenfeld & Nicolson, Michael Joseph.

Kitamura, H. Okazaki, H. and Murata, R. (1983) *Nichi-Bei Kankei o Toi Tsumeru*, Tokyo: Sekai no Ugoki Sha.

Komiya, R. Okuno, M. and Suzumura, K. (eds) (1984) *Nihon no Sangyo Seisaku*, Tokyo: Tokyo Daigaku Shuppan Kai.

Kusano, A. (1984) Tokyo: *Nichi-Bei Keizai Masatsu no Kozo*.

Kuznets, P. W. (1977) Economic Growth and Structure in the Republic of Korea, New Haven, Conn: Yale University Press.

Lawrence, R. Z. and Litan, R. E. (1986) *Saving Free Trade: A Pragmatic Approach*, Washington, DC: The Brookings Institute.

Leveson, I. and Wheeler, J. W. (eds) (1980) *Western Economies in Transition: Structural Change and Adjustment in Industrial Countries*, Boulder, Colo: Westview Press.

Lewis, W. A. (1955) *The Theory of Economic Growth*, London: George Allen & Unwin.

Lin, Ching-Yuan (1973) *Industrialization in Taiwan: Trade and Import Substitution: Policies for Developing Countries*, New York: Praeger Publishers.

Matsushita, K. (1983) *Nicho-Bei Tsusho Masatsu no Ho Teki so-ten*, Tokyo: Yuhikaku.

Morse, R. A. and Yoshida, S. (eds) (1985) *Blind Partners: American and Japanese Responses to an Unknown Future*, Maryland: University Press of America.

Motoyama, Y. (ed.) (1985) *Boeki Masatsu o Miru Me*, Tokyo: Yuhikaku.

Nakane, C. (1970) *The Japanese Society*, Berkeley and Los Angeles: University of California Press.

Nishihara, M. (1976) *The Japanese and Sukarno's Indonesia: Tokyo–Jakarta Relations, 1951–1966*, Honolulu: The University Press of Hawaii.

Ogura, K. (1984) *Nichi-Bei Keizai Masatsu*, Tokyo: Nihon Keizai Shinbun Sha.

Okimoto, D. I. (ed.) (1982) *Japan's Economy: Coping with Change to the International Environment*, Boulder, Colo: Westview Press.

Olson, M. (1965) *The Logic of Collective Action*, New York: Schocken Books.

Patrick, H. and Rosovsky, H. (eds) (1976) *Asia's New Giant: How the Japanese Economy Works*, Washington, DC: The Broookings Institute.

Patrick, H. and Tachi, R. (eds) (1986) *Japan and the United States Today: Exchange Rates, Macroeconomic Policies and Financial Market Innovations*, New York: Columbia University Press.

Pugel, T. A. (ed.) (1986) *Fragile Interdependence: Economic Issues in U.S.–Japanese Trade and Investment*. Lexington, Mass: Lexington Books, D. C. Heath.

Redborn, F. S., Buss, T. F. and Ledebur, L. C. (eds) (1985) *U.S. Competitiveness in World Economy*, Boston, Mass: Harvard Business School Press.

Reischauer, E. O. (1970) *Japan: Past and Present*, London: Duckworth.

Reischauer, E. O. (1961) *The United States and Japan*, (revised edn) Cambridge, Mass: Harvard University Press.

Rivlin, A. M. (ed.) (1984) *Economic Choices, 1984* Washington, D.C: The Brookings Institution.

Ruggie, J. G. and Bhagwati, J. N. (eds) (1984) *Power, Passions and Purpose: Prospects for North-South Negotiations*, Cambridge, Mass: The MIT Press.

Sakamoto, M. (1981) *Keizai Taikoku no Chosen*, Tokyo: Nihon Seisansei Honbu.

Schlosstein, S. (1984) *Trade War: Greed, Power, and Industrial Policy on Opposite Sides of the Pacific*, New York: Congdon and Weed.

Schoolman, M. and Magid, A. (eds) (1986) *Reindustrializing New York State: Strategies, Implications, Challenges*, Albany: State University of New York Press.

Scott, B. R. and Lodge, G. C. (eds) (1985) *U.S. Competitiveness in the World Economy*, Boston, Mass: Harvard University Press.

Shomokawa, K. (1985) *Jidosha Sangyo Datsu Seiiuku Jidai*, Tokyo: Yuhikaku.

Shinohara, M. (1984) *Industrial Growth, Trade, and Dynamic Patterns in the Japanese Economy*, Tokyo: University of Tokyo Press.

Shishido, T. and Sato, R. (eds) (1985) *Economic Policy and Development: New Perspectives*, Dover, Mass: Auburn House Publishing.

Shull, S. A. and Cohen, J. E. (eds) (1986) *Economics and Politics of Industrial Policy: The United States and Western Europe*, Boulder, Colo: Westview Press.

229

Sobel, R. Car Wars: *The Untold Story* (1984) New York: E. P. Dutton.

Soesastro, H. and Han, Sung-Joo (1983) *Pacific Economic Cooperation: The Next Phase*, Jakarta: Centre for Strategic and International Studies.

Steinbruner, J. D. (1974) *Cybernetic Theory of Decision: A New Dimension of Political Analysis*, Princeton, NJ: Princeton University Press.

Strange, S. and Tooze, R. (eds) (1981) *The International Politics of Surplus Capacity: Competition for Market Shares in the World Recession*, London: George Allen & Unwin.

Tanaka, T. and Yamazawa, I. (1984) *Boeki Nihon no Katsuyaku*, Tokyo: Yuhikaku.

Vogel, E. (ed.) (1975) *Modern Japanese Organization and Decision Making*, Berkeley and Los Angeles: University of California Press.

Wade, L. L. and Kim, B. S. (1978) *Economic Development of South Korea: The Political Economy of Success*, New York: Praeger Publishers.

Waltz, K. N. (1979) *Theory of International Politics*, Philippines: Addison–Wesley Publishing Co.

Whitman, Marina V. N. (1975) *Reflections of Interdependence: Issues for Economic Theory and U.S. Policy*, Pittsburg: University of Pittsburg Press.

Yamanura, K. (ed.) (1982) *Policy and Trade Issues of the Japanese Economy: American and Japanese Perspectives*, Seattle, Wash: University of Washington Press.

Yoshino, M.Y. (1971) *The Japanese Marketing System: Adaptations and Innovations*, Cambridge, Mass: The MIT Press.

JOURNALS

Amaya, N., 'When Fair is Unfair', *Journal of Japanese Trade and Industry*, Vol. 5, no. 1, January/February 1986.

Amaya, N., 'Keizai Masatsu was Sainen Suru Ka', *Aiia Geppo*, February 1985.

Amaya, N., 'Soap Nationalism o Osu', *Bungei Shuniu*, July 1981.

'The Automobile Crisis and Public Policy', an interview with P. Caldwell, Chairman, Ford Motor Co., *Harvard Business Review*, Vol. 59, No. 1, January–February 1981, pp. 73–82.

'Bei Koku no Kokusai Kyoso Ryoku', *Chosa Geppo*, Vol. 74, No. 8, August 1985, pp. 36–54.

Bhagwati, J. N. and Irwin, D. A., 'The Return of Reciprocitarians – US Trade Policy Today', *The World Economy*, Vol. 10, No. 2, June 1987.

Buzan, B., 'Economic Structures and International Security: The Limits of the Liberal Case', *International Organization*, Vol. 38, No. 4, Autumn 1984, pp. 597–624.

Charnovitz, S., 'Worker Adjustment: The Missing Ingredient in Trade Policy', *California Management Review*, Vol. 28, No. 2, Winter 1986, pp. 156–73.

Cheng, Chu-Yuan, 'United States–Taiwan Economic Relations: Trade and Investment', *The Columbia Journal of World Business*, Vol. 21, No. 1, Spring 1986, pp. 87–96.

Fukuoka, M., 'Nakasone Sansen ron ni Miru To-nai Shugi to Seiron Minshu Shugi Nihon Seiji wa Jiremma ni', *Chuo Koron*, May 1986.

Goldstein, J., 'The Political Economy of Trade: Institutions of Protection', *American Political Science Review*, Vol. 80, No. 1, March 1986, pp. 161–84.

Guo, Zhao-Lie, 'Ajia Taiheiyo Chi'iki no Taito to Kan Taiheiyo Kyoryoku', *Kokusai Mondai*, No. 302, May 1985. pp. 28–39.

Haitani, K., 'Japan's Trade Problem and the Yen', *Asian Survey*, Vol. 13, No. 8, August 1973, pp.723–39.

Honma, M., 'Zeisei Kaikaku no Kadai to Hoko', *The Keizai Seminar*, no. 376, May 1986.

Inoguchi, T., 'Japan's Images and Options: Not a Challenger But a Supporter', *The Journal of Japanese Studies*, Vol. 12, No. 1, Winter 1986, pp.95–119.

Inoguchi, K., Amaya, N. and Kurosawa, Y., 'Hasha naki Jidai Nihon no Yakuwari', *Chuo Koron*, August 1987.

Ito, M. and Shimomura, O., 'The Folly of Structural Adjustment', *Japan Echo*, Vol. 13, No. 3, Autumn 1986.

Johnson, C., 'The Institutional Foundations of Japanese Industrial Policy', *California Management Review*, Vol. 27, No. 4, Summer 1985, pp. 59–69.

Johnson, H. G. 'An Economic Theory of Protectionism', *Journal of Political Economy*, Vol. 73, No. 3, June 1965, pp.256–83.

Kaeda, B., 'Zeisei Kaikaku Haya Wakari 20 mon', *Bungei Shunju*, February 1987.

Kawaharada, S., 'Shin Jidai o Mukaeru Jidosha Kaigai Jigyo', *Tekko Kai*, Vol. 35, No. 9, September 1985.

Kawai, T., 'A Tentative Analysis of Business-Government Relations in Japan', *Gakushuin Economic Papers*, Vol. 22, No. 2, September 1985.

Kinoshita, T., 'Nihon Keizai to Kan Taiheiyo Keizai Kyoryoku-Ima, Nihon ni Totte Hitsuyo na Tai'o Saku wa Nani Ka', *Shukan Toyo Keizai*, No. 4627, 3 December 1985, pp.93–103.

Kitada, Y., 'Taigai Shinshutsu de Henka Suru Nihon no Sangyo Kozo', *Keizai*, No. 262, February 1986, pp.93–105.

Koganei, Y., 'Shijo Kaiho e no Mukete no Shinario', *Chuo Koron*, July 1987.

Kratochwil, F., 'The Force of Prescriptions', *International Organization*, Vol. 38, No. 4, Autumn 1984, pp.685–708.

Kuroyanagi, Y., 'Ajia Taiheiyo Kyoryoku to Rejionalism-Jijitsu, Koso Oyobi Genjitsu', *Kokusai Mondai*, No. 301, April 1985, pp. 50–63.

Kusano, A., '1980 nen 7 Gatsu: Maboroshi no Jidosha Jishu Kisei', *Chuo Koron*, November 1983.

Lake, D. A., 'Beneath the Commerce of Nations: A Theory of International Economic Structures', *International Studies Quarterly*, Vol. 28, No. 2, 1984. pp.143–70.

Lake, D.A., 'International Economic Structures and American Foreign Economic Policy, 1887–1934', *World Politics*, Vol. 35, No. 4, July 1983, pp. 517–43.

Lochmann, M. W., 'The Japanese Voluntary Restraint on Automobile Exports: An Abandonment of the Free Trade Principles of the GATT and the Free Market Principles of the United States Anti-Trust Laws', *Harvard International Law Journal*, Vol. 27, No. 1, Winter 1986, pp.99–157.

Lutz, J.M., 'Symbiosis in Manufactures Trade in East Asia', *Journal of Northeast Asian Studies*, Vol. 5, No. 3, Fall 1986.

Mack, A., 'The Political Economy of Global Decline: America in the 1980s', *Australian Outlook*, Vol. 40, No. 1, April 1986, pp. 11–20.

Matsuda, M., 'O-Bei Sho Koku to no Boeki Mondai no Ichi-Shiten: Seihin Yunyu Hiritsu Hijyo Yoso no Datosei ni Tsuite', *Boeki to Kanzei*, March 1986.

Miyazaki, I., 'Naiju Kakudai Taisaku no Dainidan o', *Ekonomist*, 18 February 1986.

Moriguchi, C., 'Nichi-Bei-O ni Ima Nozomareru 'Seisaku Kyocho' – Hoko to Kanosei', *Shukan Toyo Keizai*, No. 73, 3 December 1985.

Morley, J. W., 'Presidential Address: Japan and America – The Dynamics of Partnership', *Journal of Asian Studies*, Vol. XLV, No. 1, November 1985, pp.11–20.

Muller, R. E. and Moore, D. H., 'America's Blind Spot: Industrial Policy', *Challenge*, January/February 1982, pp.5–13.

Nakatani, I., 'Policy Coordination: An Idea Whose Time has Come', *Japan Echo*, Vol. 13, No. 3, Autumn 1986, pp.37–40.

Newton, C. C. S., 'The Sterling Crisis of 1947 and the British Response to the Marshall Plan', *The Economic History Review*, Vol. 37, No. 3, August 1984, p.391–408.

'Nihon no Zeisei Kaikau-Symposium', *The Keizai Seminar*, No. 376, May 1986.

Ohmae, K., 'Nichi-Bei ni "Fukinko" wa Nai', *Bungei Shuniu*, April 1986.

Okumura, A., 'Japan's Changing Economic Structure', *Journal of Japanese Trade and Industry*, No. 5, September/October 1987.

Olsen, E., '"Cheap Rider" e no Fuman', *Chuo Koron*, December 1985.

Reich, R. B., 'The Next American Frontier', *The Atlantic*, Vol. 251, No. 3, March 1983, pp. 43–58.

Ruggie, J. G., 'International Regimes, Transactions and Change: Embedded Liberalism in the Postwar Economic Order', *International Organization*, Vol. 36, No. 2, Spring 1982, pp.379–415.

Russett, B., 'The Mysterious Case of Vanishing Hegemony' *International Organization*, Vol. 39, No. 2, Spring 1985.

Sakaiya, T., '5 cho Yen de Nihon o sukue', *Bungei Shuniu*, April 1986.

Sakamoto, M., 'Shihyo Kara Mita Pax Amerikana no Tokushoku: Pax Britanika ni Hikaku Shite', *Sekai Keizai Hyoron*, Vol. 30, No. 4, April 1986.

Sakamoto, M., 'Pax Amerikana ni Okeru Kokusai Kokyo Zai no Futan', *Sekai Keizai Hyoron*, Vol. 29, No. 9, September 1985.

Schmidt, H., 'The World Economy at Stake: The Inevitable Need for American Leadership', *The Economist*, 26 February–4 March 1983.

Schott, J. J. and Mazza, J., *Trade in Services and Developing Countries'*, *Journal of World Trade Law*, Vol. 20, No. 3, May–June 1986.

Shinpo, S., 'Don't Blame Japan's Saving Surplus', *Japan Echo*, Vol. 12, No. 4, Winter 1985, pp.15–20.

Simon, S. W., 'Is there a Japanese Regional Security Role?', *Journal of Northeast Asian Studies*, Vol. 5, No. 2, Summer 1986, pp.30–52.

Snidal, D., 'The Limits of Hegemonic-Stability Theory', *International Organization*, Vol. 39, No. 4, Autumn 1985. pp.579–614.

Stein, A. A., 'The Hegemon's Dilemma: Great Britain, the United States and the International Economic Order', *International Organization*, Vol. 38, No. 2, Spring 1984, pp.355–86.

Stein, A. A., 'Coordination and Collaboration: Regimes in an Anarchic World', *International Organization*, Vol. 36, No. 2, Spring 1982, pp. 299–324.

Stoga, A. J. 'If America Won't Lead', *Foreign Policy*, No. 64, Fall 1986, pp.79–97.-

Tsuruta, M., 'Yen Daka Ka no Nihon Keizai-Sono Genjo to Koho', *Keizai*, No. 262, February 1986, pp.80–92.

Watanabe, A., 'Kan Taiheiyo Kozo no Uta to Shinjitsu', *Chuo Koron*, November 1985.

Watanabe, T. and Kajiwara, H., 'Pacific Manufactured Trade and Japan's Options', *The Developing Economies*, Vol. 21, No. 4, December 1983, pp.313–39.

Watanabe, T. and Hirata, A., 'Ajia Taiheiyo Keizai no Seisei-Hatten no Mekanizm to Shijo teki Ketsugo', *Kokusai Mondai*, No. 301, April 1985, pp.35–49.

Woodall, B., 'Response to the Japanese Challenge', *Asia Pacific Community*, no. 27, Winter 1985, pp.63–80.

Yamazawa, I., 'Increasing Imports and the Structural Adjustment of the Japanese Textile Industry', *The Developing Economies*, Vol. 18, No. 4, December 1980, pp.441–62.

Yarbrough, B. V. and Yarbrough, R. M., 'Free Trade, Hegemony, and the Theory of Agency', *Kyklos*, Vol. 38, 1985.

Yoshitomi, M., 'Taigai Fukinko no Nidankai Chosei', *Chuo Koron*, April 1987.

Zeisei Kaikaku Koso Nihon no Sentaku-Symposium', *Shukan Toyo Keizai*, No. 73, 3 December 1985.

GOVERNMENT DOCUMENTS AND OTHER SOURCES

Economic Outlook Japan, 1986, Economic Planning Agency, Tokyo. February 1986.

Issues Relating to the Domestic Auto Industry, Hearings Before the Subcommittee on International Trade of the Committee of Finance, U.S. Senate, 97th Congress, 1st Session on S–396, 9 March 1981.

233

Hachiju nendai no Ryutsu Sangyo Vision, Tsusho Sangyo Sho, Tokyo, December 1985.

Japan Statistical Yearbook, 1986, Statistics Bureau, Management and Coordination Agency, Tokyo, 1986.

Japanese Industrial Collusion and Trade, A Study Prepared for the use of the Subcommittee on Economic Goals and Intergovernmental Policy of the Joint Economic Committee, Congress of the United States, 31 January 1986.

Jidosha Sangyo Handbook, Nissan Motor Co. Ltd., 1985 Edition.

Kaigai Chokusetsu Toshi to sono Eikyo, Softnomics Followup Kenkyu Kai Hokoku Sho, Ministry of Finance, Softnomics Series No. 35, Tokyo, 1985.

Measures for Demand Expansion and External Economic Measures, Ministerial Conference for Economic Measures, Government-Ruling Parties Joint Headquarters for the Promotion of External Economic Measures, Tokyo, 28 December 1985.

Measures for Demand Expansion, Ministerial Conference for Economic Measures, Tokyo, 15 October 1985.

Memo on Japan–U.S. Economic Relations, Ministry of International Trade and Industry, Tokyo, January 1986.

News from MITI, Overseas Public Affairs Office, Ministry of International Trade and Industry, Tokyo, Japan.

Nichi-Bei Jidosha Mondai no Sui'i Nissan Motor Co. Ltd. Tokyo. Undated.

Nihon Keizai no Genkyo-Naiju Chushin no Antei Seicho o Mezashite, Economic Planning Agency, Tokyo, 1985.

Report of the Advisory Committee for External Economic Issues, Tokyo, 9 April 1985.

Soft-ka Keizai to Boeki, Softnomics Followup Kenkyu Kai Hokoku Sho, Ministry of Finance, Softnomics Series No. 36,Tokyo, 1984.

Statistical Handbook of Japan, 1986, Statistics Bureau, Management and Coordination Agency, Tokyo 1986.

Tsusho Hyakusho, Tsusho Sangyo Sho, Tokyo 1985.

US Trade and Investment Policy: Imports and the Future of the American Automobile Industry, Hearings Before the Joint Economic Committee, Congress of the United States, 96th Congress, 2nd Session, 19 March, 1980.

World Economic Outlook, International Monetary Fund, Washington, DC, 1986.

Yunyu Hin Ryutsu Jittai Chosa Kekka no Matome, Economic Planning Agency, November 1985.

Index